ALTERNATIVES
IN EDUCATION

ALTERNATIVES IN EDUCATION

THEORETICAL & HISTORICAL PERSPECTIVES

Val D Rust

University of California at Los Angeles, USA

SAGE Studies in Social and Educational Change Volume 6

 SAGE Publications · London and Beverly Hills

For information address

SAGE Publications Ltd.
28 Banner Street
London EC1Y 8QE

SAGE Publications Inc.
275 South Beverly Drive
Beverly Hills, California 90212

International Standard Book Number
0 8039 9980 1 Cloth
0 8039 9998 4 Paper

Library of Congress Catalog Card Number
76-56683

First Printing
Printed in Great Britain by
Biddles Ltd, Guildford, Surrey

CONTENTS

LIST OF TABLES

LIST OF FIGURES

1

THE MEANING OF MODERNIZATION

The term 'modern', as used by social scientists, possesses both a general and a specific meaning (Riggs, 1961: 61). The general meaning refers to any social processes and cultural attitudes which are deemed worthy of being emulated. This concept was in wide use as early as the Middle Ages, especially in theological and political circles. Even as the first universities were founded, the advocates of nominalism as well as realism argued their cases as being modern because they were worthy of emulation. In France newly elected local political representatives addressed themselves as modern while the old councilmen, whose 'mandate' had come to an end were considered traditional or *ancien*. Humanism and the Renaissance period expanded the concept beyond theology and politics, recognizing any new art, music and literature as modern (Anton, 1965: 8-10).

Each new historical period addressed more and more its own style, values, or inventions as modern and those who emulated its wares only reinforced the sense that that which was modern was better than that which had existed in the past. For example, nineteenth-century American educators such as Calvin Stowe and Horace Mann, who both journeyed to Prussia to learn first hand of its excellent schools and efficient pedagogical style, hailed the Prussian schools as the most modern in existence and worthy of emulation. Today, when people are barraged with appeals from the advertising media to 'go modern – go electric', or to 'modernize their home with new pile carpet', the implication is made that those who are up on the latest developments are the most modern and to be modern is to emulate those who have already adopted such living styles.

To be modern in the general sense, then, is to turn to the new or emulate some aspect of a given culture; yet, there are enduring social processes and attitudes characteristic to Western history which have in time been labelled as modern. The major early frame of reference of this sort was the Renaissance and Reformation distinction drawn between antiquity and modernity. The major cultural lines of competition at that time were between the classical Greek and Roman world and the intellectual 'modern' challenges against it. As we shall see in our study, vestiges of this conflict remain until this very day in institutions of higher learning.

But the more contemporary and specific use of the term 'modern' conceived by social scientists pertains largely to those institutions, processes, and attitudes which have evolved mainly, but not exclusively, in the West during the past two centuries, and which have been emulated by the rest of the world. We now describe this period as the 'Modern Age' and have made the specific meaning of the term so commonplace that the word 'modern' has often been used inter-changeably with the dominant characteristics of the West since the Industrial Revolution. Modernization in this sense is, therefore, synonymous with Westernization, industrialization, democratization, and so forth. It is only in this more specific sense that we can talk about a post-modern period, because here we refer to a characteristic phenomenon which took place between the mid-1700s and the 1960s rather than to any given social process which is being emulated.

As our frame of reference in this book we shall adopt this specific aspect of the term 'modern'; that is, the term shall connote the type of social change that began with the Industrial Revolution in England, and the political revolution in France, and which is rapidly coming to an end in the United States at this very time.

England was the first country to adopt the commercial and industrial processes which commonly characterize the most evident signs of economic modernity, although these processes were accompanied by far-reaching changes in the structure of social and political institutions as well as attitudes and thinking styles of individuals (Rostow, 1960: 38).

France's thrust into modernity was most evident in its political upheavals toward the end of the eighteenth century (1789-94). This revolution is usually associated with the elimination of remnants of the Feudal system; it witnessed the establishment of new social class relationships and the rise of representative government.

In spite of the difference in thrust which precipitated movement into modernity in these two countries, it is clear that enormous political changes accompanied the economic revolution in England and economic changes followed closely after the political revolution in France. Scholars have long argued that economic, political, and social variables are highly interrelated in any society and any fundamental change in one element requires adjustment of the others (Hagen, 1962: 26).

Let us illustrate by the example cited above, 'Go modern – go electric.' Such a commercial appeal suggests that families alter their means of homemaking to include a wide variety of appliances and equipment run by electric power. To do this a society must produce large sources of electrical energy and it must possess an extensive manufacturing industry which is able to supply stoves, refrigerators, vacuum cleaners, can openers, electric knives, etc. In order to manufacture such products a society must either tap its natural resources or engage in extensive import-export practices. Either of these tasks demands a vast network of road, rail, or shipping facilities. Such a process requires a large infrastructure to regulate movement and distribution of goods and includes an extensive legal structure to ensure equitable exchanges of goods and services. This system of exchange requires some universally recognized base of value – a monetary system. To ensure a full accounting of transactions a book-keeping system is necessary. This can only be satisfied if specialized educational programmes are available. We could extend this illustration as far as we wish, but we have already demonstrated a series of interconnected and interdependent phenomena, all of which are necessary to some degree in order for the whole system to function.

To be modern, therefore, not only refers to the industrial and commercial processes of life, but to the whole of social and psychic life. The interplay of values and attitudes with institutions is crucial if a nation is to be deemed 'modern'.

During the 1950s and 60s social scientists devoted enormous energy to the construction of a comprehensive paradigm of modernity. Even though certain social scientists such as Daniel Lerner (1958) and David McClelland (1961) emphasized one or two critical modernization variables, all recognized that it was a paradigm possessing multiple variables. The paradigm was attractive because it inevitably took on the character of certain nations and implied the emptiness or lack of development in most other nations. The United States was usually the 'model modern nation' because of its enormous gross national product, its pluralistic life style and its optimistic attitude that the rest of the world could be transformed into its image.

The paradigm which has finally evolved consists of a described or implied dichotomous social construct, the modern forming one 'ideal type' extreme of the construct and the traditional forming the other. This framework is reminiscent of Herbert Spencer's homogeneity and differentiation, Max Weber's traditionalism and rationalism, Emile Durkheim's mechanical and organic organization, and Ferdinand Toennies' community and society. Attempts have been made to assimilate a comprehensive catalogue of descriptors such as low-need achievement versus high-need achievement, religious versus secular beliefs, agrarian versus industrial economies, stable social structure versus high social mobility.

In any case, implicit in the theory is a linear movement between the two extremes. A nation is belived to modernize when it emulates model nations such as the United States, Germany, England, or Sweden.

In the past decade a number of studies appeared which began to provide empirical evidence that relationships between modernization variables exist. Karl Deutsch (1961: 493-514) coined the term 'social mobilization' suggesting that a number of specific processes are bracketed together as a population moves into modernity. He compiled partial data for nineteen countries which indicated a correlational relationship between GNP, population, radio audience, newspaper readers, literacy rates, work force in non-agriculture, and urban population.

A number of other studies have substantiated these and other relationships. Phillip Cutright, building on a study by Seymour M. Lipset (1959; 1963), compared political development in seventy-seven different nations. He conceptualized political development in the following manner: 'A politically developed nation has more complex and specialized national political institutions than a less politically developed nation' (1963: 255). Cutright (1963: 257) found a high communications development index which he had formed by drawing together a composite score of newspaper consumption, newsprint consumption, telephones, and the number of pieces of domestic mail per capita. It is clear from Cutright's data that as political development increases, so does communication development.

Such a finding confirms UNESCO and United Nations data on most countries of the world computed by Daniel Lerner over twenty years ago; he found positive correlation coefficients of urbanization (0.61), literacy (0.91), media participation — daily newspaper circulation, number of radio receivers, cinema seating capacity (0.84), and political participation (0.82) (1958: 51-65). Political development and communications development were also found by Cutright to be highly correlated with educational development, urbanization, labour force movement away from agricultural employment and economic development. He revealed these factors as being interdependent (Cutright, 1963: 760).

Gabriel A. Almond and James S. Coleman were able to find a positive relationship between economic development and political competitiveness of seventy-five countries throughout the world; however, the criteria used by these people was qualitative rather than quantitative and statistical (Almond and Coleman, 1960). Harbison and Myers in their study encompassing 136 countries found a positive relationship between human resource development — a composite of factors such as number of teachers, school enrolments at various levels, number of scientists and engineers, and economic development — a composite of GNP and percentage of active population engaged in agricultural occupations (Harbison and Myers, 1964).

Mary Jean Bowman and C. Arnold Anderson found positive correlations between the level of spread of education and economic levels. They found that indicators of the spread of primary education are better economic predictors than the extent of post-primary schooling. Literacy rates and post-primary enrolments are also positively correlated (Bowman and Anderson, 1967: 113-31).

There would be little value in extending this list of empirical studies since the point should be made that modernizing factors are statistically interrelated when we view these data on a global level. However, it must be pointed out that variations exist due to cultural factors. For example, Cutright shows that even though political development is positively correlated with its complete profile of national development for all countries, some countries score better than others. He found that political development in North and South American countries is much greater than in other areas of the world in relationship to the factors which make up the total national development. Figure 1 shows graphically that the relative political development in the Western hemisphere, in relationship to commmunications development, is much greater than in the rest of the world.

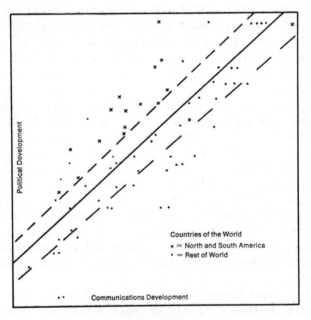

**Relationship of Communications Development
to Political Development**

Figure 1

Huntington (1968: 122-39) demonstrates in a perceptive analysis with regard to political modernization that the ease with which the United States became socially and economically modern precluded the necessity to modernize political institutions. Granted, American political processes are extensive in terms of mass participation, but the structure of political institutions is as traditional as anywhere in the Western world since it still retains a pre-industrial Tudor England form. On the other hand, Germany modernized its political structure under Bismarck and moved rapidly into an industrialized state, though it remained socially traditional. Dahrendorf (1964: 52) accords Germany the distinction of being the only Western European land which failed to change fundamental human relationships through industrialization as it became an 'industrial feudal society' in the latter part of the nineteenth and the beginning of the present century.

In spite of the empirical studies which have emerged the whole paradigm has recently become suspect, because in their enthusiasm social scientists have tended to develop a straw man concept. 'The modern ideal is set forth', suggests Samuel Huntington, 'and then everything which is not modern is labeled traditional' (Huntington, 1971: 294). Worse yet, the modern is often described and the traditional becomes its opposite, violating or disregarding all the variations which exist in the Third World (Wehler, 1975: 14). The paradigm is also under attack because it implies that all nations are destined to move toward a colossal homogeneity of social processes and structures, or if they do not, they condemn themselves to an inferior primitive state of existence.

These criticisms are accepted as having merit. The theory of modernization has enormous limitations, but in its present state of development social science has not yet evolved a more adequate theory. Christopher Lasch (1975: 34) recently reminded us that the one thing 'that can be said for "modernization" is that it serves better than no model'. By safeguarding against the major pitfalls pointed out above, the model is seen to possess great utility in the context of this book. In the first place, a distinction is made between various types of social evolution. Edwin O. Reischauer reminds us that modern variables exist in at least three different settings:

(1) in nations such as the United States and Northwestern Europe in which the elements of modernization for the most part appeared

through a relatively slow evolutionary process;

(2) in nations with highly developed, complex civilizations in which the major elements of modernization were introduced from the outside; and

(3) in nations of sub-national constitution which are undergoing their own modernization process (Hall, 1965: 34).

The traditional in each of these contexts has quite a different meaning even though all countries reflect similar modernization characteristics. Since our study will concentrate on the first of these settings, the conventional traditional-modern concept has some historical basis and will not be imposed on cultural settings which have a vastly different historical background.

We shall also avoid undue focus on the traditional, since there are variations even in the Western world; consequently, our point of concentration will be on modern variables. Finally, the major point of this book is to emphasize the historicity of the modern age. The paradigm which social scientists have developed is no longer viewed as utopian in nature but is seen as an historical era having enormous advantages but also a shadow side which is being recognized by a new generation groping toward its own world view and life style.

It remains for us to provide some overall picture of the modern world as conceived by social scientists. We do this reluctantly since any attempt to list variables becomes not only tedious but suspect. No list is comprehensive and statements which are made undergo constant refinement, but this may be of value as a point of departure. Below we provide an abstract outline of variables compiled at the Hakone Conference on Modern Japan (Hall, 1965: 20-23). We have gone back further than a decade in order to capture the sense of certainty which still prevailed among social scientists.

POLITICAL MODERNIZATION

1. Increasing allocation of political roles in accordance with standards of achievement rather than ascription.
2. Growing emphasis upon rational, scientific, and secular techniques of political decision-making.

3. Mass popular interest and involvement in the political system, though not necessarily in its decision-making process.
4. Predominance of functionally specific rather than generalized political roles organized in an elaborate and professionalized bureaucracy.
5. Broad and explicit governmental involvement in, responsibility for, and regulation of the economic and social aspects of individual and group life.
6. An increasing centralization of governmental functions.
7. Regulatory, control, and judicial techniques based increasingly upon a predominantly impersonal system of law.

SOCIAL MODERNIZATION

1. A shifting composition of population as between town and country.
2. A decline in the importance of social groups based on kinship or residence relative to that of groups created to perform certain specific functions (economic, political, religious, recreational, etc.) and joined by individual choice.
3. A wider range of individual choice between alternative courses of action, relatively unrestrained by any social sanction.
4. A growing tendency for the sanctions which do limit that range of choice to take the form of impersonal laws rather than the pressure of group opinion.
5. A lessening tendency for individuals to identify their interests with and feel loyalty toward small face-to-face groups (such as the family), with, consequently, a growing tendency for individuation, and/or identification with larger, impersonal groups (nation, class, etc.).
6. An increasing specialization of roles in the economic, political, and intellectual spheres.
7. Explicit assignment of those roles and of social prestige on the basis of achievement.
8. A tendency for relations between individuals to become (a) less often characterized by unbridgeable gaps of status; (b) more often contractually entered into rather than determined by birth or

residence; (c) more often limited to contract in a specific functional sphere (economic, political, recreational, etc.); and (d) less often charged with emotion.

ECONOMIC MODERNIZATION

1. Increasing application of scientific technology, and of inanimate energy, to enlarge and diversify the production of goods and services per capita.
2. A growing specialization of labour and subdivision of productive processes within and among firms, industries, occupations, and territories, and an increasing interdependence and mobility of individuals and groups within a network of widening impersonal markets.
3. A concomitant improvement in human skills and economic efficiency, especially at the higher technical and managerial levels.
4. An accumulation of capital goods in more productive forms and in growing amounts per worker, financed by a complex of financial institutions that characteristically divorce the savings from the investment process in order to pool liquid resources for the growing stream of investment.
5. Production, transport, marketing, and finance organized on an increasingly large scale, with concomitant tendencies to the concentration of decisions over economic life.
6. As the dynamic force behind the above processes, a society increasingly oriented to the pursuit of economic opportunity, infused (especially within the elite) by a spirit of innovation and growth, and increasingly rational in its choice of techniques and allocation of resources to achieve its economic goals.
7. As a result of these processes – and despite a characteristic increase in population – a rise in the level of material well-being, usually a widening of the range of personal choice, and sooner or later a reduction in the range of economic and social inequalities.
8. As incomes rise, a shift in the balance of employment and production from the extractive industries to manufacturing and the services, with a concomitant urbanization of the labour force.

9. The spread of wage labour as the chief form of gainful employment, and commonly the separation of ownership and management.
10. The replacement of natural hazards (e.g. weather) as the main source of insecurity by technological change, the uncertainties of the market, and the bargaining disadvantages of the individual in relation to his employer and the state.

INTELLECTUAL MODERNIZATION

1. The systematic accumulation of intellectually verifiable knowledge and the weakening of religious or cultural dogmas.
2. Acceptance of the concept of social change in human affairs.
3. An increase in the value placed upon the individual.
4. Growing attention to the vocational, social, and intellectual training of the individual.
5. Secularization and emphasis on material goods.
6. The creation through mass means of communication of new interest and belief groups with national, class, or occupational orientations.
7. A constantly widening orbit of individual involvement in intellectual communities beyond the family, village, or province to the state and to supernational ideals.
8. Improvement of means of dissemination of ideas to all members of the society.

This list has virtues not revealed in most outlines in that it is broken down according to the point of view of particular fields of study. It is helpful to draw on the contributions of political, social, economic, and ideological modernization since we are so accustomed to looking at knowledge of any sort from its discipline source. As could be expected in this type of format a good deal of variable overlap between disciplines is identifiable, suggesting the possibility of a more generic conceptual construct. The student is invited to engage in such an exercise of his/her own. For us to engage in such an enterprise of theory development would take us far beyond our goal of providng a workable framework for the dialectics of education, our ultimate interest. We will therefore be content to rely on the above concepts, allowing them to remain with their discipline home.

The advantage of remaining discipline based lies in the possibility of constructing a balanced multidisciplinary approach to the study of education; at the same time this avoids a grappling with the concepts at an unreal level of abstraction that an interdisciplinary approach would require. Consequently, we are able to place modernization concepts within a social science context giving substance to the issues and providing a broader social context for our discussion of modern education. Our framework of presentation in each of the next four chapters will be as follows. One or more critical modernization concepts are elaborated within a specific discipline context at the beginning of each of these chapters. Out of the outline will emerge a discussion of one or more critical components of modern education, which in turn will be contrasted with its traditional counterpart. Following each of these discussions we shall consider the forces of protest or breakdown at play in the mature modern world. Finally, we shall dialectically postulate general trends in education which can be anticipated in the post-modern era.

2

POLITICS AND EDUCATION

THE NATION STATE EMERGES

It seems appropriate to begin our excursion into modernity with a brief exploration of a fundamental political element of the modern age: the nation state. Its dominant position in the modern world has been through its successful efforts of rationalizing and centralizing all authority within its geographical boundaries. In fact, the most prevalent single indicator that a political unit is modern is the degree to which the authority within the territory occupied by the state has been consolidated to its administrative and legal organization.

We define authority simply as that power to which the voluntarily obedient refer to legitimize compliance to dictates or directives or which leaders or functionaries call on to bring about voluntary accommodation. Authority is probably the most crucial variable in political organization because both the type of authority and its degree of legitimacy determine in large measure the viability of any social activity including education. According to Max Weber the test of authority consolidation is manifest in terms of governmental monopolity, especially in the use of force: consequently, in a modern state 'the use of any force is regarded as legitimate only so far as it is either permitted by the state or prescribed by it' (Weber, 1968: 56).

Thus, a church may exercise certain sanctions on its members, or a labour union may act against industrial firms only to the degree that it is permitted by the state. Even the authority of a father over his son is circumscribed and prescribed by the authority of the modern state. Even though the father may exercise his 'right' to discipline his son, he does so because the state legitimizes the survival of an authority which at one time was independently exercised by heads of households.

There is a major distinction between modern and traditional authority in the West. In contrast to the distribution of centralized political authority of the modern state, Medieval European societies were highly pluralistic in nature with separate powers being held by empire, universal church, tribal duchies representing a multitude of Feudal states, other local units of authority such as village or clan, as well as custom and belief. At times these were united through power conflicts although failures of cohesion and reassertions of independent authority often disrupted the movement toward a coordinated authority structure. Life was marked for peasant and noble alike by competing and counter-active forces; authority was seemingly everywhere and yet eluded any specific identification.

Modern man has recognized conditions similar to Feudal Europe as he has come in contact with much of the non-Western world. Lucian Pye notes that as Europeans came into newly discovered areas of the world, they would inquire 'Who is in charge here?' as if some sovereign authority should exist which ruled over the territory (Finkle, 1971: 86). In actual fact, such was rarely the case since pluralism continues to be largely typical of the present Third World.

In Europe the crucial transitional state from Medieval to modern politics was monarchical absolutism which prevailed during the eighteenth century. The primary contribution of monarchical absolutism was the development of the concept of sovereignty, which in turn paved the way for a consolidation of authority in the nation state. Under the rule of the monarch, law was no longer viewed as inherent in the nature of things or retained by God, but became centred in the state itself in the person of the monarch or king.

The concept of the Divine Right of Kings which was developed in France toward the end of the sixteenth century was introduced in England by James I, who rejected the tradition that kings are servants of the law and formulated his own claims as to divine imperatives. He was to announce before Parliament in 1609 that kings are not only God's lieutenants but that they are gods in their own right who have the power to create or destroy; make or unmake 'at His pleasure', and who are 'accountable to none' (Robinson, 1904-6: 349).

The more pervasive view of this doctrine, however, was secular in nature; as political theorists such as Bodin in his *Republic* and Hobbes in his *Leviathan* argued that monarchical power was justified because the monarch embodied the state, and his authority represented a necessary violation of the powers embodied in common law. Throughout continental Europe the eighteenth century witnessed the virtual elimination of the traditional diffusion of powers and these pluralistic powers were replaced by nation states with centralized and rational authority (Huntington, 1968: 103). Absolute statism was relatively short-lived but it served as a transitional phase toward modernity as nation states continued to rationalize all authority to themselves.

NATIONALISM

In spite of the fact that the nation state is a reality, it must not be assumed that a sense of nationalism exists for that implies highly emotional and mental identification with the nation state. One of the important tasks of a nation is to ensure that a sense of devotion and awe toward itself exists. It has been stated that authority is only legitimate if voluntary compliance to dictates and directives exists. Such accommodation is only ensured if nationalism, which is usually referred to as patriotism, accompanies the objective nation state. Some mechanism must exist to ensure that patriotism is fostered in the hearts and minds of the people.

Three possibilities presented themselves to the leaders of the early nation states: socialization, education and schooling. They could have relied on the socialization process alone which is simply learning by day-to-day experiences. Socialization is the most inclusive teaching environment in any society for it includes both formal and informal learning of skills, knowledge and dispositions necessary to function as a member of a society (Brim and Wheeler, 1966: 3). By informal learning we refer to that which occurs when a child spontaneously interacts with its social environment. Most indigenous language, facial expressions, and eating styles are learned in this way. Persons learn to observe proper rules of behaviour; they model the values and attitudes reflected by parents, siblings, neighbours and others in the social environment.

England was able to rely almost completely on informal learning processes to instil a sense of patriotism mainly because it possessed its own unique identity for centuries prior to the period in which it became an established nation state. Geographically England was separated and isolated sufficiently from continental Europe to establish a sense of cultural identity. Cultural unity being a reality, the press of all social institutions was sufficient to ensure a sense of loyalty and patriotism on the part of the young.

However, such was not the case with the other new nation states. In fact the socialization process merely perpetuated traditional values and usually acted as a brake to a sense of nationalism. These states turned to more formal mechanisms of learning to do the task. Education is distinguished from socialization in that it represents systematic induction of individuals into the values, manners, morals, authority system, vocational skills, and the basic content of civil learning. Education refers to 'the inculcation of standard knowledge and skills by standardized and stereotyped means' (Cohen, 1969: 36).

The educational environments of traditional Europe were primarily nonformal in nature; education was the responsibility of institutions which did not define their main role as being educational. In pre-modern Europe, as well as colonial America, the household carried the major responsibility for the education of the young. As we shall discuss later, the household was the fundamental social unit; it was also the focus of food and manufactured products and even religious life, forming an integral web with the Church and the community (Bailyn, 1960).

With the rise of new trades and guilds, toward the end of the Middle Ages, apprenticeship became a major formalized mechanism of inducting the young into a special craft. The child was entrusted into the bonds of a household master. Criteria for admission as an apprentice were as particularistic as membership criteria for any group membership at large. Since particular families maintained guild membership, their decisions as to whom would be allowed to enter the trade or profession were generally settled on the basis of kinship. Eventually, the system of apprenticeship developed into a definite contract of service. The youth would obligate himself to serve his master for a period of time, usually from six to sixteen years.

In England, the Statute of Apprentices of 1563 established a seven-year period for all servants who would be bound to a master's house to 'serve him diligently, obey "reasonable" commands, keep his master's secrets, protect him from injury, abstain from dice, cards and haunting of taverns, contract no matrimony, commit no fornication' (Charlton, 1965). At the same time, they would be instructed in a trade or craft, and taught to read and write.

Thus, the responsibility for educating fell on the shoulders of parents and masters, though in an organic environment this task was reinforced and completed by community and Church. In the eyes of the youth, it was most difficult to discern where family ceased and community began and instruction in the discipline and values of traditional society was reinforced wherever the child was found.

This skills of a given guild were guarded and kept secret from others and each guild was associated with religious and fraternal rites that drew the young into the functions of the guild by a thorough and secret indoctrination process. If the guild were fostered and encouraged by the state, the values and devotions of the young would only be directed away from the national purposes and toward the values of the guild itself. The major nonformal educational institution, therefore, proved to be as inadequate as socialization to the task of instilling a sense of patriotism.

We turn now to formal education as an option open to early nation states. The institutions which are the site of such instruction we call schools. It is clear that schools are the most specialized of learning environments. In visual form schooling, education, and socialization may be thought of as concentric learning spheres in which education includes schooling, and socialization includes both education and schooling (see Figure 2).

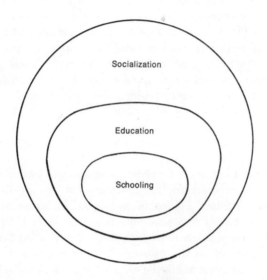

The Relationship of Socialization,
Education and Schooling

Figure 2

MASS SCHOOLING

According to Anthony Wallace (1973: 231),

> school is an institution which deliberately and systematically, by the presentation of symbols in reading matter, lectures, or ritual, attempts to transform from a condition of ignorance to one of enlightenment the intellect, the morality, and the technical knowledge and skills of an attentive group of persons assembled in a definite place at a definite time.

This is obviously a narrow definition of school. The range of deliberateness and systematization extends to the point of planlessness in some schooling environments. Although reading, lectures, and ritual are the primary symbols presented, a wide array of other sources of interaction and communication are also to be found. The objectives of schooling are often more inclusive than the various types of enlightenment spoken of by Wallace, since, for example, the school is often intended to act as a custodial institution for the young; or in highly industrialized settings its purpose includes reducing competition in the labour force by taking large segments of the population out of the labour market. The activities of the school are not necessarily confined to a specific time and place, as they often involve excursions or even community-wide participation. In spite of its narrowness, the definition given by Wallace does highlight the more common elements of schools. The process of schooling typically involves clocks, schedules, lessons, assignments, and quality judgements. The sucessful school child is the one who conforms sufficiently to the demands of this institution.

Without exception nation states have turned to formal schools in order to achieve their purposes. In fact schools are largely creatures of modernity though they existed in some form in most traditional societies. Schools intended to produce leaders and clerics have existed almost from the beginning of recorded history in the West. Other institutions which provided some limited cultural or professional training have also existed from time to time, but institutions whose sole mission was systematically to mould the lives of all the young of a culture are recent indeed.

It would be simplistic to assert that mass schooling was instituted in modernity solely to instil patriotism. The nation state took on many educational tasks which other institutions in traditional societies had carried. Wilhelm Flitner, for example, identifies four main historical roots in the German *Volksschule*. They are: (1) basic skills in reading, writing, and computation; (2) catechetical instruction, or religious and moral indoctrination; (3) enlightened learning in the vernacular; and (4) a patriotic and loyal identity with the Volk or nation state (Flitner, 1941). The primary schools in other Western lands do not have a vastly dissimilar heritage. Each of these sources reflects an historical epoch, the first three existing prior to the modern age. We will discuss briefly each of these for roots of the primary school, and in the process clarify crucial elements of contrast between traditional and modern mass schooling.

Basic Skills

Within the guild framework, schools which were designed to fulfil limited and specific tasks became fairly common. These schools were attached to the crafts which required certain writing or computational skills. In German cities in the fourteenth century, for example, writing craftsmen and notaries, who ran establishments to aid people in preparing letters, documents, bills of sale, etc. would often take youth into their care and apprentice them in their craft. Eventually, writing craftsmen also drew others to them who were interested in learning how to write, for whatever reason, and these people would study with the master until their need for writing skills was satisfied. Craftsmen who supplied computational skills to the town, usually in book-keeping and accounting, would also have their apprentices; in times others who wished to learn computational skills of one kind or another engaged the master to school them until their need was satisfied. Those masters, later to be called schoolmasters, imparted reading skills which were usually regarded as distinct and separate from writing and computational skills.

The distinctions between these different schools were jealously guarded and strict legal and corporate sanctions were established to protect the rights of one type of school against encroachments of one master into the realm of another's craft. In spite of these actions, it was difficult to prevent occurrences such as a reading master's teaching of skills reserved for the writing master (Aries, 1962: 296-97).

Prior to the Reformation, there was little or no universal attempt to systematize the teaching of writing, reading, or ciphering skills as a part of the child-rearing process. It was not expected of any child that it be sent to such a school unless and until it was necessary to use such skills. Consequently, diversity of ages was a dominant feature of all these schools and in many schools adults were often as pervasive as children (Aries, 1962: 297-301). Many children who did not attend school would, nevertheless, incorporate some level of literacy into their lives on their own either by playing with others who already possessed such skills, or by asking for help from an elder.

The main point to be drawn from the discussion thus far is that mass schooling in its early stages was not looked upon as a vital or necessary part of life unless it dealt with skills which were specifically related to the limited number of occupations demanding some capacity for reading, writing or numerical computation. It would even be a mistake to stress the importance of schooling within the total life experience context of those who went to schools. Reading, writing, and calculating were at best technical skills which contributed to the enhancement of life for a small portion of the non-cleric public.

Catechetical Instruction

It was not until the Reformation that schools were established to provide a high percentage of some populations with reading and writing skills. Salvation rather than vocation became the expressed aim of the school. Throughout Lutheran and Calvinist areas of Europe, children, especially those of poor parents, were given the necessary assistance in learning to read so that they could have access to the word of God as found in the scriptures.

Such a requirement as scriptural reading appears to have been a political device in that Luther's initial appeals were to break the bonds of the Church institution by claiming that salvation is a personal, private matter between man and his God. When this weapon turned back on Luther — some Protestants took issue with his beliefs — he resorted to the scriptures as an arbiter of disputes. That such importance was given to the scriptures had enormous implications for education, for it meant that persons must become literate in order to take advantage of the guidance which God had promised them. Luther would argue that the mayors and aldermen should support schools since preaching alone is 'sluggish and weak, and the people finally become weary, and fall away. But a knowledge of the languages renders it lively and strong, and faith finds itself constantly renewed through rich and varied instruction' (Ulich, 1965: 236). The message was clear: in order for faith to wax strong, the scriptures had to be read. Salvation itself was contingent on the ability of the individual to read and be renewed by the recorded word of God.

In spite of the fact that literacy represented an overt intention of elementary schooling at the time of the Reformation, it was almost entirely viewed as a means to a much higher end. Schooling was in no way intended to provide an institution for accumulation to worldly learning or worldly ends, but was intended to support and foster an inner growth, a spiritual awakening. The Christian religion was seen to live through the individual personal relationships with God. Even the Catholic Church believed this to be the case, the difference being that such relationships were only possible through the religious community embodied in the Priesthood and the Church. Luther challenged such authority and directed attention back to individual relationships. In theory Protestantism was anti-institutional, focusing on reflection, the inner world, and the realm of the spirit. Schooling was intended to assist the young in coming to such an awakening. In spite of this, the mode of learning became catechetical and therefore killed the intent.

In colonial America, especially in the Massachusetts colony, schools were as much a part of the scene as anywhere in Europe. Elementary schooling in America was expected to perform more than the limited functions that had been assigned to it in Europe, for the colonists were aware of their separation from centres of culture and the open frontier raised fears that 'degeneracy, barbarism, ignorance and irreligion do by degrees break in upon us' (Mitchell, 1935: 311). Colonists turned to the schools as a way whereby they might help shore up family, Church and community in warding off the threat of barbarism that was so real in the New World.

Enlightened Learning

In the seventeenth century a third mass schooling impulse emerged as a consequence of the Age of Enlightenment, which was largely rationalist, liberal and humanitarian and focused on the capacity of all people to learn and become learned. In contrast to the Reformation, the impulse here was toward learning the things of the world, not ncessarily in opposition to learning the other worldly elements, but in addition to it. The stress was on the ability of each person to become a thinker for himself as characterized by Pestalozzi's *Leonard and Gertrude* in which simple people engage in schooling and become self-sufficient thinkers.

Learning was to be directly related to the personal lives of the people. One consequence of such a focus was that the vernacular was to become the language of study since Latin was viewed as alien to the personal life experience of the common man.   These notions of the Enlightenment would be picked up by later reformers who would proclaim their possibilities within the framework of modern universal schooling programmes, but they would never be fully implemented or tested.

Modern Mass Schooling

Before moving to the unique purpose of mass schooling in the modern world, it is important to note that many elements of the traditional phases mentioned by Flitner form an important component of modern schooling. Basic skills, and especially reading skills, were considered valuable in traditional and modern mass schooling. Significantly, the West has been a party to the written word since the transition of the 'noble warrior' culture to a 'scribe' culture in Greece almost a millennium before the birth of Christ (Marrou, 1956: xiv). Harvey (1966: 628) maintains that most Athenian citizens of the fifth and fourth centuries B.C. were literate ,though evidence for this is conjectural.

The Romans inherited the Greek tradition and disseminated it throughout the empire; still, reading in Rome probably never reached the level of Athens. The so-called 'barbarians' from Germany destroyed much of the reading tradition since they neither possessed such nor appreciated its possibilities. The nobility as well as laymen were also largely illiterate and it was only the Catholic Church which retained some regard for reading during the Middle Ages (Cipolla, 1969: 39-43).

It was not until the thirteenth century as urban life, trade and low level manufacture inspired reading both for functional purposes as well as spiritual enjoyment and cultural emulation, that people attached a negative connotation to illiteracy. The Reformation inspired widespread reading among both peasant and nobility as reading became attached to salvation. Jameson demonstrated that England of the fifteenth and sixteenth centuries was by no means an illiterate society since reading instruction reached even the very small villages (Adamson, 1929). The Continent also witnessed an accelerated progress in literacy. Cipolla (1969: 54-61) suggests that the majority of the people in urban centres were literate, while most in rural areas were illiterate. In some areas literacy among adults was extremely high. Ladurie (1966: 346-947) maintains that in the preindustrial Narbonne area of France, over 90 percent of the bourgeois were literate while only about 65 percent of the urban artisans could read. In premodern United States, Americans were definitely as literate as the people in England and probably more literate than most in Europe (Anderson, 1965: 353).

European countries had generally reached a literacy level sufficient to move into the Industrial Revolution in the eighteenth and nineteenth centuries. Cipolla has suggested that by 1850, 50-55 percent of the Western European population could read, although even at that point a large proportion of those people were functionally illiterate; that is, their acquired reading ability was not terribly helpful to them in performing activities which actually demanded a higher level of proficiency (Cipolla, 1969: 71).

The figures cited by Cipolla correspond with the contemporary findings of modern and Third World areas. Anderson (1965: 357) suggests that a society must attain about 40 percent adult literacy to reach the threshold of modernity. This was largely achieved before the nation state became intensively committed to schooling. Modern mass schools are largely responsible for the further extension of literacy. Bowman and Anderson (1967: 115) have found that economically mature societies maintain a literacy level of at least 90 percent. North America boasts of a literacy level of over 98 percent while Europe is over 96 percent (UNESCO, 1972b).

The example of literacy has only been cited to stress the fact that modern schools have incorporated many aims of traditional schooling programmes. Basic skills have been common to every stage of common schooling we have reviewed. In fact, in the first phase, the major purpose of schooling was the development of such skills while the important pervasive values and learnings were left to the more general social processes. The second phase continued to stress the basic skills even while the school became an important institution to impart things of the spirit. The third phase retained the basic skills orientation while extending the realm of learning to include the mind and man's understanding of the real world.

It is important to note that the ultimate focus of learning in each of these stages includes satisfying the direct personal needs of the individual learner. In the first stage basic skills were not learned unless the individual determined it was necessary and important. There was little or no stigma attached to not learning these skills. They simply represented a peculiar skill for certain people who required them to conduct their affairs of life. Religious indoctrination also centres ultimately on the spiritual development of the individual learner. Even though the Kingdom of God or the institution of the Church may distort such learnings and demand behaviours which are not appropriate to the individual, the ultimate test of religious growth is deeply personal and intimately linked to the enhancement of the human spirit. The enlightenment, too, requires ultimate concentration on the mind. It is deeply introspective; its value cannot be directed anywhere but to the stature of the human being as a reflective, discerning, discovering being.

Quite a different picture emerges in the final impulse of mass education, which determines the unique contribution and major force of modern mass schooling. That impulse moves the importance of schooling beyond the individual, the measure of success being the enhancement of the modern nation state. In contrast to the limited, skills-specific, and diffused schooling in traditional Europe and America, modern schooling is expected to provide an extended, inclusive, and general education to a large mass of society.

Compulsory Education

The most common method whereby universal schooling has been accomplished has been through compulsory education laws which mandate that the young attend school. Even though there are instances in the West of compulsory education in early times, they were rare. The Jewish High Priest, Joshua Ben Gamala, mandated as early as 69 A.D. that every Hebrew village open an elementary school which every boy from the age of six must attend. In 826 A.D., the Council of Pope Eugenius proclaimed the canonical duty of bishops to establish 'masters and teachers who shall assiduously teach grammar schools and the principles of the liberal arts because in these chiefly the commandments of God are manifested and declared' (Leach, 1911: 21).

Scandinavian lands in the sixteenth century required that all who were
confirmed must read and thereby established compulsory reading
instruction if not schooling (Good, 1960: 158).

The main impulse of these mandates was religious. The message
was universal, its working extremely personal. As Wyclif argued,
every man must become a student of theology, not as a profession
but to awaken and to understand the inner life and man's relationship
with God and also to be in a position to read and unravel the mysteries
of the scriptures in order to warn as well as comfort his brother in the
gospel (Winn, 1929: 23).

Prussia was the first major power in Europe to attach great
importance to universal schooling. As early as 1717 King Frederick
William I had issued an edict that all parents send their children to
school. However, the first form of state-regulated schooling came
under King Frederick I who issued the *General-Land-Schul-Reglement*
in 1763, which required children from five until thirteen or fourteen
years of age to attend school and master the basic skills as well as
religion and political indoctrination (Paulsen, 1908: 138).

Following the defeat at Jena in 1806, the Prussians moved to
revitalize the state by instituting vast education reforms, both at
the higher and the primary levels. The pervasive sentiment toward
the masses was to instruct in reading, writing, arithmetic, music,
and religion. More specifically, however, were the moral virtues
of industry, piety, and patriotism which the state schools effectively
imparted to the masses (Tews, 1914).

Instruction during the nineteenth century in Prussia retained its
devotion to religion, but religion was now conceived as a function
of government which would ensure devotion to country. God, King,
and Fatherland were regarded as a trinity, and the authority of each
derived from the same source. Devotion to one reflected devotion to
all. German studies in language, history, music and religion were viewed
as instruments by which loyalty might be gained by the children of
Prussia (Reisner, 1922: 81).

The major continental rival of Prussia was France, where education
on a national scale began in 1791 when the revolutionary government
authorized an educational law with the following foundation clause:
'A system of public instruction shall be created and established, which
is common to all, without cost and indispensable to all men' (Barth,

1967: 464). Later laws mandated compulsory schooling and the establishment of schools themselves. The Lakanal Law of 1794 spelled out the purposes of primary education. Children were to be schooled in reading, writing, arithmetic, civil liberties and morals, French language, patriotism, and nature study. In spite of the fact that the above laws were on the books, slow progress was made in developing schools. In fact, in 1832, of the 38,000 communes in France, 10,400 were completely without schools of any type (Prost, 1968: 94). It was 1833 before Education Minister Guizot, who was moved by the Prussian example, succeeded in bringing about legislation that made a reality of universal primary education.

The state assumed responsibility for providing primary education for all, which was interpreted at that time as mandating schools to exist in communes of 6,000 or more inhabitants; however, compulsory attendance laws were still being resisted. The main claim against such laws was that French citizens valued their freedom too much to submit themselves to such legislation (Guizot, 1860: vol. 3, 61). Such resistance was in reaction to the highly authoritarian Prussian system of education. Compulsory attendance, reflecting traditional values, was seen as a despotic move to destroy family rights and in the process 'procure corporals and sergeants in sufficient number' (Barrau, 1857: 22). The twentieth century had almost begun before state ends became more important than family ends, at which time all children from the ages of six to thirteen were compelled to attend school (Reisner, 1922: 81).

Reisner points out that the main reason for French concern for universal education during the 1880s was a pervasive conviction that the Prussian victory over France in 1870 was because of the former's superior educational programmes. The French were determined to regain national pride and efficiency and to this end they instituted a new curricular focus. Morals and civics replaced the time-honoured instructional programme of morals and religion. All children were henceforth to be socialized toward 'French nationalism and Republican politics' (Reisner, 1922: 83).

In the United States, compulsory school attendance was accepted during the latter half of the ninteenth century. In 1852 Massachusetts became the first state to establish a law which stipulated school attendance age, the days a child must attend each year, how he

might be exempted from public school instruction, and the penalty
for non-compliance. Just as was the case in many European countries,
schools had long been available for anyone wishing to attend, but, as
a legislative commission in Massachusetts was to argue in 1847, 'for
those who, blind to their own interests . . . the State has yet to provide
a compulsory school' (Katz, 1971: 46).

Nearly one-half of the states instituted compulsory education laws
between 1870 and 1890 and shortly after the First World War this
practice was universal in the United States (Steinhilber and Sokolowski,
1966: 3). These laws were intended to ensure that the young of the
land would be educated to be 'orderly, moral, and tractable' (Katz,
1971: 48).

As emigration to the urban centres of the United States took on
enormous proportions, the schools were given the task of
Americanizing the immigrants; this involved a more direct concentration
on political socialization although citizenship training had always been
an integral part of the compulsory schooling process.

Even though the United States demands conformity to certain
basic standards, there is evidence that it does not have a history of
school indoctrination to patriotism which is as intense as countries such
as France, Germany, Russia, or Japan. At the time of the American
revolution capable spokesmen for a uniform, systematic education
came forth to call upon the leaders to remind them, as did Noah
Webster (1970), that

> our national character is not yet formed; and it is an object of vast magni-
> tude that systems of education should be adopted and pursued . . . (which)
> may implant in the minds of American youth, the principles of virtue and of
> liberty; and inspire them with just and liberal ideas of government, and with
> an inviolable attachment to their own country.

In spite of such appeals, education was not viewed by most of the
founding fathers as a necessary instrument in citizen indoctrination.

Reisner examined textbooks of the early period of the United
States and found few references which reflected a definite 'American'
feeling. He claimed the virtues appealed to were those having universal
validity in Christian lands. Political education was seen at that time to
be not American so much as international, though the ideals projected
were of political freedom and justice. As a consciousness of

sectionalism developed over the slavery issue, nationalism was once again subordinated to regional identity. The United States was a land viewed by its inhabitants in negatives. Freedom meant lack of intervention, liberty, individual expression. It was felt that patriotism could not be based on negatives but on direct action and positive forcefulness (Reisner, 1922: 358).

One of the paradoxes of modern education systems is England. The first to industrialize, it lagged behind other Western European countries in terms of state intervention in the educational enterprise. As early as 1833 the English government set aside money from the Treasury which was paid to philanthropic groups for the purposes of educating the poor; however, the government was reluctant to become directly involved and Parliament was even more hesitant to engage in compulsory attendance legislation. The Newcastle Commission report published in 1861 revealed that most of the poor children in England attended school of one kind or another over a period of six to nine years before they entered the work force at the age of twelve or thirteen. However, one-third of those enrolled attended a total of less than 100 days. The Newcastle Commission acknowledged the need for improvement but seemed satisfied that at least three-fifths of the nation's children could pick up the basic skills without conscious difficulty. Their attitude reflected general sentiment, since a survey of parents had impressed them that there was little inclination on the part of the parents to forgo the loss of wages a child could garner in order that the child be in school (Reisner, 1922: 259-60).

The English government finally assumed responsibility to provide schools for all who desired education in 1870, and the Elementary Education Act of 1876 stated that 'it shall be the duty of the parent of every child to cause such child to receive efficient elementary instruction in reading, writing, and arithmetic'. Such a proclamation post-dated a comparable law in Massachusetts by almost 250 years. The government moved quickly to the final step of government involvement in 1880 as nation-wide attendance at school was mandated and ultimately attendance was made free of charge.

English schooling is also relatively mild with regard to patriotic indoctrination. As was explained earlier, England had established a common language, common life styles, and a largely common religion. After the state intervened in schooling, it was able to concentrate more fully on skills and intellectual development than other nation states which were in more formative stages of national consciousness (Wallace, 1973: 233-35).

Those countries which have entered into the modern era during the twentieth century required that their children attend school. In the brief period between 1868 and 1895 Japan moved from a Feudal condition to attain the status of a world power. A uniform, standardized system of education under central control was established in 1886 which made four years of school compulsory (Anderson, 1959: 11).

This law was specifically intended to establish the supremacy of the state in educational affairs. The state would control education and the educational programme would ensure political socialization toward the national virtues of morality, benevolence, righteousness, civility, wisdom and fidelity (Cho, 1956: 35). With the issuance of the Imperial Rescript on Education, traditional worship, loyalty, and filial piety were translated into 'State morals and absolute virtues' whereby patriotism, religion, and family were bound into one united nationalism, and eventually militarism.

Russia was in close contact with the West during the eighteenth and nineteenth centuries and adopted educational institutions resembling European systems of a centralized character, although the level of schooling for the masses was limited. During the period leading up to the Revolution, fundamental reforms were being instituted. In 1898 the government approved a law that would have established universal free compulsory education by 1922, but the war and impending revolution slowed down that achievement.

During the 1920s the government was in constant flux and education in a state of anarchy as an enormous number of experiments were undertaken, most of which failed. As the five-year plans began defining social policy, education became a primary objective and by the time Stalin's 1936 constitution was adopted, state intervention in schooling ensured the right of all citizens to education and 'this right is ensured by universal and compulsory education; by free education up to and including the seventh grade'.

From these examples it is clear that the state now embodies the values appropriate to schooling and the schools have become institutions whereby allegiance and devotion are inculcated in the young. Such a development did not occur without resistance, but eventually the idea of state control became such an integral part of modern ideology that the quality of a nation's education was often determined by the degree to which the nation state had triumphed as the educational authority.

Even the scholars of modern nations have been so infused with the ideology that their scholarship has reflected an assumption of the more the state the better. H.G. Good, would lament as late as 1960, that the school district system in the United States, 'supported by the sentiments of the neighbourhood . . . became a formidable obstacle to educational progress', since it impeded consolidation of authority into more centralized units. Freeman Butts, yet another distinguished educational historian, wrote in 1955 that the district system eventually demonstrated 'its viability to provide adequate schools for all', and he expressed the belief that a more centralized form of control was more democratic. The state had indeed triumphed not only in its drive for power but in the minds of its most enlightened scholars.

In mature modern states we find that schooling has taken on proportions not dissimilar to the commitment of the Christian world toward religion in the premodern world. All children in the modern ᶜtate are expected to attend school for an extended period of time (Illich, 1968). To be modern is to be schooled. Although it is possible to be schooled and not modern, a social imperative of modernity is that one attends school, and the longer the better. Modern nations usually maintain between 15 and 30 percent of their population in school at any given time. In a comparative framework, those areas of the world which are most closely identified with modernity have maintained such a percentage of their population in school over a substantial period of time; whereas the developing areas of the world have not yet achieved such a status.

UNESCO figures from 1953 to 1966 (Table 1) clearly indicate this situation: we note that North America, Europe, Oceania (including Australia and New Zealand) and the USSR have maintained at least 15 percent of their population in school since the early 1950s. Those isolated countries outside North America and Europe which have reached economic maturity as defined by Rostow also maintain high schooling levels. For example, the total enrolment in Japan was 24.1 percent of the total population in 1970 (UNESCO, 1972a: V).

There is some evidence that such high enrolment ratios in modern

Table 1
Percent of Population Attending School

	1953	1957	1960	1966
World total	11.6	12.8	14.0	16.4
Africa	5.3	7.1	7.8	9.7
North America	16.3	(18.0)	24.5	27.3
South America	11.2		14.8	18.0
Asia	9.6	11.1	11.4	14.0
Europe	14.8	16.0	16.6	17.8
Oceania	17.4	20.3	23.1	20.7
USSR	17.3	16.0	17.6	22.0

Source: UNESCO (1972a).

nations are not post-Second World War phenomena. The USSR, which moved quickly into modernity, averaged less than 5 percent of their population in school in 1887, and forty years later this figure was 12 percent. Germany, England, Scandinavia, The Netherlands, and Belgium had reached 12 percent by 1850, while the United States was maintaining 18 percent of its population in the middle of the last century. The only non-Western countries known to have reached 12 percent prior to 1928 were Argentina (14 percent) and Japan (13 percent) (Easterline, 1965: 422-29).

Such gross figures, however, are often misleading for they present us little information as to the relative data with regard to actual school attendance. Since the United States has led the world in enrolment figures for over a century, it might be helpful to assess certain factors which provide greater insight than gross population figures.

Let us begin with a look at population growth since 1850. From Table 2 we see that in 1850 there were 23 million people living in the United States. During the next 50 years the population grew to almost 76 million people, which represented an average increase of over 10 million people in each decade. Even though the increase in the number of people each decade was relatively constant, the percentage of increase declined almost every decade.

With respect to percent increase in school enrolments, no solid

Table 2

The Number of Inhabitants and Enrolled School Pupils and the Percent Increase over each Previous Decade

Number of Inhabitants (in thousands)		Percent Increase	Total Enrolment	Percent Increase
1971			59,397	20.9
1961			47,025	34.7
1950	150,697	14.5	30,704	3.9
1940	131,669	7.2	29,539	0.3
1930	122,775	16.1	29,430	18.7
1920	105,711	14.9	23,876	17.6
1910	91,972	21.0	19,727	13.1
1900	75,995	20.7	17,092	14.6
1890	62,948	25.5	14,636	31.5
1880	50,156	30.1	9,983	31.0
1870	38,558	22.6	6,924	
1860	31,443	35.6		
1850	23,192	35.9		

Source: U.S. Bureau of the Census (1960, 1973).

figures are available until after 1870, since the U.S. Office of Education (known originally as the U.S. Department of Education) which was responsible for school statistics was not established until 1867. We see From Table 2 that since 1870 the difference between the percent increase of the total population and the percent increase in school enrolment fluctuated in twenty-year cycles until 1970. Even with this fluctuation the population increase percentages correspond roughly with the total school enrolment increase percentages.

Still another question which is critical in our discussion is the relative percent of youth in a given population. In Table 3 we see that the percent of population under 14 years of age and between 14 and 24 years of age has remained fairly constant during this century, and in fact, it declined slightly between 1900 and 1957.

The percent of population five to seventeen years of age enrolled in school steadily increased from 1850 to 1930. As we see in Table 4,

Table 3

Population Figures and the Percentage of the Total Population
Under 14 Years of Age and Between 14 and 24 Years of Age

	Total (in thousands)	Under 14	Percent Population Under 14	14-24	Percent Population Between 14-24
1957	171,229	49,206	28.7	25,502	15.2
1953	159,636	43,148	26.9	24,204	15.8
1950	151,683	38,605	25.7	24,458	16.4
1940	132,122	30,521	23.5	26,454	19.7
1930	123,077	33,638	27.6	24,852	20.3
1920	106,466	31,756	29.2	20,858	19.8
1910	92,407	27,806	29.3	20,024	21.7
1900	76,094	24,581	31.6	16,514	22.3

Source: U.S. Bureau of the Census (1960).

in 1850 less than half the school-aged children were enrolled in school.
By the turn of the century this figure had reached 70 percent. The enrolment figures held relatively constant through the depression and
the Second World War but began to climb sharply in the post-war
period. By 1971 an astronomical 98.4 percent of school-aged children
were enrolled in school. Most of this increase can be accounted for
by the extension of schooling. In 1870 only 2 percent of the 17-year-
olds received a high school certificate as opposed to over 75 percent
of the 18-year-olds in 1971.

From the United States experience it is impossible to speak of
optimal enrolment levels in a country. As enrolment levels were maximized in primary school, substantial growth moved to secondary
levels, and as secondary school enrolments were maximized, substantial
growth moved to higher levels. In spite of the fact that almost all the
school-aged youth were in school by 1961, the enrolment percentage
increase has continued to climb during the past decade because of
dramatic increases in higher education. In 1870 only 1.7 percent of the

Table 4

Enrolments of the School-Aged
Population Between 1850 and 1971

	Total Enrolment	Enrolment Population 5 to 17-Year-Olds (%)	Average Length of School Term	Attended/ Enrolled Pupils	Percent High School Graduates Compared to 17-Year-olds
1971	52,133	98.4			75.9*
1961	45,660	94.5			69.3*
1950	28,492	81.6	177.9	157.9	59.0
1940	28,045	85.3	175.0	151.7	50.8
1930	28,329	81.3	172.7	143.0	29.0
1920	23,278	77.8	161.9	121.2	16.8
1910	19,372	73.5	157.5	113.0	8.8
1900	16,854	72.4	144.3	99.0	6.4
1890	14,479	68.6	134.7	86.3	3.5
1880	9,867 (pub)	65.5	130.3	81.1	2.5
1870	6,872 (pub)	57.0	132.2	78.4	2.0
1860		50.6 (5-19)			
1850		47.2 (5-19)			

*18-year-olds.
Source: U.S. Bureau of the Census (1960, 1973).

18-21 age group was in college. This figure had climbed to almost 30 percent by 1950 and had almost reached 55 percent by 1971 (Table 5).

As we mentioned earlier, factors other than enrolment percentages and proportion are important in providing a complete picture of the role of schooling in the lives of modern youth. From Table 4 we see that the average length of the school year has been extended from 132 days in 1870 to almost 178 days in 1950. In other words, more children now attend school, and they expect to attend more months of the year than previous generations. If we observe actual attendance figures, the impact is even more significant. Children who attended school in 1870 were only there approximately 78 days of the year, whereas by 1950 those attending averaged 158 days per year. In other words, in

Table 5

Enrolment in College as Compared with the Number of People Between the Ages of 18 and 21 from 1870 to 1971

1971	8,116	54.2
1961	3,861	37.2
1950	2,659	29.9
1940	1,494	15.68
1930	1,101	12.4
1920	598	8.0
1910	355	5.1
1900	238	4.0
1890	157	3.0
1880	116	2.7
1870	52	1.7

Source: U.S. Bureau of the Census (1960, 1973).

1950 an average child missed only 20 school days per year as opposed to 54 missed school days in 1870. In a typical five-day school week this would amount to almost exactly two days out of school in 1870, whereas in 1950 a typical child missed only one day every two weeks.

From the United States example it is clear that schooling has not reached an optimal level but that a characteristic of schooling in this modern nation is that enrolment figures continue to expand in terms of (1) the percentage of young people who are in school; (2) the number of years children are expected to attend; and (3) the days per year children actually do attend. Add to this the traditional feature of diffusing the limited schooling through household, guild, Church and community, and we arrive at a monolithic state-dominated institution that occupies an enormous segment of a youth's life. Gone is the cohesive and organic union of education for the masses through life itself and in its place is an institution separated from anything close to natural social communities reflecting basic social necessities.

So ingrained in the minds of state subjects is the notion of extended universal schooling that it has until recently been defended as a modern human imperative. So strongly has the modern world become committed to compulsory schooling that it was included in the Declaration of the Rights of Children in 1959 by the United Nations. That declaration stipulates that the child has the right to receive schooling, which shall be 'free and compulsory' at least on the primary level. During the UN deliberations a Belgian minister to the commission protested. 'A right presupposes a certain freedom,' he said, 'I apologize for this weakness I have for logic, but how does one become entitled to an obligation.' He proceeded, however, to vote with everyone else in favour of the statement (*N.Y. Times*, 8 April 1959).

Even though attendance at school has not yet become universal, its virtues have been largely unquestioned and heroic efforts have been undertaken to achieve it. In those developed areas of the world the last remaining pockets of people who remain outside of state control are slowly being incorporated. One example will suffice. In France specific legislation was enacted in 1966 which was intended to bring the children of Nomads under the compulsory attendance regulations by stipulating that the children must attend school where they are staying 'even when their stay in said locality does not exceed half a day'. About 20 percent of the Nomad children were attending school in 1966 and it approached 100 percent within five years. The average stay of these children in each school is less than five days, and since they attend 140 days each year, they average about 30 schools a year. The state has taken the position that such an existence is a wretched way of life, and that 'leniency toward infringements of the law are not to be regarded as an indication of good will toward these families, but rather as a poor understanding of their interests' (Fohr, 1969: 12). In other words, the interests of the Nomads are seen to be best served when they coincide with the interests of the state.

EDUCATIONAL ADMINISTRATION ARRANGEMENTS

As sovereign states emerged the education came increasingly under state control, it became imperative to develop some mechanism to support and administer educational programmes. Many different administrative forms can exist within sovereign states, including those which existed in traditional societies, in which case, however, the frame of reference is unquestionably altered. The administrative forms developed within the nation state may be highly centralized, such as in France, or decentralized as in Switzerland; still, the authority rests with the state organization be it centralized or decentralized and is diffused to other institutions only in so far as the state allows or mandates others to possess such authority. The degree of administrative decentralization is secondary to the main issue of authority consolidation in the form of the nation state, but even so, it remains highly important and characterizes a major aspect of the modern schooling bureaucracy.

A most perceptive distinction as to how state administrative arrangements with regard to education might be exercised was recently made by Michael Katz. He pointed out four alternatives which were at play in the United States as it moved into modernity. These were paternalistic voluntarism, democratic localism, corporate voluntarism, and incipient bureaucracy (Katz, 1971).

Significantly, the first three of these alternatives were characteristic of different forms of educational support and control which existed in traditional Europe and which form part of the American historical legacy, while the fourth was characacteristic of modern education. As Katz fails to clarify this traditional-modern distinction, we shall attempt to do so in this chapter, by discussing briefly the four types of support and control.

Corporate Voluntarism

Katz defines corporate voluntarism as the 'conduct of *single* institutions as individual corporations operated by self-perpetuating boards of trustees and financed either wholly through endowment or through a combination of endowment and tuition' (Katz, 1971: 22). Traditional European education possesses a heritage deeply turned to corporate voluntarism as an approach pertaining to the elites who desired to perpetuate and enhance high culture. It must be remembered that most aristocratic education was informal and conducted in the household of a master or usually in the manorial household of a relative. Such a condition should not imply that little intentional learning took place, for traditional European society, and traditional societies in general, are far from primitive. The elites of traditional cultures have always fostered a 'high' culture which existed alongside or intermeshed with the more broadly based 'little' culture, as Redfield called it. High culture has usually been linked in some way to religious dogma and ritual, though not exclusively so. It was certainly not the case in classical Greece or in the pre-Christian Roman Empire. In the West during the millennium following the establishment of the Catholic Church, high culture was inextricably linked to religion.

Secondary schooling in the Middle Ages in Europe was a haphazard affair, but that which existed was largely under the control of the Church and served the clerical needs of the Church. As the Western world emerged from the grip of the Medieval world and witnessed the growth of humanism, the nobility and their courts, the feudal chiefs, and rich merchants also came to sponsor systematic programmes of cultural and personal refinements, and a growing number of boys went to these schools rather than being placed as an apprentice in another master's household.

The grammar schools and the rhetoric schools of Europe which were established from the Middle Ages to the Industrial Revolution were almost exclusively endowed institutions. The original endowments were made largely by the Church. During the Middle Ages monasteries and Bishop's seats engaged from time to time in training schools, mainly to prepare clerics to perform the offices of the Church. Such a commitment grew as Europe emerged from the darkness of the age into the Renaissance when wealthy citizens, and others, assumed responsibility for providing schools. Usually, those representatives of the Church, gentry, and aristocracy who endowed a school would become independent trustees of the school which meant that they would govern its programme, hire its master, provide facilities, and set fees for the boys, or hire someone to perform those functions. Though the school might enter into voluntary association with other schools, its trustees dictate its main structure and purpose.

In Europe, these schools eventually came under the control of the state and became the essential exclusive secondary schooling institutions, whereas in England they remained independent of the state and even moved away from religious ties. Winchester was the earliest school that has survived into the present day as William of Wykeham established a school consisting of a 'warden and seventy poor scholars', in 1379 (Carlisle, 1818: 452). In its long history it has received large endowments, the first coming from Wykeham himself, who devoted ecclesiastical revenues which he had received from several posts with the Church. Other early schools are also on record (e.g. Eton in 1440), but it was the Reformation which inspired the rapid development of schools. Over three hundred schools have been identified which would fit this characteristic. Support came from Anglican parishes, dissenting religious groups, and private endowments of wealthy, middle-class patrons.

As England entered the modern age, elite grammar schools entered a new era of expansion mainly because of the change in the structure of elite society in England. The aristocracy were forced to begin sharing their power with the emerging middle class who were no longer content to be led. Recruitment to positions of leadership fell prey to open competition among the most qualified, and in the process the endowed institution took a new major role: to ensure that the leaders of society from whatever social origin might have the values and character befitting of the elite in English society (Weinberg, 1967: 34-52).

These public schools stand alone today as the gate-keepers of the privileged classes in England. In relative terms, the state has taken over the job of mass schooling, but the endowed institutions still model English 'high' culture.

The English endowed school also left its legacy in America beginning in the seventeenth century. In the south, the notion of household education was retained for the very wealthy, but several endowed schools were also established as wealthy patrons supported exclusive schools through gifts, land, produce, and livestock. In the north, where Calvinism was pervasive, the frontier was too threatening to tolerate informal education. In such conditions as one found in Boston in 1635, there was little if any separation between Church and state. The town meetings were devoted to matters relating both to the preservation of faith and secular matters. Massachusetts instituted compulsory education, but not compulsory attendance, in 1642, and in 1647 this law was reversed as compulsory schooling but not compulsory attendance was established. This law ordered every town having at least 50 households to establish an elementary school, and every town having 100 households to establish a grammar school as well. Since there were no provisions in the law as to how these schools would be supported, a variety of mechanisms came into existence. Income from the sale of lands, private endowments, local taxes, rates or tuition fees, lotteries, liquor licences, and contributions were some

of the ways, but since most of these schools came under the jurisdiction of a town, control of the school became a governmental,
rather than a trustee, function.

In spite of the trend toward town and governmental control,
endowed schools continued to exist, though in dwindling numbers.
J.P. Gulliver, in 1857, argued strongly that endowed schools would
provide institutions of the 'highest character', led by 'enlightened
men', and secure children from contact with others of 'vulgar
manners and vicious habits', and these schools would ultimately
'contribute greatly to the growth and prosperity' of the entire
community (Gulliver, 1956: 655-94).

Thus, coincidental with the rise of public education came a
resurgence of independent schools. The academy, which had developed
in New England in the mid-1700s spread west, and in the twentieth
century the growth of country day and boarding schools continued,
though in comparison with public schools they play a rather
insignificant role. Corporate voluntarism is still evidenced in the
United States though it is found mainly in private institutions of
higher learning since preparatory schooling has been largely taken
over by the state.

Whereas corporate voluntarism was the main mechanism for
satisfying the needs of elite education, democratic localism and
paternal voluntarism were designed to satisfy the demands for mass
education and programs for the poor in traditional America and
Europe. Let us first turn to democratic localism.

Democratic Localism

Katz refers to local school districts or community schools when he
speaks of democratic localism (Katz, 1971: 15). We have already
noted that this system dominated colonial New England, but its roots
were as much in the state-Church relationship of Calvinist Protestants as
they were in the threatening New England frontier. Democratic
localism is one administrative form which emerged as mass education
became critical at the time of the Reformation. Protestantism held that
everyone should use the scriptures as a basis of abiding by God's word
and exercising faithful and public devotion. Calvin established the

model in Geneva where the Church and city state entered into a contract to govern mutually and to educate the young by cooperative administration.

In the sixteenth century Geneva was a free republic which was ruled by its own elected city council. This council, which was dominated by businessmen, invited Calvin to become the appointed head of Church. In spite of a brief interlude when Calvin was banished from Geneva, he was able to establish a close working relationship with the council and eventually became the dominant moral and conduct force in the city; nevertheless, he was there by invitation and ruled the state Church by consent of the council.

This example was retained as Calvinism moved into Holland, England, Scotland, Switzerland, Hungary, Poland, and colonial New England. The traditional-modern transition form of school support and control became one of civil-ecclesiastical partnership. Such a relationship was dominant in the Calvinist pockets of these countries through the sixteenth, seventeenth, and eighteenth centuries with regard to primary education and even affected the secondary grammar school in many regions (Medlin, 1964: 64).

Switzerland, even to this day, has retained a radical decentralization policy. All twenty-five cantons have their own director of education, but the authority is further localized as each community maintains its own school commission consisting in part of lay members who conduct regular open public hearings in which the people themselves are allowed to determine policy.

The notion that the township was responsible for education was ideally suited to the frontier situation of colonial America, because the people usually settled in small isolated areas. As the spirit of democracy and localism evolved in New England, civil demands were made, especially in settlements which were attached legally to a township, but which retained a degree of autonomy such that if they wished to establish their own school or at least if they were to support the schools, its services were to extend also to them. The typical solution to this problem was the moving school, whereby a school master would move from community to community and teach the children on a rotation basis, thus complying with the law which required a school, but providing for local schooling to take place without enormous expense (Small, 1914: 64).

Eventually, the more affluent sections of townships chose to establish their own school with a separate master. A legal step was taken as early as 1766 in Connecticut which allowed the towns 'to divide themselves into proper and necessary districts for keeping their schools, and to alter and regulate the same from time to time'. Such laws facilitated the development of school districts with their own taxation powers and their own governing bodies.

The school district system was the major authority system of town schools until the middle of the nineteenth century. A trustee or a separate board of trustees existed for each school, which was almost always a one-roomed institution. These boards maintained the broadest of powers as they levied taxes, set the length of the school year, set terms for buildings and their repairs, determined curriculum, purchased textbooks, certified and employed the teacher. Much of this changed as the district became subject to state control. The main function of the state became one of ensuring that certain minimum standards were maintained, though districts continued to work within these constraints.

Paternalistic Voluntarism

As long as the world has had monarchs with a sense of noblesse oblige, the world has been the recipient of paternalistic voluntarism. Charlemagne (742-814) exemplifies such a man who maintained that learning and religion were important, though not necessarily for himself, and so he gathered around him the most cultivated and schooled individuals of his empire and turned his court into a citadel of high culture. In England, Alfred, King of Wessex, who ruled in the ninth century also set about educating the sons of his noblemen and set into motion the establishment, through his graciousness and wisdom, of a system of schools for the elect of his subjects.

However, wide-scaled paternalistic voluntarism in schooling came about in the West mainly at the time of the Reformation. In Germany Luther appealed to the princes of the various duchies which had sided with him against the Catholic Church to assume responsibility for the civil as well as the ecclesiastical education of their subjects. These secular authorities were called upon to support and oversee schooling since Luther possessed no other means of financial support. However, the task of actually running the schools and doing the teaching was left in the hands of the pastors and even the sextons. Such an appeal indicates overtones of incipient bureaucracy, but nationalistic states were to emerge before such a concept became fully operative (Ulich, 1965: 218-49).

As the West moved toward modernity, paternalistic voluntarism became more and more linked with schooling for the poor, and with the advent of industrialism and the emergence of a class consciousness such a mode of sponsorship became linked with charity and Christian generosity on the part of the wealthy toward those who had none. The charity school movement in England exemplifies such an orientation.

This movement began in the seventeenth century in Wales where Thomas Gouge (1609-1681) had come after he had lost his pastorate in London because he had turned Puritan. He gained permission to evangelize and educate the people of Wales. Eventually, a society was formed and costs of the enterprise were met through subscription.

In Anglican circles an elite philanthropic organization which called itself the 'Society for the Promotion of Christian Knowledge' was formed in 1698 to aid in religious education for the poor, but also to help girls learn to sew, spin, and knit while boys were to apprentice in a trade. Charity schools were financed by subscription and from the proceeds of annual 'charity sermons'.

Still another expression of paternalistic voluntarism came not only in terms of education because of the compelling forces for salvation, but because of the growing industrial needs of certain lands in Europe. England was especially active in fostering industrial education for the poor, as charity schools were fostered by merchants and certain charitable foundations.

The aim of the charity schools was almost completely disciplinary: 'to rescue the masses and to ensure their obedience' (Dobbs, 1919: 91).

The mechanism through which this movement gained impetus was not only via religious philanthropy but also from merchants and fledgling industry, though federal groups did appeal to the public for financial support in exchange for certain individual rights of control of school programmes and personnel.

During the nineteenth century in England a number of Christian societies were established which provided elementary schools for the children of their followers. Government participation was restricted to grants to the largest Anglican education societies. Even though the government belatedly entered into the running of schools, a semblance of paternalistic voluntarism was retained as voluntary agencies were assured of grants-in-aid, though the grants depended on the recommendation of the state inspector. The 1902 Education Act further restricted voluntary jurisdiction as these groups came directly under the control of local education authorities, though they were allowed to provide religious instruction.

The impact of paternalistic voluntarism was felt very early in colonial America. The 'Society for the Propagation of Christian Knowledge in Foreign Parts' was by far the most active educational institution in the eighteenth century as it worked among the non-English, the Indians, the Negroes, as well as the poor English (Cremin, 1970: 341-56).

This was not the only society of that nature in the United States. The New York Public School Society was very active at the beginning of the nineteenth century in advocating free schools for the poor to be financed at public expense, but run by the clergy or Church trustees who, having no other desire than 'to serve mankind' but 'without money and without price', will ensure better accomplishment than from professionally selected people (Katz, 1971: 8-9). Paternalistic voluntarism extended beyond the early days of American educational development and has been highlighted in two major eras in the last 100 years. Emigration and urbanization were two critical factors which led to the cries of journalists and muckrakers of the 1890s to begin cleaning up the wretchedness and squalor of the large industrial city. One of the spearheads for reform was the settlement movement, as over 400 houses were created by 1910 in the heart of poverty in the largest cities. Jane Addams and Ellen Gates Starr exemplified the movement as they set up shop at Hull House in Chicago to care for the social, health, recreational, and educational needs of the immigrant poor, and they appealed to the good will of the wealthy to pay for its costs.

The second major paternalistic voluntary movement of the last century followed the Second World War as the plight of the minorities in the country entered the consciousness of the white population. By then, however, education had become the domain of the state, and paternalism pertained mainly to volunteer manpower sacrifices or efforts on the part of people to bring about a greater governmental commitment to the minorities such as the Black and Mexican-American communities.

State Bureaucracy

As we have noted, democratic localism, corporate voluntarism, and paternalistic voluntarism are all administrative creatures of the traditional West and represented the diffuse state of education in that they were all functioning to one degree or another simultaneously and did not coalesce into any meaningful whole but consisted of patchwork support and control arrangements. With the emergence of the nation state, these enterprises were eventually concentrated under the authority of the state. Various administrative models emerged which nation states adopted to ensure that public schools be established and maintained, but also to ensure that a certain standard and conformity be maintained in those schools which continued to be run outside their direct administrative jurisdiction.

France is the most obvious example of an early modern country which established a highly centralized structure. This structure came into being following the French revolution when Napoleon declared himself the absolute ruler of the land and eventually forced his dictatorship on the affairs of all of education. For Napoleon the schools were to be the instruments through which loyalty to the imperial monarchy would be ensured. He had achieved the objective entity of the nation state through a power struggle, but it would be the task of education to achieve a sense of nationalism, which could only exist in the minds of the people. Even so, Napoleon did not conceive of the schools as instruments of mass indoctrination but as training grounds for future leaders. Therefore almost no attention was given to primary schools but rather to such institutions as military schools, colleges and lycées, engineering and mining schools.

The most extreme decrees were made in 1808 at which time Napoleon declared that an imperial university was to be formed which was to govern all education throughout France. 'No schools, no establishment of instruction whatsoever', he insisted, 'may be set up outside the imperial university and without the authorization of its head.'

The school system which he conceived was patterned after the military which he had found to be so successful in propelling him to the position of emperor. As in all military systems special uniforms were devised which would symbolize membership but also rank and position. Discipline was as demanding as in the army; all members were subject to severe regulations concerning behaviour and interpersonal relationships. There were divisions corresponding to companies, battalions and regiments, with appropriate officers and drill masters who would follow directives which were processed through well-defined channels of authority.

Even though some liberalization was observed in the decades following this decree at the middle of the century, Napoleon III re-established the autocratic framework his uncle had established, though he did make greater allowance for the existence of private schooling. The French have since relied on political and Civil Servant leadership to give substance to the schools. Even today there is essentially no local lay participation in school decisions, although the process of decision-making has become more diffused because of participation of three different bodies. A permanent Civil Service staff is organized in major divisions in the government; a professional teachers association has representation in policy decisions, and a tightly supervised inspectorate coordinates programmes throughout the country. There is no question that the French administrative organization has moved away from the Napoleonic model and has evolved a more liberal working structure, but it remains a highly centralized mechanism with regional bodies whose main function is to carry out the directives of the central administration. France does not stand alone with a modern centralized administration. For example, as Japan entered the modern age she moved quickly toward centralization and by 1890 the schools were highly standardized, even to the point of lesson content and units of instruction. By 1932 all textbooks were prepared by the government and centralization reached a level comparable to that of Napoleon a century earlier. After the Second World War, however, a new system was instituted, patterned after the American system, which distributed the control to prefectural and regional communities having elected boards of education and left the central ministry of education with advisory and coordination capacity rather than with authority to issue directives (Kaigo, 1965: 116-23).

In America at the time of the revolution, education was not seen as an important instrument of citizen indoctrination, as in France and Japan, although the federal government participated early after its birth in land grant support of schools. However, by the middle of the century education had taken on extended dimensions under the authority of the individual states. The colonial tradition of local community control was retained as state legislatures delegated most powers to school districts which conducted the school programmes as a privilege; however, the individual states constitutionally retained the authority.

The structure required by such demands placed education under the control of a state central board with a supervisory and professional framework appropriate to ensure that the state aims would be met. Such a task would not have been ensured had a more traditional administrative form been adopted.

The highly centralized French structure, which emerged following the French revolution and which set about to subject Feudalistic, ecclesiastical, and aristocratic powers under the sovereign state, established the tone for new socialist and Third World nations in the twentieth century which are striving toward modernity. But the decentralized American model seems to have been more typical of early modern nations, for we find that a large number of Western nations which emerged into modernity at earlier stages have evolved decentralized systems. A review of the 110 countries which were represented in the UNESCO *World Survey of Education* of 1965-66 or 1966-67 reveals that only about 10 percent of the nations have genuine decentralized administrative structures; included in this small list are Canada, the Federal Republic of Germany, Switzerland, the United Kingdom (England and Wales, Scotland, Northern Ireland), Australia, and the United States.

Almost without exception the other modern European nations have some regionally decentralized system rather than a highly centralized one. This might be explained by historical factors. Before the turn of this century communications networks and other technical advances were so undeveloped that administrative units had to be small. Even so, as we have seen, the establishment of state control in America represented an enormous centralization process prior to the middle of the last century. England also experienced administrative consolidation as the first Board of Education was established in 1899 though it exercised little power. More important was the 1902 Education Act which replaced 2,568 local school boards by 328 local education authorities (Armytage, 1970: 186).

Once the formal administrative structure became established, tradition would dictate that little change could be anticipated. In spite of formal decentralization in so many mature modern states, the important historical process of this century has been the growing centralization of functions and administrative decisions.

In the United States, for example, federal involvement in education has become almost geometric in nature. The original Federal Bureau of Education (1868) had the sole task of statistical collection and has grown to encompass federal expenditures rivalled only by the Department of Defense. The federal government began to provide funds to subsidize schooling programmes which would otherwise have been neglected. These usually dealt with the more practical studies. The first such outlay came even before the Bureau had been established as public land was set aside for 'land grant colleges' which would foster agricultural and mechanical studies. Subsequent provisions came for agricultural and home-making subsidies in the high schools. Further funds came for activities which complemented studies, such as health, school lunches, and playgrounds; in the post-Second World War era the federal government has literally taken over the job of compensatory education as highlighted by such legislation as the Economic Opportunity Act of 1964. The Elementary and Secondary Education Act of 1965, probably the most important federal school legislation, has established the federal government as the dominant force in public schooling, even though it continues to have no legal responsibility or authority to do so.

The process of administrative centralization that we have observed in countries such as the United States and England has been accompanied by other nationalizing forces outside government. The impact of these forces has been further to reduce local, isolated control and place it in distant, anonymous hands. We shall mention three sources of such influence in mature modern systems of education.

First, a professional body has evolved which makes increasing demands on the way in which policy is determined as well as implemented. Many of these demands are self-serving, concentrating on status, security and financial advantage, while others are strictly of a pedagogical nature.

Secondly, administrators and policy-makers have come to rely on the input of specialists. These specialists do include professional educators but also researchers, management consultants, business administrators, economists, statisticians, and lawyers. The most apparent recent mechanism for specialist input is in the form of regional and national educational planning.

Thirdly, private enterprise has become interested in education as a business venture and has increasingly engaged in the production and sale of instructional materials such as audio-visual aids, books, and equipment; it also offers total instructional packages for curricular programmes in reading, mathematics, etc. Recently some business-minded people have engaged in setting up private programmes of schooling in competition with the public domain, not for ideological purposes as was the case in traditional and early modern times, but for financial gain. The examination industry is still another example of the involvement of private enterprise in education.

Each modern society has experienced some level of participation of all three forces but it has also created for itself distinctive working relationships between the various forces. One society gives greater weight to specialists and private enterprise, while another relies on specialists and professionals; still another sets an interplay in process with all factors coming heavily into play. With the emergence of these factors, one major consequence has resulted: the constellation of these forces, regardless of their relative importance, has resulted in administrative functions that ameliorate any extremes that may have originally existed in the formal administrative structure.

This is the case with both centralized and decentralized systems. Planning in France is no longer a matter of political fiat but undergoes extensive review and recommendations of specialists and educators. The Nuffield Foundation in England, as well as Ford, Carnegie, Rockefeller and countless other foundations in the United States, often determine the course of certain spheres of education as much as any administrative decree. Sweden relies heavily on pedagogical research outcomes in establishing educational policy. It should now be obvious that the formal administrative structure must be considered as a part of a total control mechanism, which in mature centralized systems has moved away from highly autocratic administrative posture toward a more tolerant, though distant, mechanism of control; whereas mature decentralized systems have moved toward a nationalization of the educational enterprise.

THE DECLINE OF STATE SOVEREIGNTY

The period of modernity is marked by the establishment and rapid expansion of nation states which have been able to centralize diffused authority to themselves within the national boundaries. It began in Europe toward the end of the eighteenth century with approximately ten nations, spread to English-speaking colonies, then to Latin America, Asia, and is in the process of establishing itself in Africa. By the end of the First World War approximately seventy nation states were in existence; with the establishment of the United Nations this figure grew to almost one hundred. Even as the trend of new nations continues, new forces are at work which give every indication that the very fabric of the mature modern political world is unravelling. Such a pronouncement does not suggest that the process of nation state development will cease. The number of new nations continues to rise as colonies and sprawling empires of the past become history.

Goodlad (1975: 249) is correct in stressing that 'many states which have not yet experienced the potency of full nationhood are not likely to sacrifice their ambitions for a blueprint of sovereignty of human-kind' or any other blueprint for that matter. It is true that the developing areas will continue to strive toward modernity. So much change has already occurred in the Third, Fourth, and Fifth World that mature modern nations have been forced to align themselves into con-stellations that have required relinquishing some state authority (Barraclough, 1964). Our concern in this essay is not with all nations, however, but with those which have achieved mature modernity. Absolute sovereignty, which is so dominant in modernity is giving way as mature modern nation states are being forced to share authority not only with international but with internal, local forces.

Internationally, the political world has already transcended autonomous nation state status and has been formed into great federations of regional blocks vastly different from large nation states of the past. For example, in Eastern Europe the interplay of nationalism, international communist ideology and Soviet hegemony have created relationships that force continual stress and compromise with regard to strict national interests in countries such as Russia, Rumania, Hungary, Yugoslavia, and Poland. We already speak of Third, Fourth and Fifth World alignments as if they were political realities. The most recent world divisions have been between oil-producing and oil-consuming nations. Each year brings about new points of difference dealing with poverty, population and pollution; these have so reduced the past ideological conflicts between mature modern nations that they appear now as squabbles between family members.

The conventional sense of nationalism is being shaken in mature countries through the inflow of immigrants and 'guest workers' who have unsettled the sense of cohesion, common language and values that have long been taken for granted. In England, the influx of immigrants from the West Indies, Africa and Asia has brought with it the most critical social dilemma of that country as it wavers between efforts of assimilation or integration.

In the past fifteen years Western Europe has witnessed the establishment of a 'guest worker' force consisting of approximately 10 percent of the labour force in the mature countries. These workers are now established and have spouses and growing numbers of children. In some German communities immigrants account for as many as one-third of all births. Schooling, with its historic indoctrination mission toward nationhood, is torn with regard to the defintion of its mission with these multitude of peoples.

The most significant element of the recent period has been the realization that the nation state as a unit was incapable of dealing adequately with the innovations brought about by science and technology. As we shall see in later chapters, the technological society, which has surpassed industrial society with its nuclear power, electronic developments, and automated production processes, has created relationships and standardization that make national autonomy seem an obsolete concept.

In spite of these developments, a single world union does not seem likely. Robert Heilbroner (1975: 110) has recently suggested that the psychology of 'us' and 'them' is probably so fundamental to human nature that such a political condition will not occur. A child tends to divide the world into two parts: 'one comprised of its subsequent extension of that family; the other nonfamilial beings who may exist as human objects but not as human beings with whom an identificatory bond is possible'. The nation state has been able to mobilize people of the most varied backgrounds into unified groups identifying one another as extended family, just as tribes and clans of traditional society were able to do. This identification process is unable to include all of mankind, however, because the world must remain, for Heilbroner at least, a division of two in some form or other. The fact that nations divide, break up or expand their boundaries is not as crucial here as the assumption that nationalism has been able to call forth a feeling of oneness with the national group and elicit a feeling of strangeness toward anyone not of that group who thus is treated as 'merely an object and not a person' (1975: 112). This does not mean that the nation state must be retained since it is only one alternative among a multitude of authority constellations that could exist and include the psychological division identified by Heilbroner.

World integration trends are not only those which are threatening the autonomy of the nation state. In many respects it is the indigenous members of the nation states who are putting nationalism to its greatest test. A movement partially tied to a psychological rebellion against the most vital factors of nationalism is now at foot. Its danger lies in the fact that if nationalism as a psychological value dies, the legitimacy of state authority would also die, which means that the state would probably continue to exercise power but its authority would be bankrupt.

It is inappropriate to discuss in detail the larger social issues whereby languages, religions, races and cultures have been vying for new recognition and expression. A type of cultural nationalism, which is often in direct conflict with state nationalism, has emerged in most mature modern states. In Canada the French Canadians, who have submerged their uniqueness for the sake of nationalism, are discovering their French experience anew; this gives them a culture apart from France but not 'American'. In the past this experience was interpreted by them and their English-speaking dominant nationals as cultural impoverishment, but a new self-awareness and appreciation is emerging calling them to become masters of their future *in* Canada but not entirely as Canadians.

France, which has been the model of administrative centralization, is finding itself shaken by a rising self-consciousness; its citizens are demanding to be recognized as Bretons, Alsatians or Basques first and as French second. These cultural conflicts are paralleled by religious strife in other modern areas. Ireland is engaged in civil war and the issues behind it are so complex that no resolution seems possible as long as an attitude of nationalism remains pervasive.

Deutsch (1969) and Fishman (1972) describe in detail the important role that language and communication play in nationalism. In spite of the fact that federations such as Canada and Switzerland face great obstacles in terms of language, they are able to cope with the problem because there are established standards for the languages in question; the schools have been able to comply with the demands of policy-makers wanting the necessary instruction to transmit these languages.

The contemporary thrust toward recognition of dialects and minority norms of the same language, as is found in the host culture, presents a far more complex and unsettling situation. The nation states of the modern age have inevitably, for the sake of national unity, chosen to root these idiosyncracies out of their systems by standardizing language requirements in schools usually based on the models preferred by the national elites. If the dialects were tolerated, they were pointed up as marks of inferiority or low class and therefore of no value.

As the modern age comes to an end a rising consciousness of the meaning of language has emerged. Minority groups have begun to see the systematic denigration of dialect as a tool of domination and as a tool of local cultural destruction. The validity of this assertion on the part of minority groups is not at issue. Once such a belief becomes internalized it becomes a political issue rather than an academic or empirical one. The position taken has been interpreted as having many Whorfian overtones (Whorf, 1956). This theory maintains that the concepts and world view which emerge from what a group sees and experiences is intimately related to the language which is used to reflect upon that experience. The knowledge which a culture accumulates and validates is a reflection of its language, even theoretical knowledge as is found in science or theology. Since minds function through language, the only objective reality which a person possesses is seen to be that which is tolerated or fostered in the structure of a language itself. Therefore, a Chinese would see the world differently from an Englishman. If this notion were applied to dialects, it would mean that a Black American, for example, would see the world slightly differently than a middle-class White because of the uniqueness of Black English. If that language is systematically denigrated, it would follow that the system of thought and reality seen by the Black American could also be considered inferior and worthy of rooting out of existence.

Minority groups have become conscious of the destructiveness of standard language policies in terms of cultural retention and are demanding that their dialects be fostered alongside the dominant languages. Mass schooling, which was largely intended to mobilize the masses toward allegiance to an elite already committed to one or another cosmopolitan language, has achieved its aim in many respects. The masses are trained in the dominant languages of French, German, English, Russian — but they are also able to express devotion to peculiar language patterns and life styles as articulately as the elites of a past age.

The international and local forces are causing enormous strain on the autonomy of the mature modern nation states. We can anticipate change in government and authority as these forces continue to build. Already new forms of government are emerging. To cite but one example, Belgium, which assumed its identity and modern political form in 1831 by accepting a rigid unitarian destiny, subsuming under its French dominant umbrella provinces in which Flemish and German were more widely spoken than French, has declared itself finished as a nation state and now designates itself as a multi-national state. Such a move opens it up for regionalization within its boundaries as well as international union. As of 1970 its constitution stipulates that the 'exercise of given powers may be conferred by treaty or an Act of institutions of international public judicial character' (Article 25b).

In 1971 Leo Tindemans, Minister of Community Matters, outlined the features of this new entity. It shall have (1) infinitely greater tolerance in the matter of language and culture; (2) tolerance in the matter of ideological and philosophical differences; (3) decentralization not only toward the various regions but further toward provinces, communes and muncipalities; (4) integration of powers with the European continent; and (5) a capital which is not dominant but with a unique status unlike typical major urban areas. In the case of Belgium we clearly see that the forces working against the nation state are both local and international. The boundaries set between nations have all too often been artificial and have not totally reflected the feelings of community and identity either locally or world wide.

These forces of protest have coalesced during the past decade to challenge state authority and have also contributed to the movement toward alternative futures in education. Formal schooling, at least in the form patterned after the typical state school model, are viewed more and more by these groups as dysfunctional in terms of the interests these groups would like schooling and education to serve.

Revolutionaries inevitably recognize that established schools are repressive in terms of revolutionary objectives and they usually set about to establish schools and educational programmes which will feature a new ideology and reorder old educational priorities. These movements are largely, though not exclusively, outside the highly developed areas of the world. West Germany, as one example of an industrial state, has experienced in recent times an upsurge of Marxist thinking with an accompanying *Gegenschule* or counterschool movement which has as one of its primary aims the rearing of children toward a conscious awareness of 'repressive' conditions that pervade modern society. These schools go much beyond the American free schools which are largely unpolitical institutions addressing themselves more to avoiding rather than encountering repressiveness. If the counterschools are successful, the child is reared so as to understand the conditions of his environment and he is aided in learning to work as a political person to free himself from intolerable political conditions (Rust, 1972: 130-33).

The nearest equivalent in the United States in recent times might be Black nationalist schools with their own leadership and ideology (Bracey et al., 1970). Although there are variations even within that movement, the strongest at this time is the Black Muslim movement which represents a separatist religious group that bases its teaching on Islam and has developed in the struggle against oppression of Black Americans. Black Muslims believe in radical cultural mores which include a strict moral code, diet, and separation from the White world. The schools they have developed separate boys and girls, divide the day between secular and religious instruction, teach Muslim duties, dietary laws, character development, the history of the Black man and the Muslim movement, English and Arabic languages, as well as some maths, and physical and social sciences. This movement in the United States has already graduated its first generation of youth completely schooled in the Muslim ideology and time alone will determine if it matures beyond the incipient stages of its development.

Various scholars have attempted to develop comprehensive categories of protests to schooling in the present condition. La Belle divides the categories of protest into three major groups 'according to their primary objective: (1) relevance, or educational responsiveness to human needs and problems; (2) efficiency, or fiscal responsibility; and (3) equality, or equal opportunity to gain access to societal resources and to participate in societal decision making' (Goodlad et al., 1975: 30). Although Hartmut von Hentig, the German educator, restricts his discussion to the school as an institution, he identifies three sources of criticism which are very similar at least in their overall content with that of La Belle. He phrases them in the following way: (1) The school reproduces the injustices of society, (2) the school is inefficient, and (3) the school must become more responsible (von Hentig, 1972: 28-41). These categories are by no means exhaustive and they overlap each other in many respects, but they do give us a hint as to the main bearings of contemporary protest. A brief glance at the table of contents of this book will show a discussion of protest within the framework of each of our four main sections and it is clear that all of these factors come into play against state-controlled education. We wish to draw specific attention here to the single most pervasive expression of state-controlled mass schooling: compulsory education.

Until very recently the attitude of mature modernity was almost unanimously that of extending compulsory education even further than it had already reached. The first break with this ideology appears to have emerged in the United States which had maintained a compulsory age limit of sixteen years in all states for at least half a century, and in fact some states had begun to successfully maintain a compulsory age limit of eighteen years. One of the original critics of such a practice was Edgar Friedenberg, a sociologists, who wrote a classic study of youth in America in his *The Vanishing Adolescent* (1959), and followed this up with the more popular study, *Coming of Age in America* (1963). In these books Friedenberg described in detail the impact of the school institution on youth, demonstrating that anything deviating from the school norms was considered, even by the youth, as abnormal behaviour. Schools taught the youth, according to Friedenberg, that the regulations of institutions should become the standards of good behaviour; morality therefore becomes directly linked with conformity to institutional standards.

Using compulsory education laws as his point of departure, he stressed the crippling effect on the lives and subsequent development of the youth. They are incapable of taking seriously or even understanding the meaning of genuine civil rights if they understand the meaning of compulsory schooling, which forces a student to participate with people 'in whose selection they have no voice, performing tasks about which they have no choice, without remuneration and subject to specialized regulations and sanctions that are applicable to no one else in the community nor to them except in school' (1963: 41). Friedenberg wondered how the young learn to participate in a democratic state when they are subject to what amounts to 'a bill of attainder against a particular age group', that did not allow them to 'participate fully in the freedoms guaranteed by the state and that *therefore these freedoms do not really partake of the character of inalienable rights*' (1963: 42).

Compulsory education was seen to fly in the face of every legal concept of services performed by one party for another. Reminding his readers that every service involves what might be regarded as legal obligations and the possibility for absolving the relationship, if there is a breach of contract, he concluded that such possibility does not exist for the young. The student 'cannot petition to withdraw if the school is inferior, does not maintain standards, or treats him brutally'. It is simply his 'obligation to attend the school and accept its services'. His message was clear. The autonomy of individual justice, even that of the young, was seen to be paramount to the authority of the state.

Friedenberg was joined by Paul Goodman, who also began to raise questions as to the value of schooling. His first book on contemporary public education, *Growing up Absurd* (1956), was complemented six years later by *Compulsory Mis-Education* (1963) which was the first major work to attack the ideology of compulsory education. Goodman's basic position was that schooling had ceased to be educative in any genuine sense but had turned into a 'baby sitting service' and at the same time was being used by the corporate structure to prepare functionaries for technological society.

Recent events have brought the issue of compulsory education to a head; it has been called into question not only as an ethical but as a legal issue. A recent Gallup Poll indicated that over 90 percent of those interviewed favour compulsory school attendance, at least in primary schools. That figure drops to 73 percent when the issue of secondary schools is raised.

The fact that such a question was asked at all is significant, for it would not have occurred to a poll-taker during most of this century in the United States, and the fact that one in four is against compulsory schooling in secondary schools is astounding. Even the one in ten figure for primary schools indicates a new consciousness emerging in the public mind. Proponents of such a point of view are armed with empirical and ideological ammunition that is compelling.

The United States prides itself in paying deference to minority views, and a recent swell of sentiment in favour of cultural diversity has resulted in one of the greatest threats to universal compulsory education laws to date. That case is over the old order Amish, descendants of the Swiss Anabaptists who emigrated to Pennsylvania almost two hundred years ago. Throughout the period in which that country adopted modernity, the Amish were able to retain their commitment to traditional values and life styles. The main overt manifestation in the small communities that still exist in the Midwest and Northeast are horsedrawn carriages, the Pennsylvania German dialect, discrete traditional drab dress and social life centred around the family as part of a highly religious communal organization. Hostetler and Huntington outline five major cultural characteristics of the Amish: '. . . separation from the world, voluntary acceptance of high social obligations symbolized by adult baptism, the maintenance of a disciplined church-community, and a life of harmony with the soil and nature ' (1971: 4).

In September 1968, three Amish residents in Wisconsin refused to send their children to high school. This was just another of a long series of incidents that had taken place in Iowa, Michigan, Indiana, and other states. The complaint was the same: the parents believed that high school would result in 'psychological alienation of the child and destruction of the Amish faith community'.

No one involved in the case denied that the school interfered with religious beliefs, but precedents had already been set as to the limits on the claim of religious freedom in the United States, anti-polygamy laws against the Mormons being a case in point. The difference in this case, however, was the claim that the Amish youth were receiving an adequate education both in terms of morals, basic skills and vocational training. There is no juvenile delinquency, poverty, crime or unemployment among the Amish. In fact, some claim that the children receive a more adequate education in their nonformal system of education than modern schools are able to provide (1971: 52).

A Wisconsin state court tried and convicted the three parents for violating the law; however, the case was referred to the Supreme Court, which reversed the decision. Although this case was ruled on narrow religious grounds, it represents the first major legal decision against the right of the majority attitudes and beliefs which are reflected in the public schools to be imposed if they do violence to personal, cultural, ethnic, racial, or religious values. A number of legal scholars throughout the country immediately launched studies of compulsory education laws as they affect other minority groups in the country. The consequence, when seen in the context of other forces, suggests a crumbling of this major standard of modernity.

Compulsory education is not just a minority group issue. It is at the heart of the contemporary rising consciousness that the nation state has systemtically drafted its citizens into school and 'has assumed the duty of enforcing the judgment of its educators through well-meant truant officers and job requirements, much as did the Spanish Kings who enforced the judgments of their theologians through the Conquistadors and the Inquisition' (Illich, 1970: 15).

The ideology which is pervasive in a particular nation state presents no great alternative. All major political systems of the world have accepted the role of school enforcer. France, Russia and the United States are alike in withholding faith in their citizenry to educate themselves if given the opportunity. The protest has no political bounds, it represents a universal crisis between 'the system' and autonomous man.

The message here is clear. State-controlled mass schooling whose charge has been to instil in the general public the values which the state has deemed appropriate, is being seriously challenged. The individual, the community, the culture to which people identify are assuming greater importance in the eyes of more and more people than are the state aims. Such a challenge is obviously not simply a school problem, but one which strikes at the core of dominance and sovereignty of the nation state.

3

SCIENCE AND THE HIGHER LEARNINGS

In all but the most primitive societies a 'great tradition', as Robert Redfield called it, is maintained which stands in contrast to the 'low culture' of folk traditions. In the first section we discussed how modernity attempted to co-opt much of the folk tradition and align it with nation state purposes. The great tradition, which reflects the hopes and ideals of every people, also played a major role in modernity, but of a different nature than folk culture.

The 'great traditions' in traditional society emanated from centres of learning in the schools and temples, and they were typically reserved for the 'reflective few' (Redfield, 1960: 40-43). In modernity the higher learnings were secularized so that they came to be found mainly in the higher schools. They also began as elitist institutions but gradually spread to broader elements of society.

The higher learnings of modernity throughout the world are distinctly Western in mode. Because of this it is not surprising that important elements of modern thought can be identified even in traditional Western history. Crane Brinton (1963: 236-37), for example, suggests that three generalizations can be made about traditional Western thought that are crucial to the modern mind.

First, Western man has historically believed the universe is ordered and not simply chaotic. Secondly, Western man has persistently felt that he possesses a special dignity that sets him apart from things and animals. Thirdly, in spite of tragedies and failures, Western man has seen life on earth as something good and valuable. These characteristics of Western thought have usually been stressed in all modern higher learnings although new modes of thought, critical to the modern mind, have also emerged since the Industrial Revolution. We wish to place these notions in some context as we briefly review the main roots of higher learnings in the West and then trace the main lines of their evolution into modernity.

TRADITIONAL HIGHER LEARNINGS

Extended higher schooling in the modern West has strong roots with the traditional Western world. Their strongest ties are with the Latin grammar schools which were so prominent at the time of the Renaissance. These schools, in turn, traced their roots to two major sources: (1) classical humanism, and (2) Christianity.

Classical Humanism

Classical humanism derives from the Latin notion of *Humanitas*, used originally by Cicero, but referring to the Greek idea of man, not in his common or typical state, but as he exemplifies the 'highest expression of an absolute and timeless ideal' (for a lexicographical discussion of *Humanitas* see Schneidewin, 1897). In spite of the humanistic focus on ideal man throughout premodern Western history, the meaning of that ideal changed several times.

The concept of ideal man in the high period of Greek culture, as expressed by men such as Plato and Socrates, aimed at balance in the development of the citizen; physical, moral, intellectual, and aesthetic sensibilities were to be won, which would distinguish educated man from the slave, the foreigner, and the barbarian. The most important function of man and that which set him apart from the animals was his potential ability to display wisdom and reason; his will and appetitive faculties were considered subservient to the higher (Aristotle, 1962). Processes such as the Socratic method, dialogues, disputations, debates, were highly developed – their value being their capacity for critical analysis.

The curricular programme of Greek higher learnings came to be based on the seven liberal arts. The liberal arts were divided into the trivium and quadrivium; the former was composed of grammar, rhetoric, and logic and was considered to be well suited for the training of public leaders and the best training of the intellect. The quadrivium was composed of arithmetic, geometry, astronomy, and music; these studies were usually related to the more practical crafts and domestic economy although their importance to the development of the mind was also recognized.

Within the liberal arts studies there was great room for variation and emphasis. The Greeks displayed two mainstreams of schooling, the one being philosophical and reflective, the other being rhetorical, characterizing man by grace, polish, and eloquence in the public arena.

The Romans being of a more practical bent than the Greeks adopted the mode of educating the orator rather than the philospher. The Roman concept of humanism, which also formed the basis of Renaissance humanism was less speculative than the Greek, and it did not draw to itself the notion of human perfection so much as it turned to the purposeful powers of language and literature. The Latin language became the central focus of cultural possession and transmission. Education became almost synonymous with competence in the Latin tongue, for it provided the avenue to eloquence, communication between men of state, and literary fulfilment. To speak well was to be cultivated and to live the highest expression of human life.

With the advent of Christianity into Western life, humanism was to recede into the background until the Renaissance at which time, through the efforts of men such as Petrarch and Bocaccio, a whole school of thought emerged which brought forth still another variation of the human ideal. Renaissance humanism represented in many respects a revolt against feudal and ecclesiastical authority and an attempt to focus on man as the centre of attention. His sense, feelings, rational faculties, sense of self, all captivated the attention of the Italians and later the Northern Europeans. In terms of literature education and learning, a new principle was established for ideal man which called for a recapturing of the spirit of antiquity with no interest in the dynamics of living in the contemporary world. Greek and Latin texts were learned by rote and even the teacher commentaries about their grammatical and literary significance were also memorized. The young were expected to write as the ancients had written, think as they supposed the ancients had thought, and even feel and sense as the ancients had done (Burckhardt, 1958: 211).

The grammar schools which emerged at this time became deeply entrenched in reproducing classical and religious artifacts of the ancient world, and although there were adjustments over time, the humanist tradition in these precursors of the secondary grammar schools was to carry all the way into modernity before significant changes were made.

Christianity

The second root of the classical grammar school was Christianity. Various forms of schooling are identified during the Medieval period, which were almost completely Christian in terms of its 'great tradition'. Their different identities are more a function of who sponsored them than of their structure and content. Monastic schools were conducted under the auspices of the monasteries; cathedral schools were run by the bishop in conjunction with his cathedral; the chantry schools were conducted by priests who helped the young learn the chanting of masses as well as the conventional learnings of Christian schooling.

The Christian leaders during the Medieval period had adopted the grammar school of ancient Rome but had subsequently adapted it to their own special purposes. As we have already mentioned, grammar schools had earlier been the vehicle by which the Romans had prepared citizens and leaders of the empire, but the Christians transformed these schools to train intelligent and devoted leaders of the Church. The priests of the universal Church were the mainspring of the Latin tongue, which served as the instrument for the transmission of God's word and facilitated communications between men for theological disputation and study of the Holy Word. The ultimate purpose of the schools was singularly common. They were training grounds for the clerical profession and when the most prominent monastic schools of the

Middle Ages blossomed into universities at Paris, Oxford, Padua, and Bologna, this goal was retained, although law and medicine were also studied.

Theology, the highest Christian science, was built upon a liberal arts foundation. The trivium came to dominate the curriculum as the lower levels concentrated on Latin grammar, conversation, composition, and Latin writings along with scriptural training; at the higher levels studies in Greek grammar and literature were initiated together with some Hebrew.

During the time of the Renaissance, the cultivated classes of the Western world revived classical humanism in order to educate their youth, but the soul of the schools, at least in Northern Europe, was more clearly reflected in the hymns, creeds, and masses of Christianity. During the period prior to the modern age, some secularization emerged since schools on the Continent came more and more under the control of civil authorities, but they remained closely tied to religious forces which formed the basis of traditional life even in the West.

In summary, we see that traditional higher learnings consisted of a special set of teachings reserved for a select circle. In antiquity these teachings concentrated on the physical, intellectual, and artistic centres of man; this rounded education did however eventually give way to a dominant literary and intellectual set of teachings in spite of the fact that the trivium and quadrivium remained at the base of teachings from antiquity until the modern age. These teachings were not intended for the masses because of an assumption that their perceptions were generally obtuse and their intellect limited. To benefit from the higher learnings it was necessary to possess keen and delicate moral perceptions, bright and subtle intelligence, and a sensitive sprituality. There is no indication that the higher teachings were held secret or even unavailable to the masses, but a belief was maintained that they were unfit to be touched in mind, heart, and soul by these teachings. On the other hand these would lead the elect toward the highest expression of man, or toward what Marrou has termed 'individual culture'. That is, a belief was maintained that through the higher learnings, men of select ability would be led to a perfected state not only culminating in a fully developed mind but signifying an individual who had truly become a man (Marrou,

1956: 137-46). Though this training concentrated on developing an artistic and scholarly class, it was also utilitarian in that the recipients of this training were to become clerics in the broader sense of the term.

In time, the vitality of classical study began to fade. The Latin tongue remained the lingua franca of scholars but its use in everyday affairs was superseded by the vernacular as English, French, and German became respectable for serious writing. The grammar schools, with their vast interests and narrow focus, were unable to adjust to changing conditions and they suffered what might have been a slow and painful death. In fact, in colonial America, the classical grammar school became so dysfunctional that it disappeared from the scene and was replaced by a completely different school by the middle of the nineteenth century.

In Europe, however, the grammar schools witnessed a reawakening as the modern age emerged and eventually they evolved into exclusive secondary schools which persist to this day in forms such as the Great Public Schools in England, the *Lycée* in France, and the *Gymnasium* in Germany. Their classical orientation has, to some degree, been contaminated by modern learnings, but in many respects they remain true to their traditions.

MODERN HIGHER LEARNINGS

The prestige of the grammar schools was so great that they were able to perpetuate their existence throughout the whole of the modern age though, in order to do so, it was necessary to reorient the utility of the schooling which was offered. We are reminded that the grammar schools were ancient instruments for training leaders of the Roman Empire, and with the spread of Christianity during the Middle Ages these schools became the training grounds for Church leaders. Although more diverse publics took advantage of schooling in the early stages of the modern age, the traditional aims were retained, for these schools were once again intended to train leaders even though these were more leaders of state than of Church. However, during the nineteenth century the rationale for such purposes was altered radically; whereas the main goals of the schools were once directly related to leadership tasks (e.g. in Rome rhetoric was necessary for the statesman and in the church the scribe was necessarily a man of letters), and thus vocational in nature, the purpose of academic schooling in early modernity became one of general development, *culture générale*, or *Allgemeinbildung* of boys destined for high station.

This 'liberal education' attempted to provide the young with a unified summary of total cultural content and implied as much a moral or character training as the transmission of information. Its purpose was to awaken the inner spirit, the creative energies in man. It was general not because it was superficial but because it was to open and foster a harmonious human development. It was not to be seen as specialized or one-sided, but broad and comprehensive, and especially not vocational or practical. The entire nineteenth century is a history of the attempt to preserve the meaning of liberal education in the higher schools while accommodating the programme of the schools to new content that was forcing its way into the picture. We can trace the evolution of academic schooling in modernity through two distinct phases. One is the attempt to define all studies in the secondary school as liberal education. The second, appearing in the twentieth century, is an active accommodation of schooling to science and technology and the collapse of the humanist tradition.

Liberal Education Phase

At the beginning of the nineteenth century, in spite of elaborate justifications, to obtain a liberal education simply meant that a person had gone through a course of studies which focused on the language components of the liberal arts as they had been passed down from the classical era. This course of studies varied somewhat from country to country. In Prussia, Wilhelm von Humboldt, who was most responsible for Prussian educational reforms at the turn of the nineteenth century, considered languages as the particular means by which one was liberally educated. Though Humboldt recognized some value in modern languages, he gave priority to the study of the languages of antiquity since he felt that the thought and languages of the Greeks and Romans would convey more perfectly than any other medium that essence which liberalizes and humanizes.

In France, following the Revolution at the end of the eighteenth century, a new political order came into being which determined that the schools would act as an agency for the promotion of a national culture. The grammar schools were thus transformed to provide special preparation for those who would ultimately move into the professions, and although these schools contained courses in scientific and social subjects, they retained allegiance to logic, rhetoric, ethics, and languages, all a part of classical education. However, the main impulse was national culture and enormous time was devoted to a study of the French language and literature as well as French history. Thus, a liberal education in France was largely identified with French culture.

In England, through the efforts of such men as Thomas Arnold at Rugby, an education for the 'complete gentleman' was developed in the 1820s and 1830s. Arnold drew upon the 'timeless' principles of linguistics and the classics and combined these principles with Christian purposes to create a liberal education for the future Civil Servants and leaders of the British Empire. In the process the Great Public Schools, which had reached their lowest point almost a century earlier, were revived; still, it is clear that these schools largely retained their cleric heritage even after they had lost their cleric purposes.

The higher schools which emerged so forcefully at the dawn of modernity could almost be characterized as having little modern content; they had mainly redefined their purpose but remained true to their content origins. Long before this, however, an intellectual break with the past had already taken place. The most critical intellectual innovation in the West in the past three centuries was the development of the scientific method or reliance upon observation, description, and verification as a means of accumulating knowledge. Through the scientific method, knowledge is believed to be best intellectually verified by reducing all distinctions to quantitative or measurable terms.

Emergence of Science

The methods of observation and experimentation in modern life are so commonplace that it is difficult to imagine a life style without them. Through Western interactions with the non-Western world, some

people are beginning to become more sensitive to the fact that modern
man perceives his relationship with Nature in a way which is distinct
from that of traditional man. It took several centuries for such a mind
to develop. Probably the most important element of Western thought
which contributed to scientific thinking was the separation of man
from Nature. Brinton (1963: 234) claims that the dualisms of the
West were highly instrumental in helping natural sciences flourish.
Without the tensions of the real and ideal, of this world and the other
world, and of mind and body, the intellectual apparatus necessary to
'devise the incredibly complex order of things we call science', would
not have been possible.

The philosophical tradition of the West from the fifteenth century
onward provided the intellectual tools necessary to deal with the
growing opposition between man and Nature. Such an opposition had
several sources: the newly-discovered literature from the Greek world;
the breakdown in the class structure in which the aristocratic tradition
had been able to divorce itself from material considerations and manual
work; Protestantism with the resulting competitiveness of religion
which required the individual to begin to make choices about fundamental questions rather than merely accept them; the rise of
technology which was prior to, and distinct from, science, and which
brought man's focus on inventions and things, all contributed to the
scientific mentality (Hooykaas, 1968: 211-39).

Natural science was first made respectable in the West in the
sixteenth and seventeenth centuries as prominent scholars provided
it with a philosophical base. In France, Descartes forged a new
theory of cognition as he exclaimed the certitude of self-consciousness
through rational thought and doubt, but it was in England where
the inductive method of modern experimental science was given its
greatest philosphical respectability. Francis Bacon attacked the
scholastic disciples of classicism who continued to concentrate fully
on deductive thinking even after the most obvious fallacies of fact
in ancient thinking had come to light. Copernicus had already
revolutionized man's concept of the universe by demonstrating in
his work *On the Revolutions of the Celestial Spheres* that the Ptolemaic
universe was untenable. New astronomical verifications were joined
by navigational discoveries which demonstrated old views to be
absurd. Studies of the human anatomy showed earlier concepts to be

far removed from reality.

Bacon appealed to his countrymen to accept the evidences of sense perception and in his *Novum Organum* he outlined how experimentation and observation might be employed to derive true knowledge. By the use of inductive thinking and testing of particulars, general axioms would be uncovered. The source of all truth lay ready for all men who were willing to organize and classify scientific knowledge. Bacon even envisaged the application of science for practical purposes with such potential as to even create a new Utopia, as glorious as that envisaged by his contemporary Thomas More.

Bacon was one of the first visionaries to see the impact science had to have on education. A severe critic of the schools of the time, he anticipated the new humanism of the twentieth century with its rejection of the classical ideal of man and its focus on the pursuit of learning for the benefit of mankind and the improvement of his lot on earth (Bacon, 1876-1890: Vol. 3, 413-17).

Bacon was joined by the Moravian educator Johann Comenius who advanced the notion that all the physical senses should be brought to bear in learning. Until this time formal schooling had become so oriented to the mind and to words that the contribution of other attributes of the human being to learning had fallen into disuse. The most vivid illustration of his concept of instruction was his book *Orbis Pictus* in which he demonstrated the value of identifying real objects visually in the process of learning. His more inclusive work, *Didactica Magna* lays down the rules whereby all learning should take place through the medium of the senses.

At this point we are at the stage in which consideration is being given as to how to instruct more efficiently. In fact, Comenius had been so influenced by the claims of the newly emerging scientific world that he set forth to apply his concepts of pedagogy. Recognizing that invariant laws of heavenly bodies and physical forces were being discovered, Comenius dreamed of discovering the invariant laws of method in education. He was to declare:

> As soon as we have succeeded in finding the proper method, it will be no harder to teach school boys, in any number desired, than with the help of the printing press to cover a thousand sheets daily with the neatest writing (in Keatinge, 1931: 50-51).

Infatuated with the practical possibilities of science he would continue, 'It will be as pleasant to see education carried out on my plan as to look at an automatic machine of this kind, and the process will be as free from failure as are these mechanical contrivances, when skilfully made.' Both Comenius and Bacon believed that an encyclopedic science-based curriculum would provide all men with all knowledge.

Science Education Beginnings

A few schools accepted the challenge of science at an early date. In Germany, August Hermann Francke (1663-1727), while remaining true to his commitment to pietism, established a system of education which did emphasize closely monitored and rigorously controlled religious instruction but which introduced modern languages as well as practical and natural science studies. Julius Hecker (1707-1768) established the first *Realschule* in Germany in 1747, the forerunner of practical oriented institutions that included economics, architecture, the physical sciences and mathematics in their curriculum. Johannes Bernhard Basedow (1724-1790) was also to establish the *Philanthropinum* in 1774 which introduced practical studies. However, it would be 1900 before any schools which stressed the *Realen* would be accorded the right to qualify pupils for the university.

In England a main thrust toward modern subjects came from outside conventional institutions. Since the nonconformists in England were excluded from grammar schools and universities, they set about building their own institutions which differed from conventional grammar schools 'both in aim and accomplishment' (Parker, 1914: 124). The nonconformists were not encumbered with the schooling tradition as they established their own institutions; they 'paid more and more attention to science and to modern languages and later to "commercial" subjects' (Parker, 1914: 132). They lost their own classical orientation between 1690 and 1750, by which time they had established separate degrees for modern subjects such as history, geography, sciences and modern languages. Eventually the dissenting academies disappeared; it would be more correct to say the classical schools absorbed them and their programmes than to say they ceased to exist.

In spite of modern subjects being taught in the more formal schooling programmes of dissenting academies, the most typical science study came from educational activities which were at play completely outside the sphere of formal institutions. These activities were more vital to the modernization process than those which took place in formal institutions, including the dissenting academies. One of the major impulses for education came with the invention of the printing press, which in itself was a modernizing agent. The notion quickly developed that knowledge was to be shared for the benefit of all. As the printed word in the vernacular became available, texts for general consumption soon became a ready tool for mass education; 'teach yourself' manuals, adult self-education books, and pamphlets rapidly became, in England at least, a major instrument for instruction in literature, history, geography, science and technology (Charlton, 1965: 298-99).

In Britain, the Royal Society of London for the Promotion of Natural Knowledge was formally chartered in 1662 after having met informally for almost two decades. These men had been inspired by figures such as Francis Bacon and were intrigued to inquire into the 'New Philosophy, or Experimental Philosophy'. Fortunately, King Charles II saw fit to grant such a charter even though he failed to grant an endowment.

Royal societies were not only societies established during this period. In England a number of chemical research societies were established as well as private laboratories. Wealthy patrons were deeply involved in this enterprise as well as in others. Priestley and Wedgwood, for example, set out to establish experimental farms and a pneumatic institute. Cavendish sustained a large research library at Clapham and encouraged his friends to avail themselves of it. Priestley was engaged by the Earl of Shelburne to run a library (Armytage, 1970: 382-90).

Such societies were not restricted to England as comparable groups were established in many countries prior to the 'take-off' stage of economic development. In France, men such as Descartes and Pascal had met in informal meetings since the 1640s, and the statesman and exponent of mercantilism, Jean Baptiste Colbert, had established the Academie des Sciences in 1666. In Germany, regular scientific papers were published by the Academie Naturae which had been founded in Leipzig in 1652 and the more official Berlin Societas Regia Scientarium which was later called the Deutsche Academie der Wissenschaft was established in 1700. In Russia, Peter the Great's wife, Catherine, fulfilled his wishes for a scientific society by being instrumental in establishing the Imperial Akademiia Nauk in 1725.

In America, Benjamin Franklin took the lead in helping to establish a copy of the Royal Society 'whose example the American Philosphical Society think it their honor to follow in their endeavors of enlarging the sphere of knowledge and the useful arts' (Meyer, 1967: 111). The society aided in studies and experiments in physics, medicine, mathematics, astronomy, etc., as well as more practical tasks such as farm development, and improvements in utilizing natural resources.

If we return to England, we note that other types of non-institutional educational arrangements included the multiplication of cheap coffee houses which served as centres where such groups as 'scientific clubs', 'conversation clubs', and 'literary and philosophical societies' could meet and exchange information and points of view (Armytage, 1970: 378; 390). These establishments also served the purpose of general enlightenment. Since workmen habitually began their day with coffee in the coffee houses, they had the chance to purchase a daily or weekly journal or receive a political tract or paper gratis.

As was mentioned, most of this activity in England took place outside the walls of the established schools, which aligned themselves with the static force in breaking down the absolute notions of knowledge and truth during the centuries prior to modernity. Since negation is at the heart of empirical investigation it tended to break down standards which tradition and Christianity had perpetuated simply by the force of authority and faith. Thriving in an atmosphere of controversy and dissent, science became a secularizing force since Christianity, as with all religions, was affirmative and tended to define conflict only in terms of deviations from indisputable norms which derived their authority from outside the human intellect and concrete experience.

Within this atmosphere it is clear that the classical programmes of schools could not long maintain their exclusivity. In fact, in the nineteenth century, the pure unified schooling orientation that existed was soon lost as other subjects of study made their way into the curriculum of the schools in all of Western Europe. The dominant curriculum spheres which challenged the domination of the classics in the nineteenth century were modern foreign languages and science-mathematics. These subjects were taught in the classical schools but so little attention was given to them that they might have been considered frills in comparison with the classics. Contemporary foreign languages were then taught as though they were classical languages. In Germany the study of English, for example, meant the study of English philology with a stress on the classical roots of the English language. *Beowulf* was, therefore, more important than any contemporary English literature. The same was true of French studies as the *Song of Roland* was better known than any recent French literature. The instruction methods used were also those of the classicists. The spoken foreign languages were not taught nor were the customs and setting of the people emphasized; grammar and translation were deemed appropriate. This is not to say that modern languages were not learned. One of the main informal educational modes of elites in traditional Europe was to engage their children in The Grand Tour, whereby the young would travel the well-worn circuit through Europe seeing the people, becoming boarders with a family, and learning some language. The main purpose of these travels was to acquire those learnings necessary to assist the youth in his public and commercial activities, but it also took on important social significance. French and Italian were the most popular cultures to visit, though German areas, Spain, and England often formed part of the circuit (Charlton, 1965: 199-226).

A sharp division emerged in modern nineteenth-century countries between the 'translation' method of language instruction and the 'natural' method found in newer schools in some countries. In fact, Germany in 1886 saw the emergence of a modern language association with its own professional journal, *Die Neueren Sprachen*. This group did not affiliate itself with the modern language section of the established General Philological Congress which continued to rely on classical content and methods of study.

In spite of the more liberal attitude taken by the newer language teachers, their struggle was a struggle for equal recognition rather than destruction of the humanistic tradition. The language advocates claimed modern languages studied through the more natural sight and sound avenues were as valuable in acquiring a liberal education as were the classical studies. Eventually, newer schools concentrating on modern languages were either accorded the right to prepare school-leaving certificates or the classical schools expanded their programmes to provide for modern language study equivalent to the classical studies.

More important in terms of its ultimate impact on the meaning of liberal education in modern schools has been science-mathematics. Mathematics has always been viewed as an important discipline though its marriage with empirical science awaited the modern world. Science advocates also defended science study as having the same potential as classical studies in imparting a liberal education. Thomas Huxley was to reject the premise that a purely classical education was necessary to cultivate the future leaders of England. In fact, if the purpose of such education was to attain 'real culture', then there was no question that 'an exclusively scientific education is at least as effectual as an exclusively literary education' (Huxley, 1895: 141). He did not argue for exclusivity, however, but rather for the inclusion of science as an equal to classical studies. Herbert Spencer (1820-1903) was to ask, rhetorically, in the latter part of the nineteenth century what knowledge was of most worth; in answering the question he determined five major areas in which education would be necessary in order for a person to live completely. They were: 'That education which prepares for self-preservation; that which prepares for indirect self-preservation; that which prepares for parenthood; that which prepares for citizenship; that which prepares for the miscellaneous refinements of life.' The ideal education would deal with all five areas and Spencer demonstrated resoundingly that science 'is the best preparation for all these orders of activity' (1897: 84). This is not only the case with knowledge, but with conduct; indeed with the whole of civilization. Science was proclaimed as the highest study both in worth and beauty.

In spite of these appeals, English schools were more resistant to change than those in countries on the Continent. This can be partially explained by the heavy national overtones of science in that day. Alexander Williamson, of University College, London, shed some light on these variations in 1867 as he contrasted English, French, and German scientists. He saw in England that science was practised by different classes of society and of the most different occupations which was 'the source of its practical fruitfulness' (in Tilden, 1930: 239). Indeed the English who were captivated by science came from different classes, some being closely associated with Protestant dissent, others being middle-class tradesmen and craftsmen who connected science with trial-and-error attempts at gaining some useful knowledge; still others were liberal political elites. On the one hand science was associated with artisans and its value was seen in practical fruitfulness rather than anything which might be attractive to the scholar or humanist. Science of a different sort was recognized as a potential element of liberal education. Oxford and Cambridge provided science lectures, but when these courses were taught they were in the style of classical studies, being theoretical and descriptive, involving at best an occasional demonstration. Laboratory work was still too akin to the work of labourers and dissenters to be seriously considered part of an education fit for a scholar or gentleman. This perhaps explains why such dismal interest was shown by university students toward courses such as chemistry and anatomy. The actual number of students even declined in number during the first half of the nineteenth century (Haines, 1957: 17). The sixth Science Commission Report of 1875 declared that an examination of 128 endowed higher schools had been made and less than one-half were found to have taught any science at all. Only thirteen possessed a laboratory and only ten gave more than four hours of science instruction a week. Forty 'first class schools' were surveyed. Of 461 Oxford and Cambridge examinations candidates '438 boys took up Latin, 433 Greek, 455 Elementary Mathematics, 305 History; only 21 took up Mechanics, 28 Chemistry, 6 Botany, 15 Physical Geography' (*Nature*, 1875: Vol. 12, 594).

Natural science promised no reward either socially or economically for it was considered to be a sport run by eccentrics and non-conformists both religious and otherwise. England, as in so many things, presented a picture of science as an avocation or an amateur enterprise. Haines describes it thus: 'It was a peculiarly local, provincial activity, modest, without the pretension of a professoriate to authority . . .' (1957: 20). Of course an occasional genius would come forth providing an original contribution or two, but the value of science in England lay particularly in its potential because of its practical orientation. Its marriage with technology would produce wonders but such a union was not to occur until later in the century.

On the Continent Williamson found quite a different prevailing condition. Scientists 'belonged always to a peculiar class, more isolated from other classes of men, more connected by its interests and occupations' (in Tilden, 1930: 239). The English were seemingly at a stalemate because any proposal for scientific advance was so connected to political and religious rivalry that opposition was immediate no matter what the issue; and even the scientists were so disparate that they could not act as a body. The Continent did not suffer from this condition. German universities, for example, had encouraged the development of science and staffed their institutions with men of relative economic security having social protection through the practice of *Lernfreiheit* which pertained more to the scholars than the students. Professors of all sorts possessed the social distinction of being Civil Servants and their professional journals received strong public financial support ensuring their widespread availability.

The orientation of the Continent toward science itself provided additional advantages. Williamson suggested the Frenchmen, having a devotion to theory and conceptual constructs 'turned more to the methodical and refined elaboration of detail' within the theoretical frameworks which existed. The French advantage over England was, however, overshadowed by the commitment of the Germans to science, who were the scientific leaders of the world during the century. Williamson explains the reason for this being because 'partly driven by the native tendency, partly by the social and political consequence of [their] long religious struggles, turned more to the first principles of knowledge in general, and of scientific theories especially' (in Tilden, 1930: 239).

Such a radical stance with regard to science domination in German higher studies can be explained by comparison. The singular notion of science in France and England relates only to the order of Nature known as *Naturwissenschaft*. The German concept of science, however, includes an additional order called *Geisteswissenschaft*, which deals with the world of mind, culture, and spirit. Thus, there existed a mechanism through definition which allowed the Germans, in spite of the expansion of science, to retain the cohesiveness of liberal education. Such a retention was successful because science had been tied to philosophy, which, in idealistic Germany after Kant, stressed the existence of a universe in which the idea, the spirit, the absolute, was pre-eminent and all things, including natural science, were a part of this unity. The science disciplines that had emerged were also considered to be part of this unity and the role of the scientist was nothing more than that of one who systematically searched for truth. The material world was seen as a realization of the spiritual and therefore not just inert matter to be manipulated and used. The spiritual and material were seen to participate in a dialectical interaction, each being at once both product and process of evolution and change. The true scientist could only deal with the material universe, if he at the same time engaged in considerations of the inner spiritual forces of the universe.

In spite of the deeply mystical elements of science study, the crowning achievement of Germany was seen in its practical contributions. Their shocking victory over Austria in 1866 and France in 1870 awakened the world to the emergence of Germany as a world power and this distinction was laid to its schooling commitment. Their victory over these lands had been attributed to the superior schooling of the soldiers and officers (Rust, 1967: 24-25). We must remember that higher education in Germany was already synonymous with *Wissenschaft* or science. As early as 1856 the Prussian ministry of education had declared that the old distinction between languages (classical studies) and sciences (modern studies) that had crept into the humanistic discourse was no longer meaningful. Ludwig Wiese, the minister at that time, was to declare that Latin, Greek and also German language study had themselves become scientific. Philology no longer dealt with poetry, eloquence, or rhetoric, but it had become a science in itself (Blättner, 1960: 129).

Since higher studies were linked with science in Germany, any consideration of education reform using Prussia as its model would involve science. During the debates as to national education in England in the 1870s, science was a large issue as the leading scientists of the country argued persuasively for a ministry of education *and* science with subsidies for construction of laboratories and a heavier commitment to science studies at all levels of education. The next phase of science was already budding as its importance was seen in its industrial and commercial rather than its liberalizing potential. Its supporters maintained that if science and education were neglected in England, its status among nations would be in danger (especially Science Commission, 1875).

Even so, the main argument for the inclusion of the new studies in elite education was still on their liberalizing potential. Advocates of the newer studies maintained only that modern language and mathematics-science were as legitimate as the classical studies in instilling in man those traits which were befitting a man of high station in society. Advocates of the newer studies won the battle, but in the process destroyed the concept of a liberal education as it had been known in early modernity. Courses of studies were already so differentiated that by the turn of this century liberal education in the elite schools of Europe could only be defined as that course of studies which was sanctioned by the secondary schools to qualify for admission to the university.

The definition of a liberal education took a slightly different turn in the United States, where the classical grammar school had lost its viability during the colonial period. The frontier and rapidly evolving social conditions demanded an education which would address itself directly to the emerging needs and interests of the new nation. Whereas in Europe those practical and science institutions could be singled out as isolated instances, the main secondary schooling institution to replace the grammar school in the United States during the eighteenth century was the academy.

The first academy was established by Banjamin Franklin in 1751 in Philadelphia. Its programme was an amalgam of classical studies with more directly vocational and practical subjects. With the swell of the American common school movement, the academy also became largely extinct and was eventually replaced by the American high school which by the end of the century was a reality though it was not until the 1890s that it took a specific form and definition. The Committee of Ten appointed by the National Education Association of the past century, maintained that the high school should serve all the students of the land and assist in preparing them for life. In the process, however, those few students who qualified for college should also be adequately prepared.

These two goals were accomplished by requiring all students to engage in a college preparatory course which consisted of various combinations of Latin, Greek, English, German, French, chemistry, geology, physics, mathematics (algebra I and II, geometry I and II, trigonometry), life sciences, geography, history, English literature, physiology. There were certain required courses of study (e.g. English and mathematics), but a number of options were available, so long as the student had 'spent four years in studying a few subjects thoroughly' (Tyack, 1967: 385). Thus, America evolved its own definition of a liberally educated person: one who has studied any core subjects intensively. Even in America these options were not unlimited; however, they were restricted to 'solid' subjects such as those listed by the Committee of Ten in 1892.

Although the definition of a liberal education in America at the turn of the century provided much greater flexibility (or depending on the point of view it might also be interpreted as having been more superficial or even more specialized), it continued to possess the same intent: education was potentially liberalizing in quality.

Americans were as precise as any European in declaring the liberalizing value of education. William James claimed that the empiricist attitude, which was linked by James with pragmatism in his day, turns 'away from abstraction and insufficiency, from verbal solutions from bad *a priori* reasons, from fixed principles, closed systems and pretended absolutes and origins . . .' to the 'open air and possibilities of nature' (James, 1943: 45). This open air toward Nature promised to liberate men from shackles of traditon and rule by unquestioned authority. Its claim was to strip life of myths, fantasy, and legend, and to replace it by knowledge based on fact and truth. John Dewey was to join James and proclaim that the function of science is 'emancipation from local and temporary incidents of experience, and the opening of intellectual vistas unobscured by the accidents of personal habit and predilection' (Dewey, 1916: 269). It is clear that for Dewey 'science represents the office of intelligence, in projection and control of new experience'.

These were more philosphical statements than scientific, but the critical attraction of science, at least in the schools prior to the twentieth century, was its philosphical dimension. As we have seen, this explains in some measure the reason why science was so readily incorporated into German education. It gave the Germans a new means of discovering scientific principles, of excursions into theoretical system building. Science was for the Germans as metaphysical as it was factual and utilitarian. It represented an avenue to wisdom, to knowledge, to truth. The value of science in the liberal education phase was its illuminating potential; it not only worked on the individual student of science, but provided other students with access to its secrets. It represented a new educative process and was successful if it achieved the ideal proclaimed by Fichte of a 'transformation of knowing in action'. Ultimately its value lay in the private sphere and educational enhancement of the student of science.

There is some vestige of this attitude in the present world although it has largely been overtaken by a new maturely modern orientation. I.I. Rabi, Nobel prize winner from Columbia University, still to this day exemplifies this position as he describes physics as his nearest equivalent to God, including its mystery and wonder. Physics for him is not a profession, something to make a living from, but is something to 'follow and admire'. It has been a pursuit possessing a 'deeper emotional quality' which has moved him 'to see the world as something that is tremendously important beyond himself, to be able to appreciate the human spirit' (Bernstein, 1975: 50-53).

Polanyi, who also today reflects the more philosophical orientation of science, has described the difference in originality between science and technology. Originality is appreciated in both but in science 'originality lies in the power of seeing more deeply than others into the nature of things, while in technology it consists in the ingenuity of the artificer in turning known facts to a surprising advantage' (Polanyi, 1958: 178).

The twentieth century was to witness a shift in emphasis away from the liberal and philosophical qualities toward the utilitarian. The modern world came to characterize the value of science not so much by its impact on the individual personality as by its potential to translate scientific knowledge into practical technical use. Its value is not so much personal as it is social and material. Let us turn to that phase of science.

Social and Material Phase

Science is so bound to material and technological conditions that it is difficult for us to realize that this relationship is little more than one hundred years old. The Industrial Revolution was achieved without the help of science. Polanyi points out that the great London exhibition of 1851 contained only the Morse telegraph as an example of 'devices of products based on the scientific progress of the previous fifty years'. At that point in our history the 'appreciation of science was still almost free from utilitarian motives' (1958: 182). By the end of the nineteenth century all that had changed.

Barraclough sees the first major relationships between science and technology arising through the use of electricity as a source of light, heat, and power, and in its electrolytic contribution to chemistry. Chemistry itself also had a profound impact on medicine, especially pharmacy, as well as hygiene and nutrition. These were pre-twentieth century starting points of the new phase in science which led to the final dissolution of the humanist tradition in modernity (Barraclough, 1964: 46-50). Barraclough is correct, however, in determining that this collapse was long delayed in formal education (1964: 235).

Even as the world revolted against the elitist ideals of the humanist tradition and moved to correct injustice which existed, the elite schools perpetuated, to a great degree, the classical tradition. We have already observed that science and modern languages were admitted as appropriate to advanced studies because they were seen as liberal in nature. So strong was the humanist tradition that the advocates of vocational and technical studies who argued successfully that these become a part of formal schooling, also made their demands within a liberal education context.

Let us turn to America, where the gap between liberal and technical education was never as great as in Europe. At the turn of the century John Dewey emerged as the foremost spokesman for a new education.

In a classic statement made to the parents and supporters of his laboratory school at the University of Chicago in 1899, Dewey (1899) argued that society had undergone a thorough transformation through industrialization. 'If our education is to have any meaning for life', he said, 'it must pass through an equally complete transformation' (pp. 23-24). He reminded his readers that in the traditional world, 'the entire industrial process stood revealed, from the production on the farm of the raw materials, until the finished product was actually put to use' (p. 107). In the process of living, children came to understand how their culture perpetuated itself from generation to generation and they especially understood the meaning of the moral qualities and skills which would be necessary for them to function productively. In modern society the Gestalt of the traditional world was lost. The child is separated from the processes of raw material acquisition and production and sees the world in a segmented, piecemeal way. For Dewey the schools were the institutions which could perform the educative process necessary to give the child a sense of social organization. To do this, however, the school had to alter its form, and he envisaged it being orgnized as an embryonic community which would help the young integrate the processes of society into a meaningful whole.

The school would be so structured as to replicate the major spheres of industrial society: a textiles centre, a wood and tools shop, and a cooking centre would form the basis of learning. Through interaction between these centres at the school and interaction with critical segments of society, the child would come to grasp the structure and processes of modern social environment.

As the child studied, it would be very likely that he would develop skills which might be vocationally useful, although the educative process would fall far short of its potential if this were all that was accomplished. The studies engaged in would serve mainly as a departure whence children shall be led out into a realization of the historical development of man' (Dewey, 1899: 19). Even at this stage in his conceptual development, Dewey saw the school as educative in a liberal sense. Some years later, in his more philosophical statement, *Democracy and Education,* Dewey would develop more fully the argument that occupational training and technical skills development are 'truly liberalizing in quality' if learned within the framework of scientific inquiry (1916: 235).

The work of Dewey and other progressive educators paved the way for formal education to be considered both liberal *and* practical. To accomplish this it was necessary to shift the meaning of a liberal education since utility had always been considered to be illiberal. This shift had a philosphical as well as a practical dimension.

Philosphically, we have observed that science had undermined the truths and values of traditional society and had promised to provide a more certain avenue to reality. It had dismantled the certitudes of the traditional world, but toward the end of the nineteenth century we observe that it had already begun to dismantle its own certitudes. Scientists such as Ernst Mach in Austria and Wilhelm Ostwald in Germany drew implications from scientific work which made the philosophical assumptions of materialism and naturalism suspect and in turn attempted to translate the activities of science into the realm of ideas. Henri Poincaré, French mathematician and physicist, saw science as nothing more than an illumination of conventionalisms rather than a genuine key to reality. He turned away from any attempt at philosophical illumination and discovery of absolutes, claiming the important role of science was establishing relationships between things. 'Discovery consists precisely in not constructing useless combinations', he maintained in his *Science and Method,* 'but in constructing those that are useful . . .' (Poincaré, 1914: 51). We shall see later on that the scientific belief in absolutes was indeed retained and resulted in one of the major protest actions against it, but at this stage the value of dismantling certitudes in the traditional sense was to reduce the value of philosphical pursuits in the context of a liberal education.

The most starling developments came from the United States with the rise of pragmatism which utterly redefined the meaning of truth, moving it away from its traditional relationship with reality toward instrumentalism. The ultimates in life were so illusive that it was foolish to look at 'first things, principles, categories, supposed necessities', as William James was wont to say, 'and only fruitful to look toward 'last things, fruits, consequences, facts' (James, 1943: 47).

The philosophical thought as developed by the pragmatists had actually raised the processes of science to the level of philosophical reflection. 'Dewey, Schiller, and their allies, in reaching this general [pragmatic] conception of truth', declared James, 'have only followed the example of geologists, biologists and philologists.' Science itself had become the model for what was considered to be the highest ideals of modern thought. The successful stroke of science was to 'take some simple process actually observable in action . . . drawing relationships between the parts and then generalizing from the observations' (James, 1963: 49-50). Science, which had once promised access to more secure certitudes than the traditional avenues to truth had become instead an expanding intricate network of relationships and functions, the source of which 'was beyond common experience and could only be conceptualized abstractly' (Barraclough, 1964: 237-38).

The practical dimension of the new liberalism emerged by attempting to redefine liberal education in a context of a new scientific humanism that was to replace the classical idea. Schooling was no longer to be viewed as civilizing in terms of the Greek ideal of *Humanities*, F.C.S. Schiller, John Dewey, and other rejected the traditional humanist desire to mould the ideal man and turned instead to humanitarian ends rather than personal aggrandizement as reflected in the idea of human perfection (Schiller, 1907). Those studies based on literature and linguistics were seen to have lost their focus, if they had ever existed, on 'liberating human intelligence and human sympathy'. The prophets of a new humanism thought the scientific world had opened the way whereby man might devote himelf to function productively in a world based on humanitarian service and brotherhood. The marriage of science with technology had given a vision of a world in which the basic human wants might be satisfied.

These scholars had correctly assessed the direction science was moving, in that scientists had begun to see science 'as a system you can do things with . . .' (Bernstein, 13 October 1975: 50). The world had come to place its faith in a utilitarian mode of operation and science promised to be the source of its utility. The new humanists assumed the scientist would be willing to allow himself to become an instrument of social progress by devoting his specialized skills to the improvement of the lot of man.

The progressive schools would have a multiple mission. They would help the young find identity and meaning in the complex industrial world; they would give the young the intellectual and practical skills necessary to function productively, and they would serve to correct the injustices and inequalities of man. This new humanism has failed to evolve but it has contributed to the slow death of liberal education even though lip service has been paid to the latter during the course of our century. Liberal education, with its focus on the development of the individual personality, was being replaced by the concept of an education whose worth would be measured by its practical, useful consequences which were social rather than personal or individual.

As modern societies have reached full maturity, it can be seen that scientific and technical studies have not only won the battle for a place in the curriculum, but they have also won the war. Not only have technical studies and science become a mainstay of any modern curriculum, but the 'scientific mode of inquiry' has invaded every facet of modern schooling programmes. Schooling has lost its liberalizing goals and we have reverted to a purpose in schooling not dissimilar to the traditional institutions, for schooling has once again become vocational training, but with a difference. No longer are the vocations intended to elevate man to a transcendent state. No longer is schooling viewed as a civilizing agent, but it is viewed as a tool of modern technological society.

Gone too is the belief that the higher learnings are appropriate for only a few individuals. The industrial state requires a general level of education that extends beyond basic schooling requirements. Some nations have been able to cope more appropriately than others in actually implementing the kind of schooling system demanded by scientific industrialism. According to C.P. Snow (1964: 34), of the powerful nations, America and Russia have made the most dramatic changes.

Since the Soviet Union is attempting to place society on a scientific foundation within the framework of Marxist thought and since total planning is an integral part of its structure, the programme of the schools throughout the country is both highly unified and strongly oriented toward basic education in mathematics and natural science. Approximately one-third of the student's time in the ten-year school is devoted to polytechnical studies (Medlin, 1960: 44). Aside from two main differences, specialists from the U.S. Office of Education who have observed programmes in both the United States and Russia find roughly comparable programmes in mathematics, physics, chemistry, and biology. First, all young people in the ten-year school in Russia receive the same theoretical training; in the United States much of this training falls into elective categories. Secondly, the Soviet programme is accelerated as it lasts ten years rather than twelve (Medlin, 1960: 203).

One might easily conclude that the Soviet children receive even a better grounding in science-mathematics than American children. However, it must be remembered that all Russian schools have uniform programmes while U.S. schools provide a high percentage of its students with comparable programmes and many schools even offer a richer and broader programme. Nevertheless, the Soviet Union is the most extreme example of a land in which there is no formal negativism against science and technological practice. Soviet education is synonymous with qualification for work. To be educated is to possess 'relevant economic potential'. Even the concept of liberal or general education has been co-opted to mean that a person has been scientifically educated, and polytechnically oriented within the socialist tradition (Zänder, 1975: 246).

The Soviet Union does not stand alone. In America there is little pretence of a general education of any sort. The statement, *Industrialism and Industrial Man,* by Kerr et al. (1964) best characterizes the full role of advanced education in modern society. According to these men, education is not an end in itself; it is not liberalizing but it is the handmaiden of Industrialism. Industrialization requires an educational system functionally related to the skills and professions imperative to its technology. Ironically, the overt concern of the technocracy is not with values and meaning, since those are taken for granted, but with skills. The technology sets into motion its own imperatives and the educational process is designed to satisfy these demands. In terms of values, technological education must be change oriented. Those being educated must be oriented in such a way as to be capable of continually adopting new techniques new skills and even new disciplines.

The higher system must stress 'natural sciences, engineering, medicine, managerial training — whether private or public — and administrative law'. Since a study of the classics serves to orient one toward conserving traditional values and a static view of society, humanities and arts receive relatively little consideration. Social sciences, on the other hand, are highly valued because they are obviously related to the 'training of managerial groups and technicians for enterprise and government' (Kerr et al., 1964: 19-20).

The humanities, literature, the arts and even theology are fostered and continue to exist although they are usually deemed valuable only in so far as they help fill the void created by the increased 'leisure time of industrialism'. Though a multitude of disciplines and specialized fields of study have emerged as a consequence of the modern age, the trend is unmistakable. To be credible these disciplines, including the arts and humanities, must adopt the mode of inquiry defined by science and technology.

A single example from contemporary West Germany would illustrate the above situation adequately. The state of North Rhine-Westphalia recently adopted a programme to eliminate the elitist tradition in education whereby the studies of Gymnasium pupils were separate from all others. All advanced nations in Western Europe have struggled with this type of reform measure, which is more socio-political in origin than pedagogically determined, in that equality of educational opportunity and equality of vocational professional recognition are at issue. The classical separation between 'formal' and 'vocational' studies is no longer tolerated, and model experiments are under way to establish an entirely new institutional form. In spite of the fact that these reforms are just now taking place in Western Europe, it may be of value to note that they are one of the final steps toward full modernization and not the beginnings of the post-modern era. Such a condition indicates how strongly traditional values and institutions have been embedded in Western culture and what an enormous task modernization set for itself.

The crucial element of the German reform in this discussion is the qualitiative criteria which the West Germans have selected to determine if a field of studies, whether it be vocational or general, is to be counted as 'higher' in nature. The Germans are explicit in maintaining that the worthiness of any study to be included in the curriculum of the upper secondary school, regardless whether the sphere is 'nature, technology, language, politics, economics, religion or art', is the degree to which it possesses a scientific or pre-scientific orientation. A field of studies is seen to possess a scientific orientation if it employs explicit 'standard methods of observation' and a theoretical framework. Such fields stand in direct contrast to studies having a foundation in 'poetical intuition, religious relevation, ideological derivative, or such' (Strukturförderung, 1973: 25-31).

Methodologically, the Germans maintain that all higher studies must reject a teaching process based on a formal presentation of a body of knowledge and instead concentrate on educating toward critical thinking. All students, regardless of discipline or level of studies, are expected to learn to develop, on the basis of tentative data interpretation, systematic thought and action schemes, appropriate categories, and hierarchies. The important focus of all studies would thereby be with fundamental scientifically oriented cognitive processes.

The demands of industrial society are accepted as given by educational policy-makers in North Rhine-Westphalia, which means the students are not only expected to learn to think in a scientifically appropriate manner, but that they should also prepare themselves for the world of work in the industrial age. Study profiles are now emerging in the schooling organization which are intended to give the student an opportunity to engage in the development of some form of saleable skills.

The kind of skills development opportunities which would be available are open-ended and limited only by the condition that a given course of studies possess a scientific orientation. If, by chance, studies are engaged in which do not yet have the above requisites, i.e. work orientation or science base, the student is expected to participate in science oriented exercises sufficient to ensure that he or she is able to work and think appropriate to the demands of the industrial society. Science work for secondary students is placed in such an important place because almost all students move from secondary school into one of two spheres:

(a) Should study in higher education take place, students are required, regardless of realm of study at universities or technical colleges, to engage in a learning process that is science based.

(b) Should the person move into the work world, that person would confront a social condition that is largely determined by science or technology and he or she would only survive productively if he or she were able to cope with its demands.

A number of study profiles are anticipated to emerge in the upper level of the secondary school since the demands of modern society continue to expand. Consequently, the German planners have declared any attempt to adhere to a conceptualization of 'system' or 'unified studies' found in traditional general courses to be nothing more than a romantic notion which is doomed to failure since it would be based on romantic ideology rather than realistic critical assessment. In spite of the fact that profiles of studies are expanding, the rhetorical question is asked as to whether there is a limit to the number of study profiles possible. Such a question allows the planners to argue the nonsense of such a concern since an expanding scientific world would expect it to take place, but it is stressed that a new way of viewing the expansion of fields is necessary. An assumption to the entire plan is that there is no denying movement toward both specialization proliferation and also interdisciplinary cooperation, which corresponds to progress in specializations. It is further assumed that the student must come to understand the meaning of the expanding scientific process as the means of production in the society. It becomes necessary for the student, at least at the propaedeutic stage to concentrate his science learning on that which belongs to fundamental scientific-technological civilization. It is forecast that a convergence of learning processes at the propaedeutic stage would occur even as fields of study increase. This means the possibility of a radical shrinkage of disciplines even as the number of studies specializations emerging out of the discipline increase. Bearing this conception in mind we see that general education becomes science education. The mature modern world finds itself grouping to evolve a programme of studies which is science based in terms of content and methodology and which will also qualify the young who work in a scientific-technological world.

THE ATTACK AGAINST SCIENCE

This is a growing assault on science that has rocked this mode of inquiry to the point that it is often viewed as being on the defence or in total retreat. The claim made by defenders of science is that this assault represents a revulsion not just against science but against all rationality and objectivity and a move toward intuition and extreme subjectivity (see, for example, Scheffler, 1967).

The 'hippy/flower-power subculture' has usually received high criticism for being the culprits who reject science since they are seen as

> conscientiously irrational, deliberately making language opaque; comprehension is sought instead through mystic experience supported by hallucinogenic drugs; a meta-language system is sought to describe the oneness and unity of man with nature, which bypasses the scientific job of analyzing it rationally; nonrational states of mind, typically schizophrenia, are glorified'
> (Rose and Rose, 1969: 260).

Defenders of science are correct in determining that at least objectivity in the conventional sense is under attack, but this challenge is left unanswered as long as slur tactics are resorted to. What these defenders usually fail to observe is that it is not the value of objectivity that is being challenged but rather their claim that science itself is objective. The attacks are levelled against the two modern phases of science which we have discussed. We noted that its first phase was its philosophical and its second phase its social, utilitarian value.

With regard to the first phase, we observed that science promised to provide surer access to the secrets of Nature and reality. So successful have been the sciences in transforming the world that modern man has come to believe that the promise of science with respect to the basic questions of reality were being fulfilled. Modern man, according to Theodore Roszak, has come to view premodern and traditional cultures in the contemporary world as systems of mythology juxtaposed against one another. When one culture replaces another its myths are merely replaced by a new set of myths: 'a *re*mythologizing of men's thinking'. Science promised to do better, for it intended to '*de*mythologize' men's thinking, to bring people's ideas into clear unadulterated focus with regard to a person's relationship to reality, truth, and beauty (Roszak, 1969: 210).

The modern world became so socialized to the truths of science that individuals were unable to see the world in any other way than that in which science had defined it. This world view is now under attack and the symbolic empire on which it was built is crumbling. The central message in the attack is that reality is as much in the eyes of the beholder as it is in the thing in itself — a simple message, but an awesome one. Social sciences, being the least established, have come under the most direct attack.

Sociologists such as Peter Berger and Thomas Luckmann demonstrate persuasively 'that reality is socially constructed'. As a matter of fact, these man suggest that the intellectual antecedents of the sociology of knowledge have long reflected such a position. Marx, who established the root propositions of the sociology of knowledge, maintained that man's consciousness is determined by economic structure; he was followed by other thinkers such as Max Scheler, Friedrich Nietzsche, and Karl Mannheim who in one way or another were to recognize that knowledge must always be knowledge reflecting some bias or position.

They maintained that ideas have a relational quality or relativism from which we cannot escape (Berger and Luckmann, 1966).

Anthropologist Carlos Casteneda studied for ten years under an old Indian named Don Juan and used psychotropic plants during most of this time only to discover that such plants were not a part of Don Juan's life but that he had used them only as an aid to help Casteneda gain glimpses of a reality to which he was otherwise deaf and blind. Considerations with regard to the relativity of values in cultures had long been implicit in anthropology. From Boas had come the challenge that other civilizations may exist, 'based perhaps on different traditions and on a different equilibrium of emotion and reason, which are of no less value than ours . . .' (Boas, 1911: 208). From Ruth Benedict would come the admonition that even in man's philosophical probings he cannot go behind his own cultural bias: 'his very concepts of true and false will still have reference to his particular traditional customs' (Benedict, 1934: 2). Melvill J. Herskovits, who has been active in this field for over thirty years, carried the concept as far as anyone by establishing a working definition of cultural relativism (Herskovits, 1973). These early anthropologists concentrated almost exclusively on values and attitudes, but it was Casteneda who came to respond to 'perceptual solicitations of a world outside the description we have learned to call reality', and in the process awakened a whole generation to the possibility of eliminating their own blindness and finding new, more meaningful world views (Casteneda, 1972: 103).

Anthropological linguists, who support the so-called Whorfian hypothesis that cultures using different languages interpret reality differently, have gained new visibility. Benjamin Lee Whorf originally postulated the thesis that the very structure of languages determines the way in which individuals interpret experience (Whorf, 1956). Edward Sapir had earlier made a claim similar to that of Whorf and would undoubtedly have agreed with Berger and Luckmann that language, probably the greatest socializer that exists, actualizes the tendency to see realities symbolically and colours reality not only between languages but even between dialects (Sapir, 1964: 1-44). This notion has been tempered somewhat in recent times but men such as Jerome Bruner continue to demonstrate that language does critically influence cognitive processes (Bruner et al., 1956).

Psychiatrists such as Ronald D. Laing challenge using the concept of schizophrenia as criteria for determining sanity or insanity. According to Laing, the concept might be used as a standard for measuring capacity of humans to adapt to the external world, the world of objectivity and rationality, but it prevents persons from exploring their inner world without being characterized as mentally ill. Society in this context has defined the substance of reality and hospitalizes many who explore elements of reality outside its domain (Laing, 1967). Laing has made us aware of the social context of our own reality structure and has caused thoughtful people to reassess judgements which may be passed on others who venture outside conventional reality.

Even though the challenge to objectivity has touched the soft sciences just mentioned, hard natural sciences pretend to remain aloof. Scheffler has pointed out that even though the ideal of objectivity is partially applicable to 'history, philosophy, or human affairs', the demands physical scientists make on a 'staggering range of issues of natural fact' as they subject these issues 'continuously to the joint tests of theoretical coherence and observational fidelity' lead rational people to conclude that, through natural sciences, modern man is at last beyond his fantasies and somehow in touch with ultimate nature (Scheffler, 1967: 3).

However, from the ranks of natural sciences themselves have come men who challenge such a frame of reference. Michael Polanyi strikes at the core of the issue in his contention that scientists attempt to 'seek at all costs' to eliminate from science those elements of man which are deemed subjective, that they strive to play down all but an 'objectivist framework even though that cannot account for the intellectual powers, passions, personal, human appraisals of theories (Polanyi, 1958: 15-17). Indeed, Polanyi not only suggests the role of subjectivity in scientific theory building, but he also maintains that it is essentially an intuitive and mystical enterprise. 'Like love, to which it (personal knowledge) is akin', states Polanyi, 'this commitment is a "shirt of flame" blazing with passion, and also like love, consumed by a universal demand. Such is the true sense of objectivity in science . . .' (1958: 64). And it seems that this commitment is that which structures the inter-subjectivity which we call objectivity. Thomas Kuhn suggests that the basic difference between the hard sciences and other enterprises is that the work of scientists is 'based firmly on a settled consensus acquired from scientific education and reinforced by subsequent life in the profession' (Kuhn, 1963: 343). The utter subjectivity of the hard sciences is therefore masked; the scientist is so socialized to the assumption that the scientific community knows what the world is like, that he concentrates his efforts on completing the picture of the universe which has been handed down to him. In the process he learns to suppress any novelties which are subversive to that commitment.

Such a declaration flies in the face of typical descriptions of open mindedness, creative work, theory development, hypothesis testing and the like which we read in the introductory chapter of most science textbooks or in the complex treatise of science. Margaret Masterson recently suggested that Kuhn had been so widely read and positively regarded among scientists themselves because he has actually described how scientists are trained and what they actually do rather than perpetuate the philosophy of science myth that science is a critical, dynamic process. He appeals to scientists because his 'material is recognizable and familiar to actual scientists, they find his thinking about it easy to understand' (Masterman in Lakatos and Musgrave, 1970: 59).

We shall concentrate here on the education of the natural scientists in order to demonstrate how they are socialized. Kuhn points out that 'the single most striking feature of this field is that to an extent totally unknown in other creative fields it is conducted through textbooks' (Kuhn, 1963: 344).

Textbooks 'address themselves to an already articulated body of problems, data, and theory, most often to the particular set of paradigms to which the scientific community is commited at the time they are written' (1962: 135). These are reinforced by writers of popular science publications for laymen and by philosophers of science who analyse the logic and structure of the scientific body of knowledge. In contrast, students of music, arts, and literature gain their education 'by exposure to the works of other artists, principally earlier artists' (1962: 164). If textbooks are used, they play a secondary role to the direct exposure to the art forms themselves. In the social sciences, which serve as half-way houses between the arts and science, the textbook has greater significance but the student struggles with the 'classics' of his field or secondary literature. Consequently, the students of the arts and social sciences are constantly confronted with the conflicts, the contrasting methodologies, the alternative theories, and the unique terminologies in their fields. More importantly, the student deals with 'competing and incommensurable solutions to these problems, solutions that he must ultimately evaluate for himself' (1962: 164).

The natural science student goes through a much different process: typically, the undergraduate student of chemistry, physics, astronomy, geology, or biology acquires the substance of his field from books written especially for students. Until he is ready, or very nearly ready, to commence work on his own dissertation, he is neither asked to attempt trial research projects nor exposed to the immediate products of research done by others, that is, to the professional communications that scientists write for each other. There are no collections of 'Readings' in the natural sciences. Nor is the science student encouraged to read the historical classics of his field — works in which he might discover other ways of regarding the problems discussed in his textbook, but in which he would also meet problems, concepts, and standards of solution that his future profession has long since discarded and replaced (1963: 344).

What Kuhn has outlined, and what any former student of the natural sciences immediately identifies with is 'a narrow and rigid education, probably more so than any other except perhaps orthodox theology' (1962: 165). It is of little consequence which textbook or which teacher science students encounter, for they inevitably 'differ in no way in terms of substance or conceptual structure'. The student is rarely if ever confronted with problems which confront the profession, but he is exposed almost exclusively to problem solutions which have become standard examples of the conceptual structure of the discipline. The entire enterprise is deliberate in its socializing endeavours and when engaged in over a period of several years it is almost certain to produce the frame of mind in the neophyte deemed appropriate by the profession (Kuhn, 1963: 344-45).

The advantage seen by Kuhn of such a programme is that there is no chaos in the profession because essentially everyone works with the same scientific world view. However, as scientific work progresses, anomalies or findings emerge which do not fit the contemporary theory. This accumulation process actually eventuates in recurring scientific revolutions since the exceptions to the rule pile up until they become intolerable under the existing world view. It is then that a reconceptualization is forced on the scientific community and another generation begins a new indoctrination process into the new 'paradigm'.

It is evident under the conditions outlined above that science is a mythologizing process, and perhaps it is the most dogmatic of mythologizers. Let us cite one example as an illustration. The Kpelle of Liberia maintain a highly traditional world view which defines knowledge as the 'ability to demonstrate one's mastery of the Kpelle way of life'. Truth is the 'conformity of one's statements and actions to that way of life'. The Kpelle recognize that different cultures have different standards with their own inherent knowledge and truth. For them there are no ultimate standards; instead the culture defines the standards. That Americans boil their water determines nothing for the Kpelle. That the Chinese can gain greater yield from their rice crops determines nothing for the manner in which the Kpelle should grow their crops. To the frustration of the developers the Kpelle see little reason to change their ways because their standards, being profoundly relativistic, are self-validating (Gay and Cole, 1967: 89-92).

In contrast to traditional orientations such as the Kpelle, modern scientists assume universals which transcend cultural variations and relativism, and have turned their notions into a world-wide intellectual colonialism far greater than political colonialism of the past. Before one disparages over the commitment of scientific ideology, we might mention a point of view expressed by people such as Joseph Pearce, who suggests that the relationship between what people think exists 'out there in the world' and what they actually experience are highly symbiotic. In fact, the asking of questions and the passionate concern for their answers eventuates in making the answers possible. For Pearce, conversion to a frame of reference, be it science or religion, is a necessary antecedent to actualizing anything. The objectivity of science becomes another blind subjectivity to which a whole community gives its allegiance; nevertheless, that allegiance is critical in bringing forth effects (Pearce, 1973).

Those reacting against science argue that its claim of being objective and therefore more nearly akin to nature is not warranted. Science is seen as nothing more and nothing less than another faith attempting to impose its wares on the world community in the name of objective truth and logical thinking.

The scientific community is also being told that science teaching is almost entirely indoctrination into the faith. It is seen as a process where hypotheses are taught but not tested beyond their own self-validating procedures. Scientific education is condemned as a process in which scientific 'laws' are not discovered but in which they are learned; this learning is then set forth in textbooks and validated in carefully designed laboratory experiments.

In spite of this situation, even men such as Kuhn defend science, arguing that it is the one sure field of inquiry that leads to progress. Scientific revolutions, and therefore scientific progress, is a product of the very manner in which scientists work. In contrast, the arts and philosophy in their traditional mould are fields which fail to progress as disciplines mainly because the nature of their work is one of breaking away from the traditional, the past. These areas are characterized by 'constant criticism and the proliferation of new modes of practice', but in no obvious sense is there linear progress as there is in natural science (Kuhn, 1970: 244).

The second contemporary protest is levelled against the very progress science claims for itself. Materially, scientific progress has led to an increase in physical resources and energy production, while socially, its contribution has been to diminish the sense of personal significance of the individual. We shall look briefly at both of these trends and explore the reasons why they have led to a disenchantment with science.

We shall mention but three historical examples of scientific explorations leading to important conceptual constructs which have been responsible for the decline in man's sense of self-worth. The first major blow came when the Ptolemaic concept was replaced by the theory of a heliocentric universe. The Ptolemaic system, which existed throughout Christianity, placed the earth and therefore man at the centre of everything, but in 1514 Copernicus published a short report which postulated that the sun is located at the centre of the universe and that the planets including the earth form orbits around the sun. This theory, which became the accepted view of the scientific world, forced man to abandon much of his egoism and place himself in a more 'objective' diminished perspective, since the universe no longer revolved around him.

Darwin provided the next major blow to man's self-image by postulating a theory that all life, including human life, is a product of organismic evolution. In the Darwinian concept of evolution, man did not hold a unique place separate from animals, but was related to all animal life. Although Darwin saw man as the highest expression of the evolutionary process, man could no longer see himself as special or unique.

Freud was to serve still another blow to man's crippled self-image in that his theory of the subconscious destroyed the faith of man in his own rationality and consciousness. After Freud, man saw himself driven by forces over which he exercised little control. Man was neither special nor was he controlled by forces within himself since they were beyond the reach of his own rational faculties.

In traditional society man had held himself in an elevated position. He had maintained what Crane Brinton called a feeling of his own dignity which set him apart from other forms of life. He considered the world to be his to subdue and conquer. The march of science had wrenched man from his special position in the universe, had thrown him into the throng of all life, and had even robbed him of the belief that he was master of his own self.

We are able to chart an inverse relationship between the decline in man's sense of relative importance in the universe and the rise of energy production and power. It would be pointless to outline the obvious increase in energy and its consumption. It is also unnecessary to describe in detail problems related to this increase since it has become so apparent that we need only mention a few examples: Hiroshima and atomic warheads as a consequence of nuclear fusion and fission; IBMs as a part of space exploration; pollution and a world energy crisis in relation to modern modes of travel; soil depletion and erosion in conjunction with agroindustry; bodily disturbances and ills related to refined and preserved foods. A major share of the protest against science can be seen against this backdrop, since the problems science has created for the modern world often tend to outweigh the advantages. I.I. Rabi describes the impact on him of Alamogordo where he participated in the detonation of the first atomic bomb:

> At first I was thrilled. It was a vision. Then a few minutes afterward, I had gooseflesh all over me when I realized what this meant for the future of humanity. Up until then, humanity was after all, a limited factor in the evolution and process of nature. The vast oceans, lakes and rivers, the atmos-

phere, were not very much affected by the existence of mankind. The new powers represented a threat not only to mankind but to all forms of life; the seas and the air. One could foresee that nothing was immune from the tremendous powers of these new forces. My own concern was to join in any efforts to contain these dangers (Bernstein, 1975: 58).

Robert Oppenheimer, who possessed the greatest American scientific mind at the time of the development of the atomic bomb, was led to confess in 1948:

> In some sort of crude sense, which no vulgarity, no humor, no overstatement can quite extinguish, the physicists have known sin, and this is a knowledge which they cannot lose (in Harris, 1976: 67).

Alfred North Whitehead could hardly have dreamed of the significance of his statement 'that the world had got hold of a general idea [science] which the world could neither live with nor live without' (1926: 63). Scientific progress has implicitly resolved to 'denature the vital facts of our existence' to the point that we view ourselves as little more than the simplest of expendable organisms (Polanyi, 1962: 141), and at the same time, scientific progress had provided mankind with the potential to utterly destroy not only his own existence but that of all higher forms of life.

We are unable to stop here. The protest penetrates scientific ideology further. We have observed that the advocates of science education legitimized the study of science as a part of higher schooling by arguing its potential to liberally train its subjects. It was argued that science could transmit a set of higher values, train the mind to think critically, and help its recipients appreciate beauty in its highest forms. Scientific inquiry now dominates modern education and has even had a profound impact on the most critical and reflective of studies such as philosophy. It has also long since dropped any pretence of being liberal in any traditional way. Disregarding the conventional aspirations of liberal educators to seek higher values or appreciate beauty, we will look at the capacity to think critically. In one respect, scientists are prepared to deal competently with the puzzles or problems that exist within the framework of their personal scientific specializations; however, according to Kuhn, this training is deficient, in two major respects. First, the rigidity of training ill prepares the scientists to cope with the scientific revolutions that occur. Scientists as a body usually hold to the paradigm which they were taught as students; therefore when a revolution occurs, an entire new generation must be indoctrinated into the new scientific truths. Secondly, science education does not prepare the scientist to conceive scientific paradigms. The training is so thorough that, as anomalies accumulate, the scientist is unable to break away from his old paradigm and consider new, more adequate scientific explanations. Even so, science has gone through enormous revolutions. We have observed that the rigidity of science ultimately provides the source of its own revolutions by producing evidence that the old paradigm is not adequate to cope with accumulated findings. Kuhn claims the new theory is usually conceived by 'a young man or a new one to the field'. It seems science itself does not suffer from its orientation and 'the loss due to rigidity accrues only to the individual' (Kuhn, 1962: 165). Such a conclusion is harmless enough as long as we restrict ourselves to science itself. But if science permeates all fields of inquiry, it may produce victims of the most narrow indoctrination and the highest dogmatism, who are unable to deal with genuine alternatives or critical dilemmas. If we do not halt the trend toward a total take-over of science in education, where will we train those critical minded decision-makers who will be able to weigh adequately the issues that bear on civilization?

4

TECHNOLOGY IN EDUCATION

We might pause briefly to note that our major focus in earlier chapters was on goals. Chapter 2 concentrated mainly on purposes of mass education as required by the nation state and Chapter 3 discussed the changing purposes of the higher learnings. We now turn away from these and focus our attention on the delivery system – the technology, which has been established to achieve these ends. A word of caution is necessary because distinctions between ends and means are in many ways artificial constructs and can never be completely separated from one another. In fact, we shall see that the modern technology which we have developed to achieve our ends has become an end in itself.

TOWARD A TECHNOLOGICAL SOCIETY

Technology means the systematic application of knowledge to accomplish some goal; consequently, it can exist in every sphere of human life. The most dramatic manifestations of technology have been felt in economic and especially industrial development; these have become so pervasive that it is impossible to conceive of modernity without conjuring up a vision of continual technological advancement.

An economy is considered modern if it demonstrates its ability to enlarge and diversify the production of goods and services per capita over a sustained period of time. In order for any economy to accomplish this task, it is necessary for national income substantially to exceed sustained population growth. A necessary but not solely sufficient condition for such a process to occur is the establishment of a dynamic technology. When technological development is great enough to allow an economy continually to reinvest a percentage of its savings back into the economy, it has reached what Walter Rostow has called the 'take-off' stage of economic growth (1960: 7-8).

Britain was the first country where modern economic conditions developed. During the first half of the nineteenth century France, Belgium, and the United States passed into the stage of economic development and by the end of the century they were joined by Germany, Sweden and Japan. Other Western nations, including Russia and Canada, have also achieved such a status though most countries of the world are still trying to balance disparities between population and economic growth. A thorough analysis of economic modernity would take us too far afield, but we do wish to draw on certain technological concepts which have been important to the development of modern educational technology.

Our first major point has to do with a frame of mind which social scientists refer to as rationality. Although rationality reflects elements of philosophical rationalism, it pertains more nearly to Max Weber's notion of *Zwecksrationalität* or the rationality of means and ends. It involves considerations of appropriate means (technology) to achieve 'discrete individual ends' (Weber, 1947: 115). A number of means and ends are usually rationalized together, their relative importance or priority being weighed as well as the potential positive and negative consequences of alternative courses of action. Modern technological thinking involves the application of scientific and rationally organized knowledge to achieve the ends sets forth and usually involves operationalizing the ends to specific practical outcomes.

Enormous human energy has been invested in an attempt to rationalize modern societies to increase the efficiency level of production to its maximum. In fact, we have arrived at a point at which technique has become an ideology. This ideology has permeated every sphere of modern social life and in many respects forms the basis on which the quality of any endeavour is judged. Technique ideology simply suggests that means toward all ends have become conscious, clear, deliberate acts, the intention being to apply the most efficient means possible to achieve a given end. With the intervention of rational judgement, technical operations which are based on convention or tradition are subjected to the scrutinizing efficiency assessment. Ellul suggests that we arrive in the mature modern age at a point at which we do not simply test the relative efficiency of traditional practices, but look for new 'better' alternatives. That is, given variations of a technical means in a given cultural milieu, such as catching fish by hand or net, it is no longer sufficient to select the better operation within the limited range of two possibilities, as in this example, but to move toward 'the best means in the absolute sense, on the basis of numerical calculation' (Ellul, 1964: 21). This would involve considerations of all possible methods, even those not yet in practice; the method selected would be that which could stand up against all other means in terms of its absolute effectiveness.

Marion Levy maintains that the two most important innovations of the modern age in terms of efficiency considerations have been the development of new tools and reliance on new energy sources. 'In general the higher the multiplication of the application of energy by tools', states Levy, 'the higher the level of modernization.' The corollary to this is 'the greater the ratio of energy from inanimate sources to that of animate sources the higher the modernization' (in Hall, 1965: 25). Except for aids such as the windmill and water wheels, premodern societies, even in the city, relied heavily on human beings and animals to lift water, till the soil, grind grains and transport materials. There is an efficiency limit to all techniques and as long as traditional societies depended on the use of animals and people, they were restricted to optimal use of very low level energy sources (Sjoberg, 1960: 196).

It would be incorrect to suggest that Europe did not possess technical understanding prior to the eighteenth century, since the industrial era only signalled the blossoming of a long technical maturation period; it had been without decisive checks and had failed to thrive among peasants and low skilled labourers (Ashton, 1948: 12). For at least 750 years a slow fermentation had taken place in Europe with no immediate consequences. With the emergence of shifting populations, the development of a malleable social milieu, increased emphasis on systematic thought, the application of scientific technology, and reliance on inanimate energy sources, the Western world broke through the bonds that had confined man for thousands of years and the industrial age was born.

Ashton has identified two distinct phases of the early Industrial Revolution in England. First, during the period just prior to the 'take-off' point spoken of by Rostow, the efforts of the English were directed mainly toward harnessing forces external to man. The thrust was therefore to replace human labour-saving mechanisms by exploiting the energy of coal for smelting, atmospheric pressure for pumping, and gravitational power for turning water wheels. Toward the end of the eighteenth century, however, the nature of the problem had changed, for the ways in which these technologies had been developed were extremely wasteful. The shortage of coal and other sources of energy forced the English into the second phase of the Industrial Revolution in which they concentrated on the development of canals, power engines, power transmission techniques, and other energy-saving processes (Ashton, 1948: 74).

Very similar stages are to be observed in other lands as modern man rationalized economic systems by moving away from the animate toward the adoption of more sophisticated tools and devices which increase the efficiency of inanimate sources of energy. The technical applications which were so crucial to economic development have become a part of all spheres of modern life. The 'science of education' which is more correctly a 'technology of teaching' has also come into full maturity in modern lands. Our task here shall be to outline those aspects of modernity which bear heavily on this technology.

We have selected two major examples for discussion. First, Germany developed instructional technology which has remained labour-intensive. Secondly, England and America adopted a different labour-intensive scheme at the beginning of the modern age with America then moving away from this scheme toward inanimate instructional sources.

INSTRUCTION IN MODERN GERMANY

Although its beginnings were just the opposite, a modern instructional tradition has evolved in Germany that has relied almost exclusively on directive teacher influence. The original roots of modern German instructional practice can be traced to eighteenth-century humanitarian liberalism which, peculiar as it may seem, was best exemplified in French political philosophy. Jean Jacques Rousseau, whose writings are probably the most representative of this orientation, rejected the scholastic tradition of the past which concentrated on the mind and word, and turned attention to the physical senses. Rousseau challenged many contemporaries, such as John Locke, by maintaining that children are barely capable of reasoning and any consideration for abstractions must therefore come at the end of a child's educational experience. 'Childhood', he insisted, 'has ways of seeing, thinking, and feeling peculiar to itself' (Rousseau, 1962: 38-39).

Rousseau claimed the teacher had to be cautious, because most of the instruction of the past would prove to be invalid. In the first place, the new teacher had to concentrate on motives rather than methods. If the child wished to learn, any method would be suitable, for the inner drive in small children was the critical determinant. The task of the teacher was to create a fertile environment which would not hinder the child in his personal development.

Rousseau was the first to conceptualize a notion of self-actualization or the full development of physical, intellectual, and emotional nature of the human being. In rejecting the directive structured educational patterns of his day, he probably went too far in stressing that the child has the inner resources spontaneously to move toward a self-actualized state, if placed in an environment which will not prevent but foster native activities; he was, however, able to tilt the balance of teaching again toward the whole child.

Central to Rousseau's philosophy of education was the idea that external intervention could not accelerate the process of natural development. It could inhibit and thwart growth, but the inner workings of the child were seen to have their own schedule and time. Any attempt to short-circuit Nature's schedule would not be of advantage: 'Do you not see that in attempting to improve on her work, you are destroying it and defeating the provision she has made' (1962: 17).

Nature would take the child through infancy, boyhood, preadolescence, adolescence, and finally manhood in its own most efficient, peculiar way because 'each age and state in life has its own proper perfection, its own distinctive maturity' (1962: 65).

A final major point stressed by Rousseau was that each child possesses its own distinct, inherent temperaments. No matter how much the teacher may wish or even attempt to change them, the child possesses certain inclinations and teacher intervention only becomes a barrier to growth. This 'inner fire' of youth was in no way viewed by Rousseau as a hindrance to learning, for it was seen as the source of the drive toward fulfilment and self-realization. If the temperaments of the child did become a hindrance, then the orientation of the teacher had to be at fault and the change that took place had to reside in the indiscriminate, and probably dull, uniform, programme offered to the child.

The impact of Rousseau's ideas was immediate and far reaching. Rousseau, in 1762, had written his *Emile* in the form of a manual for a tutorial relationship, maintaining that a single person should have charge of the child throughout his education in order to avoid conflicts of authority within the child. It was Johann Pestalozzi who modified the ideas of Rousseau, making them applicable to the school setting. His practices, even though they took place in Switzerland, ultimately became the model for the Prussian primary school reforms at the beginning of the nineteenth century.

Pestalozzi had emulated Rousseau by maintaining that his school would extend beyond the verbal and intellectual tradition of the past and become a social environment which would foster the peculiar ways of seeing and feeling that existed in childhood. The teacher would not be able to impose himself into the lives of the children but would operate on the basis of mutual respect and allow spontaneous self-activity to occur.

Pestalozzi's distinctive contribution came by designing a learning environment in which the child was both able to express spontaneity and conform to the demands of a school environment. Pestalozzi's school became centred on 'object lessons' or 'observation experiences' which the teacher would introduce. He believed as did Rousseau that Nature had its own way of development, but he further believed that the teacher had a special role in the process. For him, sense observation was the external expression of, and the point of departure for, natural drives. The teacher could assist nature by removing the confusion of the sense impressions that were bombarding the child, separating objects out, and allowing their distinctiveness to manifest themselves, and placing them together to help the child see relationships and similarities. If done correctly, the number, form, and word of particular phenomena would become clear to the child. It is obvious that the notions he developed could be incorporated into the scientific and technical training of the modern age, but it is also important to point out that Pestalozzi was as much concerned with social habit formation as physical sense acquisition. Observation of devotion, faith, trust, thankfulness, and love were seen to provide the doorways to social efficiency.

Through the efforts of liberal reformers such as Diesterweg, Zeller, Harnish, and Froebel, the ideas of Pestalozzi were carried into the Prussian primary school programme and soon became the guidelines of all worthy schooling for the masses. Prussia was one of the few places in the West which attained universal primary education prior to the period of 'take-off'. We can attribute this anomaly to the Germany insight concerning political socialization advantages which would accrue to the state. Since the focus of mass schooling was forthrightly political, the German states were more than willing to provide the resources necessary to establish an extensive, labour-intensive programme of instruction. Needless to say, the optimistic and vital notions of Pestalozzi's followers were soon twisted into a total concentration on the 'social efficiency' side of the schooling programme; this came to mean indoctrination of the masses with the virtues of industry, piety, and patriotism (Tews, 1914).

In an attempt to find people who were qualified to instil these virtues, the Prussians established a policy early in the nineteenth century of placing non-commissioned military officers in the schools and teaching seminaries as teachers. In this position they proved to be most dependable because they accepted with pleasure the counsel and directions of their superiors and maintained the schools, as they had the military institutions, in a state of 'orderliness, proper conduct, cleanliness, and industry' (Tews, 1914: 116-17). Even though the practice of appointing non-commissioned officers as teachers was not widely spread, it does represent the conceptual model which Prussia relied on in spite of the honour they gave Pestalozzi for establishing the model teaching mode.

Once the technique of social efficiency was well established, the next step was to bring all aspects of learning under the efficiency label. It was under the influence of Herbart that Germany moved as deliberately as any country from 'intuitive to scientific understanding of the process of learning' (Ulich, 1961: 204). Although Herbart, who claimed to have discovered the key to the 'science of education,' died in 1841, his influence was paramount for a number of decades. Reble (1951: 209) attempted to attribute this influence to the 'clear structure and simple applicability' of his theory. Such a tribute is rather generous since his attempts to develop a general system by intertwining philosophy, psychology, and pedagogy resulted in a disarray of extensive, cumbersome, and pedestrian materials. Herbartianism in its 'clear structure and simple applicability' came rather from people who were usually too young to have known him personally and who drew from Herbart only enough to give authority to their own schemes of instruction (Dunkel, 1970).

Tuiskon Ziller in Leipzig and Wilhelm Rein in Jena became the two major Herbartianists in Germany, both of whom dropped Herbart's philosophical involvement and concentrated more on two 'improved' pedagogical notions. The first notion was that the end of education was ultimately moral in nature, an idea that had infatuated Herbart throughout his life. Ziller did little more than use Herbart to justify his own quite traditional curricular programme stressing biblical and ecclesiastical history. Herbart had conceived the idea that all instructional material must recapitulate the cultural-historical stages of evolution for the child. He maintained, therefore, that every subject matter must be grouped around epochal stages. Ziller developed a programme for the *Volksschule* which would essentially take the child through the Bible and end with the Catechism in the eighth year (Ziller, *Allgemeine Pädagogik:* 1892). Rein complemented Ziller's concern for faith in God with a programme to instil faith in the sovereign state. Consequently, this first Herbartian idea only served to perpetuate the Protestant faith and patriotism in the new German Empire.

The second Herbartian pedagogical notion — the theory of formal levels of instruction — is that which is related to technological thinking. They were considered formal because they were deemed appropriate for any level of the curricular programme and within any subject matter. Herbart's original conception consisted of four levels:

(1) Clearness, or the precise grasp of subject matter particulars which would be achieved only if the teacher would break the subject matter down to the smallest possible parts and clarify each element in its totality.

(2) Association, or the establishment of ties between each element with already known, related, or similar elements.

(3) System, or the placement and role of a particular element within the context of the whole system within which it functions.

(4) Method, or the ability to practically and usefully apply subject matter.

Ziller adopted Herbart's concepts of association, system, and method, but he divided the concept of clearness into two steps: analysis and synthesis. It was Wilhelm Rein, however, who made the system practical and sensible by simplifying Ziller's five steps and calling them Preparation, Presentation, Association, Generalization, and Application. Here was a neat and tidy outline, almost in checklist form, which the average teacher could rely on in making certain no steps were forgotten as he worked through his instructional programme. Even so, the average teacher was seen to need more technical assistance than a mere checklist, and Rein, with the help of assistants, worked out a full eight-year course of study published in eight volumes. Rein provided the teacher not only with a framework but a comprehensive, detailed, ready-made programme. It regularized the process into a formalized and mechanical format which could be easily controlled and evaluated by the school bureaucracy. Through the encouragement of the new German state the Herbartian format became deeply set in professional training and was carried into the schools with ever increasing detail. Even though the major focus of Rein was on the Volksschule, his impact also reached the Gymnasium and became a model for all instruction in Germany.

The reform movement at the turn of the twentieth century represented a challenge to Herbartian teaching technology since Pestalozzian and Rousseauian ideals were revived in the New Education Movement. The teacher was expected to move into the background and rely on the free activity of the child. The movement did indeed have an impact on teaching. However, the limits of valuable spontaneity in children was rather narrowly defined and almost completely eliminated with the emergence of National Socialism. The instructional process which had been so efficiently formalized during the previous century was restored and carried to the point of depersonalization of the teacher himself. The creative impulses of the child were no longer tolerated, the individuality of the teacher was restricted; thus National Socialism actually carried Germany and her schools to new levels of formalism.

We see in Germany the development of teaching technology which remained almost completely human oriented; however, the instructional process became systematic and regularized to the point that its workings could almost be described as machine-like. Labour-intensive instruction could be described as typical of modern educational processes which use Herbartian-type models as their basis. We shall see that America was somewhat influenced by Herbart and that Japan relied heavily on Herbart in bringing about a modern revolution within a generation.

Since formalistic pedagogy is labour-intensive, it quickly reaches a point of peak efficiency; therefore, it soon became necessary for the new world to consider possibilities for utilizing inanimate energy sources in the instructional process. Before we examine these attempts let us look at the labour-intensive phases of instructional technology in early modern America and England.

INSTRUCTION IN MODERN AMERICA AND ENGLAND

At the beginning of the nineteenth century certain groups and individuals in America and England attempted to popularize the idea that schooling would be of value not only for the leaders and elites of society but for the poor and middle classes. Schooling had also become both a welfare and an industrial issue because concern was growing as to what to do with the children crowding the streets of developing urban areas.

The monitorial system in England and America initially guaranteed that some level of education could be provided for the masses in the cities. Its main attraction was the claim that effective schooling could be accomplished without enormous financial investment. Governments had not yet recognized the potential of schooling in terms of national advantage, so it was necessary that any claim toward universal schooling include the provision that it could be accomplished without levying taxes.

Monitorial instruction, developed by Andrew Bell who had experimented with the system while serving in India as an army chaplain, and copied by Joseph Lancaster who was also British consisted of a single teacher administering education to hundreds of children. The model resembled the operations techniques that had been worked out for the early factories in England. It represented a creative attempt to structure a largely social environment so that it replicated the organizational features of the factory. Such a similarity made it attractive since that type of education was specially tailored to the future factory worker.

Up to 1,000 children would assemble in a large hall where the master would call the best children together and teach them some simple lesson or task. The children would then be sent to their stations as instructors of perhaps ten of the slower children. Their task was to give directions to the small group and to monitor the ability of those children in performing the assigned task. The master would give commands to the monitors who would in turn give commands to children, who were expected to follow the instructions in precise detail. In this way all children might go through procedures such as the following: ready the writing slate, pick up their writing instrument, place it on the slate and write a figure, put the writing instrument on the desk, turn the slate around and hold it up, all in unison. The monitors would give orders when to do the acts and they would inspect the written work of their group. Everything was carried out in a mechanical and orderly fashion with no extraneous behaviours tolerated. If successful, the instruction would proceed 'by the numbers' from task to task, in educating the children. It was claimed to cost as little as a pound or even less per pupil per year and be effective enough to accomplish its objective: education in no more than two years.

Accompanying the instructional programme for master and monitors was a creative array of teaching aids. These represented the first stages of non-book inanimate energy sources devoted to the instructional processes. Wall charts, maps, writing slates, sand boards were but a few ways in which the monitors were assisted in helping their charges learn the assigned tasks. These aids were looked upon as supplementary rather than primary since teaching was still viewed as labour-intensive.

The monitorial system soon spread throughout England and was transported with great success to the American continent. Two English societies were established by their authors. The Lancasterian Society established its own teacher preparation programme and within a quarter of a century about 3,000 schools were set up to employ these teachers. Bell's Society centred more directly in and around London but was able to set up about 500 schools. These groups claimed to have placed more than half of all working class children in school by 1835.

The Lancasterian system had already been introduced in the United States by 1806 and had a significant impact on New York City and many smaller cities (Reigart, 1916). A teacher training institution was set up in Philadelphia in 1818 and many of the prominent schools of today, such as the University of Michigan, trace their origins to Lancaster's system.

Probably the most significant impact of the monitorial schools was the seed it planted in the minds of the people that universal education was possible without much expense. Such a notion is Utopian in nature and defies common sense, not to mention economic reality. The monitorial system failed in its claim and as historian Henry Holman (1898) suggested, the outcome was more nearly 'to teach poor children next to nothing for next to nothing'. The system did pave the way for the advent of a modern school system, as the public was persuaded to support public education even if it would involve great expense.

The United States and England chose separate paths after each had given up the monitorial model. Publically-supported education in England was relatively slow in developing and, in contrast to the rapid adoption of common schooling in America, England experienced an intermediate phase between the monitorial system and compulsory education. Holding to the tradition that 'government is a necessary evil', the English moved rather cautiously toward public support even when it became apparent that large numbers of young people were without schooling under the voluntary system. Attempts at nationalization by James Kay-Shuttleworth, the first secretary of the Committee of Council, essentially a national department of education, were aborted in the 1840s (Barnard, 1947: 111). In 1858 the first national education commission was appointed to 'inquire into the state of popular education in England, and to consider what measures, if any, were required for the extension of sound and cheap elementary instruction to all classes of people'. Three years later the Newcastle Report was issued and even though the commission recognized alarming deficiencies in existing schools, its members were satisfied that most of the children were able to receive some schooling and did not deem it necessary to alter significantly the old system which had evolved.

One recommendation was to have striking consequences, however: the scheme for assisting the private enterprise with public funds. The funds would be distributed according to a system of 'payment by results'; that is, public funds would be distributed to private schools according to the number of passes the school was able to attain on external examinations. 'We have been living under a system of bounties and protection', the Secretary of the Council of Commission Robert Lowe was to declare, 'now we propose to have a little free trade' (Lowe, 1862: 165), which meant that schools would go into competition. for the funds available. Under the new system a child entered Standard I usually at the age of six. At the end of the school year he was examined, and if he was successful he would advance to the next standard. The school would be given a grant for its achievement. If he was not successful, he would be held at the same standard for another year and the school received no compensation. The successful child completed six standards in fulfilling the minimum elementary instruction programme.

The consequences for such a system appear to have been twofold. First, its proponents failed to recognize the learning deficiencies of the lower classes and this practice resulted, therefore, in nothing more than public support of the higher classes. Secondly, the external examinations concentrated on the three Rs and therefore forced an artificially narrow, fact, and drill orientation.

It required a quarter of a century to correct, to some measure, these consequences. 'Payment by results' was finally done away with and replaced by a system of block-grant payments in 1900. Robert Lowe had claimed earlier: 'If it is not cheap, it shall be efficient; if it is not efficient, it shall be cheap' (Lowe, 1862: 229). The latter hypothesis proved true: the system deteriorated since the number of teachers and the level of their morale declined at the same time as greater numbers of the young began to enter the schools.

When the block-grant system was adopted, the programme of external examinations and support for private institutions was incorporated into a system of universal schooling for all. The criteria for success of teachers and schools was to revert to more qualitative factors although the students continued to be judged on examination performance. As we turn to America following their monitorial phase, we find that mechanization came to play a much larger role than in other modern lands.

Publicly-supported   universal schooling was soon accepted as a priority factor of modernity in America and by the middle of the century the common school was a reality. By this time the Lancasterian system had fallen into complete disfavour, and it became necessary to devise a mechanism whereby schooling would be conducted efficiently enough to meet the requirements of having almost all children in school.

In spite of the famous changes in industry that were taking place at the beginning of the nineteenth century in which greater sources of inaminate power were being applied to spinning and weaving, locomotive transportation, etc. little attempt was made to devise instruction in a similar way. The monitorial experience had demonstrated that one kind of labour-intensive factory model for schooling was not appropriate: educators did not even consider the possibilities of mechanical devices for instruction beyond a few visual aids. Since schooling was labour-intensive, it became necessary to find a vast human resource of 'manpower' which had hitherto been considered largely inappropriate for the world of work: women. It is true that women had a history of participation in teaching of sorts in the old dame schools of earlier centuries, but such activities were more a welfare service than professional participation. American women had also tended school during the critical months when all men were needed as work-hands in the fields.

But with the rapid expansion of schooling, the men available could not satisfy the demand and the salaries they expected usually exceeded the income from local school tax levies. Women were willing to do school service for very little money and social conditions had reached a point at which it was acceptable to hire them. The economic value of women had already been recognized on the expanding frontier of the United States; the growing industrial settlements were also opening the way for women to move out of the home into the occupational sphere. Philosophical justification for women was also beginning to emerge.

Horace Mann and Henry Barnard both commended women as more adequate to handle the needs of the young since their emotional and moral make-up was deemed more appropriate to teaching than the more worldly, abstract world of the man.

The hero of Pestalozzi's classic books *Leonard and Gertrude* and *How Gertrude Teaches her Children* was the mother and the model teaching environment was, for Pestalozzi, the home. Indeed, if school was to be redeeming, it had to pattern itself after the affectionate and secure environment established by the mother in the home, who was able to demonstrate the true art of teaching. The father of the *Kindergarten*, Friederich Froebel, whose influence was most pronounced at the time the common school was establishing itself, accentuated the mother model even more than Pestalozzi in that he saw the basis of all education in the mother-child relationship. The instructional process consisted mainly of the songs and games they were to play together (Froebel, 1840). These notions gave ample justification for the entrance of women into the teaching profession.

By the middle of the nineteenth century women in America were quantitatively competitive with men. By 1880 almost 60 percent of all teachers were women and this figure rose to 70 percent by the turn of the century. So pronounced was the presence of women that the pronoun for teacher shifted from the masculine 'he' to the feminine 'she'. The increasing proportion of women was to continue for another two decades and would reach its peak when approximately 85 per cent of all teachers were female (Woody, 1928).

With the rapid growth of schools, many teachers found they did not have much more schooling than the children they were teaching; consequently, sophisticated teaching techniques could hardly be expected. Teachers lectured and admonished as best they could, but they relied most often on the technique of recitation which had been passed on from traditional institutions. This approach consisted of calling pupils, individually or in small groups, to the teacher's desk where they were expected to recite the lesson which had been presented in a text or which may have been dictated. Horace Mann estimated that with this method the child was engaged in recitation about one-eighth of the time and sat quietly, apparently memorizing the lesson, the other seven-eighths of the day (Brubacher, 1967).

This situation was to change somewhat during the last half of the nineteenth century as normal schools began to convey more adequately the pedagogical ideas of Pestalozzi and Herbart. Just prior to the Civil War, Edward Shelden was successful in introducing some Pestalozzian ideas, especially the so-called object lesson, into the normal school at Oswego, New York. Object lessons consisted of collections of objects or tangible demonstration materials of every sort. Within a decade the 'Oswego system' became a fad in American schools and teaching itself was to be significantly altered.

The impact of Pestalozzian principles appears to have resulted more in the collecting of teaching paraphernalia than in the development of concepts of object or sense instruction. Teachers were industrious in collecting artifacts and specimens for the school museums which sprang up throughout the country. Laboratories in schools can in large measure be attributed to the object lesson principles that had been imported. Schools were deemed adequate only if they possessed wall maps, globes, solar demonstration kits, dictionaries, abacus equipment, cones, cylinders, balls, and cubes. The child was expected to learn from actual handling and observing real objects.

Americans appear to have made as much use of this type of material as the Europeans. The American display at the international exposition in Vienna in 1873, consisting of maps, charts, textbooks, and some equipment, won some admiration. The school display in Paris in 1878 proved to be even more impressive (Oliver, 1956).

If Pestalozzi was largely responsible for the increase in material teaching aids in instruction, then Herbart was to provide inspiration toward concrete steps in teaching. Literally scores of educators journeyed to Jena, Germany, during the 1880s and 1890s to learn the 'science of education'; American educators transformed this concept into nothing more than a technology of teaching.

The concentration on method already forecast the third phase of instruction in American modernity. Compulsory education had been realized in all but the most backward states and the vast manpower requirements were largely met; therefore, it was time to concentrate on the effective use of this manpower. For all the changes that had taken place in education, the instructional process was not that dissimilar to that in traditional institutions. This was all to change as the United States approached the twentieth century. Educational measurement was born and if it promised anything, it promised efficiency. As early as 1888 Charles Eliot had delivered a paper to the National Education Association entitled, 'Can School Programs be Shortened and Enriched?' (Eliot, 1898: 51-76) and in 1911 the Association appointed a select committee on the Economy of Time in Education, giving it a special charge of eliminating waste in the school programme.

It was no accident that Frederick Taylor's famous statement, *The Principles of Scientific Management,* appeared that same year, for educators had been caught up in a national efficiency craze that was being preached by businessmen, industrialists, doctors, and laymen of every sort. Taylor's programme became the centre of the push because he claimed to have fashioned his methods from the exact sciences. He turned to experimentation, measurement, and generalization in order to discover laws of management as exact and impartial as the laws of Nature. Taylor's initial interest had been to turn the factory into a giant machine with all its parts functioning with the precision and harmony of a clock. It would, of course, be necessary for the workers in the factory to engage in activities which were not arbitrary but which would be reduced to specific, simple routines.

Raymond E. Callahan, who has written the most thorough statement about the impact of Taylorism on American educational administration, identified five major elements of scientific management relevant to education (1962: 28-34). First, time and motion studies were conducted in which a worker's job was divided into its simplest components, and the seconds or minutes required to complete each component were recorded. These were compiled to give a total profile of the worker's activities over time. The same procedure was followed with regard to the tools and machines that were being used by the worker in order to get a full description of a particular job.

Secondly, standardization was then introduced so that fundamental elements would appear time and again in any job. Theoretically, once all fundamental elements were identified, it would be a simple task to describe what usually appeared to be complex activities. Elements were intially identified rather arbitrarily, but as descriptions accumulated they were perfected in such a way as to reveal better and faster fundamental elements.

Thirdly, specific and measurable tasks were established daily for every worker, who received an instruction card describing in minute detail what was to be done, how it was to be done, and the exact time allowed for doing it. A second aspect of this element was a so-called 'bonus plan' which paid the worker according to the pace that he was able to maintain: the faster the pace the higher the pay.

Fourthly, functional foremanship was instituted which consisted of supervisors who were assigned to teach the workers how to carry out their jobs. Written instructions were provided but the foreman was responsible to help the worker both understand and carry them out.

Fifthly, a planning department was instituted which was responsible for the entire operation. It would do the time-and-motion studies, develop the ever changing job descriptions, establish the rules, all 'on a scientific basis'.

Great energy was expended between 1911 and 1930 to apply the above principles to education. 'Educational efficiency experts' and 'human engineers' emerged in ever increasing numbers. Ellwood P. Cubberley, one of the leading administrators and educational historians in the country at that time, described scientific management as 'one of the most significant movements in all our educational history' (Cubberley, 1916: 325). The concepts of Taylorism were applied to all facets of schooling, fulfilling the dream of modern administrators that the school would finally rid itself of the ascriptive, traditional moulds of the past and become a truly modern institution patterned after the most advanced institution of modernity — the factory.

The most popular school organizational structure to emerge was the platoon system as developed in Gary, Indiana and New York City. Since platoons of students were working, studying, playing, and eating in constant rotation order, all facilities were in constant use. Plant efficiency was obtained by almost doubling the hours the school was open. The efficiency of teachers was increased by making them specialists of specific learning sequences which allowed them to repeat the same activities many times with different groups of children. The physical learning capabilities of all children were increased by caring for their health and nutritional needs. The total programme was geared to process the 'raw material' according to differing individual capacities and inclinations (Bobbitt, 1912: 260).

The instructional process, being an integral element of the school factory, was also subjected to the rigours of the managers. Joseph S. Taylor, superintendent of schools in New York City, outlined the relationship of his teachers to scientific management principles:

> (1) the state as employer must cooperate with the teacher as employee, for the latter does not always understand the science of education; (2) the state provides experts who supervise the teacher, and suggests the processes that are most efficacious and economical; (3) the task system obtains in the school as well as in the shop, each grade being given a measured quantity of work to be accomplished in a given term; (4) every teacher who accomplishes the task receives a bonus, not in money, but in the form of a rating which may have money value; (5) those who are unable to do the work are eliminated either through the device of a temporary license or of a temporary employment; (6) the differential rate is applied to the teacher, quantity and quality of service being considered in the rating; (7) the result ought to be a maximum output at a low relative cost, since every repeater costs as much as a new pupil; (8) the teacher thus receives better wages but only after demonstrated fitnesss for high position; (9) hence we ought to have the most desirable combination of an educational system − relative cheapness of operation and high salaries (Taylor, 1912: 350-51).

Following Frederick Taylor's principles New York, and other cities which adopted the programme, relieved the teacher of all burdens with regard to the way in which they should teach since the 'burden of finding the best methods is too large and too complicated to be laid on the shoulders of the teachers' (Bobbitt, 1913: 51-52); This burden was performed by the 'expert staff in the central office' (1913: 54-55), which became the 'planning department' conducting time-and-motion studies, determining objectives, assigning tasks to the teachers, and supervising their performance.

Once a method was developed, the teacher was expected to follow its dictates in detail. Teachers were not permitted to follow caprice in method and as clearly superior methods were discovered, the teachers were expected to employ them. It was maintained that these limitations on teachers were not according to 'personal arbitrary authority', but 'those of law' (1913: 93).

In summary, we might stress that the efficiency movement of the early part of the twentieth century accepted as given the necessity of teaching being labour-intensive. Although there were systematic attempts to reduce the number of teachers to an absolute and economical minimum, there was almost no consideration of the possibility that teachers were interchangeable with inanimate sources of instruction. In contrast to industry, which had moved to high levels of material sophistication with assembly line operations, communications technology including high speed printing, telephones, radio, and even television in the latter part of the period, instruction had not been appreciably affected by these innovations. There was an occasional statement such as that attributed to Thomas Edison in 1916 that the motion picture would replace the teacher (Finn, 1960: 386), but the introduction of technical equipment was still in its infancy.

However, a subtle change had already occurred in teaching in America which corresponded in some ways to the broader change in industry and business, i.e. the relationship between the worker (teacher) and the machine (material aids). During the modern age the nature of labour itself underwent a qualitative change in that the worker came to be perceived as an appendage to the machine. It was the worker's task, both in the factory and commerce, to do what the machine could not do. The worker was replaced as quickly as technology could eliminate his job. The consequences of this evolution have been to create a broad stratum of semi-skilled workers, doing varied tasks which require widely differing ability levels. The semi-skilled worker has replaced the skilled craftsman and has become a dominant craft category in modern industry. In fact, changes in production and work modes are gradually obliterating the traditional divisions between unskilled, semi-skilled, and skilled occupations (Schelsky, 1957: 43).

The teacher as worker was not yet perceived by Americans during the progressive era as 'an appendage' to the educational machine, but the efforts of school administrators were clearly intended to place them in just that position. For them the 'science of education' had clearly come of age and though the teacher would resemble the workman more than the educator, she would fit comfortably into the mechanistic organization conceived by the administrators.

One wonders why the teachers did not rebel against this threat. There is some evidence that they had already willingly become an appendage to a different aspect of the apparatus. European visitors were acutely aware that they had already given up their own autonomy. Americans had come to advocate the importance of 'educating to books', investing great sums in interesting children in books by building libraries in every secondary school and in the smallest communities. But the foreign visitors who visted the schools observed a negative side to the American focus on books. Instruction was seen to be determined less by the teacher and even her supervisor than by the textbook the teacher used. The German, Ernst Schlee, lamented the fact that textbooks contained a series of questions with answers which the teachers used during the discussion time (Schlee, 1894: 15). Friedrich Nüchter was even more alarmed than Schlee when he discovered that the content of the textbooks was now the 'absolute ruler' and in fact the 'textbook was the real teacher' in the American schools (Nüchter, 1915: 16). It follows, then, that it would present little difficulty to replace the textbook with a human engineer.

It has been impossible to include in this discussion the role of humanists during the progressive era. Many of the progressives jumped on the band-wagon of science and supported the efficiency movement, while the more reflective expressed grave reservations as to its potential (Yengo, 1964). The progressive side of the American scene, however, represented at best only a threat to the established schooling programme, and enough to stifle the efficiency movement during the late 1920s and 1930s.

Even at the time when progressives were enjoying their 'heyday' other events were occurring which would be more decisive in the stream of history. American technology had reached a stage in which it was not just characterized by smoky steel mills, the assembly line, and the dirty working environment. The electronic age and other advanced technological processes were ushering in a new type of industrial environment characterized by clean, silent, working conditions all run by a limited number of highly qualified engineers and technicians. The word 'technocracy' emerged for the first time in the public debate in America in 1932, although it had been coined some thirteen years earlier by William H. Smyth. Americans, finding themselves in the middle of the depression, were becoming disillusioned with the promise of modern industry. The high levels of unemployment, the waste, and lack of economic coordination in industry needed some explanation.

One logical explanation for it all was that technology had grown too complex for the simple politician or businessman to handle. The main spokesmen of this particular point of view joined together in groups such as the Technical Alliance, Technocracy Incorporated, and the Continental Committee on Technocracy, and set out to right the faltering machine of state. Economist Thortsen Veblen's essays and books almost represented a technocratic manifesto in declaring the beauty of the 'specialized, complex, and interdependent productive and distributive mechanism' which, however, called for a 'discipline of the machine process' since it could not tolerate obsolete notions such as business leadership or private ownership. The technocracy could only fulfil its destiny of providing for all human wants if human passions and selfishness were not allowed to intervene and disrupt its processes. For Veblen, the saving grace of mechanical technology was that it was impersonal and dispassionate, because it served human needs, 'without fear or favor or respect of persons, prerogatives or politics'. But it was susceptible to interference, breakdown or sabotage from the ignorant, undisciplined leaders of industry. Since technicians and engineers were the builders of and organizers of the various parts of the technological system, they were the only ones with the knowledge, objectivity and competence to run it.

The orginators of the concept of technocracy interpreted it in rather narrow terms, believing that its success or failure depended on the leadership value of technicians and engineers (Veblen, 1921). As the modern age came to full maturity, this point of view was superseded by more penetrating analyses. This is not to minimize the dominant role these people have assumed, but the meaning of technocracy has gone beyond a certain group of specialists and now represents the whole rationalized, mechanized, efficiency-oriented apparatus of modern societies. Within this framework the worker is an element of the system who is viewed more and more as an appendage of its operations. Such a point of view invaded all systems after the Second World War, including the schools.

Once a teacher is viewed as an appendage to the operations of schooling, it is only a matter of time before the activities she engages in are eroded and replaced by a more reliable, objective instructional apparatus. This has not yet happened, but the technological ideology of America after the Second World War pointed unreservedly in this direction. Full mechanization of the schooling process would await the introduction of automation into schooling. The main characteristics of this period were mainly applications of pre-war industrial and communications technology, mainly of the mass media variety. In the school setting, films, duplication materials, and radio were considered supplemental to the main thrust of instruction; that is, they were still considered as audio-visual aids to the teacher. The only use of mass media as a primary instruction tool was in areas where no 'qualified person' was available. *Encyclopaedia Britannica* Films, for example, put together 300 half-hour films on physics and chemistry which were intended to cover the material high school students were expected to learn. Where no science teachers existed, these films became the course of studies for isolated pupils (Finn, 1960: 388).

Television also became an important mass media tool. Finn has outlined four major types of television instruction: (a) broadcast on an educational channel, which means public agencies in cities or states provide funds for non-profit educational and public service purposes; (b) broadcast on a commercial channel, where the main interest is advertising and profit; (c) closed-circuit television, which involves live instructors who provide supplemental instruction, or primary instruction 'exclusive of classroom teachers'; and (d) closed-circuit television in which filmed lectures are circulated 'as replacement for classroom teachers' (1960: 388).

In recent years television for instructional purposes has reached staggering proportions. Programmes for young children, such as Sesame Street (pre-school age) and Electric Company (Lower-Primary grades) cost millions of dollars to produce and are viewed by high percentages of all American children. So pervasive is their impact that the major problem evaluators encounter is finding children for control group purposes who do not watch the programmes.

At the other end of the educational continuum television is being used for the most advanced instructional purposes. Several television sets exist in most large lecture halls at American universities so that the professor can lecture and show demonstrations of the greatest detail to hundreds of students simultaneously. Often, films of previous performances are taped so that the professor is not even present at many of the sessions. These films can be made available in areas where people of high competence are few or the newest techniques of a craft are not yet known.

So long as instructional technology is oriented as a mass media tool, the teacher has remained a preferred instructional element; however, in the past two decades a new orientation toward education has gained prominence. If taken seriously, it implies a mode of instruction which economically can only be tolerated when conducted by mechanical devices. This is the idea of individualized instruction.

Most forms of individualized instruction stress diagnosis of a person's individual requirements and abilities and the assignment of the student to a programme of studies which will best satisfy these needs. Let us refer to a single example of a conceptually well-developed individualized instruction programme which represents most of the elements of contemporary efforts. Harold Mitzel recently summarized five primary concepts. First, the learner is allowed to proceed on a learning continuum 'at a self-determined pace that is comfortable to him'. Secondly, the learner can work on a given learning sequence at times convenient or appropriate to him. Thirdly, the learning begins on a learning continuum at a point which is appropriate to his past achievement rather than at one which the teacher finds appropriate for the majority of the class. Fourthly, the learner should be allowed to detour from the learning continuum in order to undertake remedial efforts for skills or knowledge necessary to continue in the learning sequence. Fifthly, the learner has a wealth of instructional media from which to choose which will assist him in learning the same intellectual content as every other learner (Mitzel, 1970: 434-39). We would add one other component to this outline: the instructional programme will be so designed as to give the learner a feeling of success as he proceeds along the learning sequence and yet will be rigorous enough to be a challenge.

Although the concepts of individualized instruction as outlined are simple, it is most difficult to operationalize them on a mass basis without the assistance of a vast electronic technology. The implications of these concepts to teacher-dominated instruction are that they would only be able to cope with them if they were responsible for a very small group of learners. The first four principles noted above would only be possible if the teacher relied exclusively on instructional devices which did not demand human interaction, or if the teaching mode reverted to a tutorial situation; but even then the teacher would be at the mercy of the student's personal, often capricious, learning schedule. The fifth would only be possible if each child had at his disposal a range of teachers having differing teaching styles. Yet the concept would not be completely fulfilled because the live teacher represents a single type of instructional media and cannot play the role of a film, book or tape recorder. The final point might be viewed by the naive as the main advantage of teacher-based instruction since human beings think they are not replaceable as reward agents. B.F. Skinner, has argued that experimental studies involving reinforcement of behaviour are greatly influenced by the 'personal mediation of the experimenter'. In these experiments mechanical and electronic devices were constructed and used. They were mechanical because humans were unable to monitor literally millions of observations necessary to define the appropriate programme for the learner. Skinner maintains that 'the most effective control of human learning requires instrumental aid. The simple fact is that as a mere reinforcing mechanism the teacher is out of date' (Skinner, 1968: 21-22).

On all counts, if a better way is to be chosen, mechanical devices appear preferable to the live teacher. Experts assure us that an appropriate technology is already available in impressive quantity in the form of teaching machines. We usually identify teaching machines with those highly flexible, computer-assisted, private electronic tutors, those of the more sophisticated variety. Finn reminds us, however, that less complex usable equipment exists (Finn, 1960: 389). These include:
(a) individual reading pacers and similar devices;
(b) individual viewing and listening equipment for existing slides, filmstrips, motion pictures, and recordings;
(c) language laboratories of all types; and
(d) specifically programmed printed verbal materials . . . scrambled textbooks . . . the programmed textbook.

It is rare to find a school which does not have most of these materials available. Of course language laboratories would only be found at the secondary level, but it is expected that a 'good' school have one.

It is recognized by all experts that even though teaching machines can replace the lecturer and can 'be more efficient' in the use of a single teacher's time, since it is possible to reach much larger audiences, technologists concede that as of now machines can only be used for a portion of the school day. The ratio of teacher-machine teaching is ever changing and the teacher is relieved of instructional burdens as quickly as technology is able to assume the teacher role. No one argues that the teacher should be totally eliminated. 'The whole objective . . .' declares Simon Ramo, 'is to raise the teacher to a higher level in his contribution to the teaching process and to remove from his duties that kind of effort which does not use the teacher's skills to the fullest' (Ramo, 1960: 372). What this usually means is that the teacher is taken from the classroom and becomes what Ramo describes as a 'teaching engineer' or one who devotes his time to preparation of teaching materials and audio-visual presentations (1960: 379). The limited energy of a single person as teacher has finally been recognized and inanimate energy sources are thus being applied to expand the impact of that person's contribution to education.

TECHNOLOGY UNDER ATTACK

Historically, modern countries have expressed optimism about the possibilities of technology since it promises nothing less than the possibility of gaining genuine control over the natural and even the social environment. Societies see the potential of applying technology to alleviate man from the misery of want, the pain of scarcity, and the hurt of social and material disadvantage.

The role of technology in early modern schooling is also viewed positively since it is seen as a tool which can more effectively help the young become contributing members of state and humanity. Those technological innovations with regard to instruction which we have discussed in this chapter were rarely viewed in negative tems, but as liberating and joy-producing. S.J. Curtis, British educational historian, concluded that the employment of psychological studies and especially ability tests had such 'striking repercussions on classroom practice' in that schools which predated Binet were far different from the new schools which 'had become bright and pleasant places, pervaded by a friendly atmosphere . . .'. In contrast to the dismal environments imagined to have existed in earlier times, these new schools endeavoured to suit their teaching to the abilities, experience, natural interests, and outlook upon life, of the child at different stages of development. It was commonly believed that this improvement evolved because modern society had been able to develop a higher level of technology and was able reliably to test children and predict more accurately their capacities and needs (Curtis, 1948: 369).

How is it possible that such optimism would turn sour? Critics such as Jacques Ellul would even overlook the mechanization of instruction and the objectification of testing and cite the *techniques de l'école nouvelle* in his homeland of France as a striking example of the evils found in technological society. These schools with their 'bright class-rooms, understanding teachers, and pleasurable work' functioning in 'relaxed' and 'balanced environments', where no 'force' or compulsion exists, manifest technological society at its efficient 'best' in exercising 'a highly refined technique, detailed and rigorous' (Ellul, 1964: 344-49).

By the end of the past decade a feeling had emerged that a 'curious automatism, human in origin, but not human in action, seemed to be taking over' (MacLeish, 1968: 14). Humans had lost control of their lives and were beginning to ask why. The brunt of hostility directed against the modern age has been toward technology, not only because it is so pervasive and visually present, but because it is integrally linked with human values. Modern man has come to recognize that its potential to shape his environment and his personal life has negative as well as positive consequences. The exact nature of technology in its mature form is open to various interpretations, and we shall explore the three major points of view which are reflected in the literature.

Technology as a Tool

Advocates of the first position maintain that civilizations from the dawn of recorded history have adopted a certain technology by using tools and mechanical processes to assist in work performance. Modern tech-nological society is simply viewed as a more sophisticated extension of the tool-using society. Two of the crowning achievements of industrialism are that it has provided labour-saving devices and simul-taneously supplied the masses of the people with material goods. It is not happenstance that the West would evolve a technique orientation that would bring about such a high producitvity, since the prerequisites for technology are built into some of our most fundamental values. Capitalist and socialist societies alike have assumed that rationality and efficiency should be exercised in our collective and personal lives and what could be more rational and efficient than the calibrated, standardized, machine processes of industry.

Industrial mechanisms were so successful that they came to serve as models for almost every aspect of modern organization. We have discussed in this chapter how advancing technology has been applied to instruction, but we must be conscious that industry provided the model for all aspects of mass schooling in modern countries. Alvin Toffler (1970: 400) declares in vivid terms 'the whole idea of assembling masses of students (raw material) to be processed by teachers (workers) in a centrally located school (factory) was a stroke of industrial genius'. We noted earlier that the administrative structure of education in the twentieth century replicated industrial administration. We shall see in the next chapter that the whole school plant (an industrial term in itself) is a mirror image of the factory.

When we observe the superficial structure of school with children marching from work station to work station, bells ringing to signal when to change stations, teachers ensuring tht each child goes to the assigned work desk, the image of a factory comes into focus. If we probe beneath these organizational factors and inspect the structure of learning as outlined in the lesson plans, the structure of knowledge as developed in the disciplines, the structure of assessment as manifested in grades and examinations, then the industrial model is just as evident.

It is a beautifully rationalized system and was undoubtedly the only alternative in its day for delivering education patterned after the industrial model. That price exacted from Western man sacrificed still another highly valued tradition – the belief in individual freedom; for concurrent with the value of rationality is the belief in freedom of choice. The individual is recognized as being able to make choices as to the type of life style he leads, the material objects he acquires such as home, automobile, clothes, and the type of career he follows.

The critics who hold that technology is only an extension of a tool society claim the problem of our age is the relationship between rationality and freedom. One the one hand those rationalized systems of industry have given man enormous opportunities of choice which never before existed. At the same time certain choices have been systematically reduced. We now have the opportunity to acquire automobiles, telephones, etc. but those 'personal, experimental, workmanlike' aspects of products are increasingly being replaced by the 'abstract, mathematical, and industrial' (Ellul, 1964: 146). A crude analogy may suffice. Horses, in their unique infinite variety, are being replaced by automobiles which, though they provide variations in colour, size, and horsepower, all still reflect a standardization which is not found in natural variety.

Critics of a modern tool society are the least fearful of technological consequences since they usually recognize the value accrued by industrialization. Who would not be willing to endure the humility of owning an automobile like our neighbour's if the choice is between having that automobile or having no automobile at all? Who would pass over standardized schooling in lieu of no schooling at all?

We must be very clear about the nature of the protest within this orientation. It is generally recognized that standardization exists in terms of outcomes or products, but we have already stated that modern schooling compensates for these losses by opening up educational product possibilities that were not possible in preindustrial times. There is still belief at this level of criticism that we are in the driver's seat and are using schooling as a tool for our own futures. The revolt here is not in terms of outcome choice restriction, but in terms of process rationalization. We shall give some attention to this process.

Technological advancement is achieved when one method proves to be superior to another. Its superiority in modernity is only demonstrated to the degree that a difference is noted in terms of quantitative measure. Once this difference is noted, the 'rational' thing to do is to select the superior method. To the degree that we measure differences mathematically, we also forgo real personal choice between methods since the choice becomes self-determined. That is, if one method of teaching French requires 3,000 hours and another method requires 2,500 hours to achieve the same competence, the method to be selected has already been determined if we make a rational choice. In general, methods have proved to be superior if their processes take on more precise definition, the limits of freedom are narrowed, and the mechanism is made to perform its function more exactly. In mechanical devices such achievements could be heralded as progress. In educational establishments, where the raw products are humans rather than metal, wood, or fibre, and the more sophisticated production line is intended to produce educated human beings rather than mechanical devices, the activities of those individuals functioning in the system must also be more precisely defined. Individual discretion is tolerated only so long as it does not go beyond the bounds of anticipated events within the system. Capricious acts result in system malfunction and breakdown and must be eliminated in preference to predictable behaviours which conform within the limits of freedom allowed by the system. It is in this sense that C. Wright Mills (1959: 169) could write: 'The increasing rationalization of society . . . lie back of the rise into view of the man who is "with" rationality but without reason, who is increasingly self rationalized and increasingly uneasy'.

We might illustrate this process in education. We noted earlier that programmed instruction has become increasingly important in the United States. It is entirely rationalized because it attempts to anticipate every possible learning path the learner might be required to take. The learner can only function within the constraints of the instructional programme and it loses its intended efficiency if he breaks out of the system or uses it for some unexpected purpose.

The teacher role is also so closely defined that it too disallows unorthodox or unique behaviours. In the experimental programme at Pittsburg led by Robert Glaser, the teacher role is described in the following manner. The teacher cares for the placement and the pretesting of the learners, diagnoses their needs, fills out the work prescription (based on the tests results and other information), follows learner progress, provides motivation, administers the post-test, and establishes learner achievement level.

All of these behaviours are familiar to any teacher because teachers of all eras have engaged in each of the activities listed. The difference lies in the fact that the individually prescribed programme relies only on the teacher to process it rather than on him to interact directly with the child as learner. The pretest instruments are administered according to instructions. Diagnosis is nothing more than calculating the scores on the pretest and referring to the programme index which gives the appropriate prescription according to the pretest outcome. In other words, prescription is predetermined for each possible pretest score or profile. Motivation is not a matter of personal choice or teaching style, but is designed to be applied to particular behaviours. The post-test, being a part of the programme, is simply administered and scored by the teacher. The teacher does only that which the programme requires and, if it is not followed in detail, it will experience some process breakdown.

We have directed our discussion toward student and teacher as part of the mechanical process because the contemporary revolt stems mainly from them. Hartmut von Hentig has characterized their protest against the technological, systematic, effficiency-oriented curricular programme as a revolt against a system that does not deal with the person but with a 'standard learner'. From the point of view of 'me' the learner, it is no longer to be taken seriously because 'it does not deal with me, but with an abstraction of me' (von Hentig, 1970: 32).

The Technique Ideology

Representatives of the second position accept all the criticisms of the first, but take the impact of technology beyond its tool function. Quantitative change in technology is seen to have reached a point at which a qualitatively different nature of the phenomenon emerges. Jacques Ellul is the most extreme spokesman for this position, and he maintains that the multiplication of techniques has 'caused them literally to change their character'. Technique was at one time only a means, a tool, a mechanism for achieving some end. In mature technological societies it is no longer seen as a means, but has actually 'taken on substance, has become a reality in itself' (Ellul, 1964: 63).

We saw the first stages of this position in our discussion of pre-Second World War technocracy in America. Technology was seen to have progressed to the point that it could not be left in the hands of amateur businessmen and politicians but could only realize its destiny if run by engineers and technicians. Their competence lay in running the machine at peak efficiency, but thoughtful consideration of the implications of this demand reveals that their leadership can only be justified if the efficiency of the machine were more important than other considerations. Whereas traditional cultures had used tools for some end, modern society was beginning to give such allegiance to the tools that they were taking on the character of being ends in themselves.

As modern societies have moved to full maturity, they have progessed even futher than the followers of Thorsten Veblen envisioned. Helmust Schelsky, interpreter of contemporary technocracy in West Germany, believes that even the experts of technological society have lost control of the apparatus which has come to serve exclusively its own material requirements. Technical imperatives and material rule have become the first cause of all social phenomena including politics

(Schelsky, 1961). Schelsky is joined by the modern prophet of the counter culture, Herbert Marcuse, who sees all institutional authority in modern societies receding from the grasp of individuals and groups and become 'increasingly impersonal, objective, universal and also increasingly rational, effective, productive' (Marcuse, 1966: 89).

The technical apparatus has altered the organic and vital functions of human life since they have also become mechanical and standardized. All aspects of life and Nature have been made predictable and calculable to the point that man appears to have lost control over the system which he set in motion. Technology is seen to have emancipated itself from human control and has set in motion its own imperatives. Those loosely-defined aims of modern culture have been overtaken by technique itself which has come to integrate all rationality to itself.

Hasan Ozbekhan (1968) does not accept the pervasiveness of technocracy claimed by Ellul, Schelsky, and Marcuse, but he does admit to the autonomous rule of technocratic systems. He claims the aims of technocracy are no longer determined by forces outside the system but are determined by the possibilities available. In this context technical 'know how' becomes an imperative for the establishment of goals which allow the 'know how' to find expression. Thus we go to the moon, build freeways, and super transports because we are able to build them. Education too has become an outlet for new professions such as systems analysts, who have the ability to spell out in technically appropriate language, the objectives, the evaluations procedures, the grouping criteria, and the components of instruction. These competencies having been mastered, the systems analyst is plugged into the assembly line called school which adjusts itself to allow those competencies to find expression. One example in instruction will suffice. In order to realize the possibilities of individualized instruction mentioned earlier, it was necessary that the concept of individuality take on new meaning. It became nothing more than a time factor in the rationalized school. Individualized instruction came to be that which allows the gifted child to accomplish the learning tasks more quickly than the average child, who accomplishes the learning tasks more quickly than the slow child. The mechanized educational train simply provides opportunity for children to move along the track at varying speeds. We are not in a position to ask where the train is going.

The teacher in this system has also been transformed. The teacher is not a person, but a role, a set of competencies, an element in the system having no individuality since the system can only function 'rationally' if every element in it is tightly coordinated and harmonized with every other element. We noted that the slightest malfunction or deviant aim can send the entire system into disarray. Such a rational system has been a powerful instrument of progress and teachers are now at the stage at which their own alienation is accepted as a psychic condition necessary to maintain the standard which technocracy has produced.

Not only are teachers subject to a systematic manipulation and control of their psyches, but all participants, directly and indirectly related to the educational enterprise, are made to reconcile their mode of existence and relationship to the schools with the conditions imposed on them by the system. It is necessary that this reconciliation involve an enormous emotional investment in the value of schooling as a product to be acquired or sold, in the 'services' it provides for use or performance, in the 'fun' all participants have in it, and in the 'status symbols' it carries with it.

The triumph of industrialism is viewed by its critics as having developed the capacity to achieve its purposes through careful manipulation rather than compulsion or force. Marcuse (1964: xv) summarized the state of things very well in a single paragraph:

> . . . in this society, the productive apparatus, tends to become totalitarian to the extent to which it determines not only the socially needed occupations, skills, and attitudes, but also individual needs and aspirations. It thus obliterates the opposition between private and public existence, between individual and social needs. Technology serves to institute new, more effective, and more pleasant forms of social control and social cohesion.

Marcuse claims the productive apparatus has been able to accomplish its objectives by rationalizing its irrationality. 'Its productivity and efficiency, its capacity to increase and spread comforts, to turn waste into need, and destruction into construction', give modern man the illusion that he is extending his mind and body to ever greater accomplishments. In reality he is only identifying himself with his commodities. Modern men's souls are 'in their automobile, hi-fi set, split-level home, kitchen equipment (1964: 9). Schooling is viewed as indispensable, an institution which must continue to grow as a force of production and consumption. The rationality of domination is not a conspiracy, not conceived by a small group of self-selected despots, not standardized, but it is diffused through society as a manifestation of pre-formed psychic tendencies.

If the technological protest were contained in the two positions which have been outlined, it is unlikely that it would have moved beyond the esoteric circles of critical scholars and a minority of disenchanted students. The material pay-off was too great to risk destroying technocracy for the sake of potential freedom. The situation had also reached a stage that the protest would have been directed against the self as much as against the technocratic institutions.

Inefficiency of Technology

The crucial difference in the third position is the claim that the effectiveness of modern technique is an illusion. It is this protest point of view which has stirred the feelings of anger beyond the bounds of those perennial critics of society. If this point of view is correct, it would mean that we have given ultimate value to processes that are not valid in terms of their claims.

Robert Presthus has pointed out that rational organizations 'exude an aura of "efficiency"', since they typify all that Max Weber found to be good in them: they have explicit goals, expert personnel, precisely defined lines of authority, leaders who function in accordance with prescribed rules; however, they are often efficient only in a tautological sense. That is, everything runs smoothly but little is accomplished. These might be symptoms of bureaucracy rather than technology, but Hasan Ozbekhan has observed that the dynamics of technology suffer from deep internal contradictions or force contradictory consequences on man's mind and his environment (Ozbekhan, 1968: 60). This being the case, technology is never able to achieve efficiency in an overall sense since improvement in one sphere usually requires deterioration in another.

Ozbekhan gives three examples to illustrate this phenomenon. First, technology 'tends to feed on itself and expand'. As in a chain reaction it moves beyond the original intended use and invades other realms until it is impossible to determine when it is appropriate to use and when not. Planning has become necssary because of this situation but the planners themselves are unable to 'go behind the undefinable cloud which blocks our vision of future consequences. (1968: 60).

Secondly, there are built-in costs in terms of money and physical well-being, against which technological effectiveness is pitted. We have already mentioned examples such as radiation, pollution, soil depletion, bodily disturbances, and mental illness.

Thirdly, when we add up the costs of technology in terms of the total environment, 'the gains never seem to add up to system wide improvement or betterment'. In fact, Ozbekhan is emphatic that the imbalance created by technology has actually led to a deterioration of the 'quality of life' (1968: 61). This is an enormous indictment and one that cannot altogether be validated, but we can gain some perspective as to its implications when we look at the world-wide universal formal schooling situation.

Schooling has expanded at unprecedented rates throughout the world; yet the demands for formal schooling remain largely unfulfilled. Most countries have expanded their educational systems almost to breaking point in terms of money, energy, and time given to the system. Brembeck (1973: 3) reminds us that the motives for such expansion have varied from political response, to rising expectations, to humanitarian recognition of the value of literacy. As a consequence of the relationship of these efforts and national development, some sobering questions are being raised. The developed areas in the modern era are committed to universal formal schooling and the developing areas accepted this mode of education as a means of overcoming the differences in national income. How is that possible when we understand the desperate financial disparities which are growing and which will continue to widen if the present course is maintained?

In the United States in a typical year the increase alone in GNP is equivalent to the whole of Africa's yearly income and half that of Latin America, even though there are more people on both continents than in the United States (Ward, 1966: 54). There is no possible way for Africa to emulate the United States and expect to compete. A different and viable solution has not yet been found, but we are being forced to ask what can be done.

Efficiency considerations which challenge the headlong rush into universal compulsory schooling come mainly from the developing areas of the world. This thrust must be distinguished from the efficiency ideologues in the modern world who discuss subtle ways to help children read a little faster or who call for reorganization of school programmes into modules, year-round schooling, etc.

These programmes have usually been instituted because they were thought to be more 'efficient', but they have reaped sobering results. Ralph Kaplan, in a careful review of mechanized instruction was forced to conclude that it has been a poor investment in terms of its original intent. Harvard computer expert Anthony G. Oettinger also concluded in his popular book *Run, Computer, Run* (1969) that investments in computer-assisted instruction have not paid off. The greatest indictment of technological innovation would come from people such as William Kvaraceus, who were willing to concede that technology was effective, but the gains added up to a deterioration in the overall quality of education. He maintains that instruction has become embodied in 'the formula' whereby modern man has become a victim of a deepening and fast recourse to formulae which promise 'a fast liberal education', or 'instant enlightenment'. The impact of technology, with its slick, professionalized banalities in 'canned and frozen instruction' is seen by these critics to be effective and destructive at the same time (1965). The issues raised in this debate are, at this point, over subtle issues which are only possible to debate when universal formal schooling already exists. These issues are in no way comparable to the desperate situation in the developing world.

However, questions have been raised even in the mature modern world which are more fundamental than subtle methodological debates. During the past two decades, a growing protest, initially polemic in nature but gradually empirical in substance, has emerged. The first protest was stirred by a 'gut level' feeling that something was wrong with the schooling establishment. In America, Paul Goodman (1963) was one of the first to attack the school as a waste; he believed its main function was to keep kids under control for twelve years since he believed any normal child could learn all schools had to offer in about one-third the time. This means it might take about four years to learn what is expected in primary and secondary school if the child really wanted to learn it. Criticism of Goodman, Edgar Friedenberg and others have received some empirical support which is undermining the notion that the more schooling the better. Thorsten Husen recently published information concerning a Norwegian experiment which was conducted in the 1950s. Two parallel groups of students 12 to 14 years of age were chosen, the one was taught full time and the other half time for two years. Such an experiment was important because these children lived in the long, narrow, fjord area where travel was difficult, necessitating that they live away from home during the week. The half-time group was given home studies and reading assignments to compensate. There was only slight variance in the achievement scores recorded between the two groups. Husen (1972: 32-35) points out that similar evidence is available in Sweden which has undertaken experiments of achievement levels of children in remote areas since the 1940s.

In the United States a number of schools are providing evidence of the same sort. Charles Rusch in Los Angeles has established a mobile school which takes advantage of community resources to educate by visiting businesses, industry and governmental institutions. His children devote approximately eight hours a week to the study of basic skills. On the basis of standard achievement scores, the children have remained on grade level or higher, and are able to devote more than two-thirds of their time to other modes of inquiry.

The most substantial evidence against the notion, the more schooling the better, comes from the International Association for the Evaluation of Educational Achievement, which recently launched multi-national studies in various subjects. Mathematics was the first subject selected and the study tested the relationship between achievement at age 13 and a number of variables. One cluster of variables included length of the school week, time given to homework, time even to maths instruction. These variables only account for about 3 percent of the total variance in achievement of 13-year-olds. When broken down, the time devoted to mathematics instruction ranged from 4.3 to 8.9 hours. There was no relationship between instruction time and achievement. Similar findings on the other variables was also evident (Husen, 1967).

On the national level some countries, such as England and Wales, begin formal schooling at age five, while other countries, such as Sweden and Denmark, begin formal schooling at age seven. The achievement studies show no relationship between the time a child begins school and the achievement level at age 13.

In summary, essentially all critics of technology assume it has rationalized away enormous freedom in our lives. Many of these critics also assert that a technique ideology has led to a society in which 'know how' and efficiency have taken on ultimate value, and still others see the claim of efficiency itself as illusory. The outcome of these protests has done much to undermine the myth that extended formal schooling alone is the most efficient mechanism to educate the youth of developed and underdeveloped nations. Schools are now seen as obsolete and wasteful and requiring too much time to accomplish their objectives.

5

STRUCTURAL ORGANIZATION
OF SCHOOLING

Our final major consideration shall be to explore the characteristics of modern school structures. We begin with a brief summary of conventional social science perspectives on the evolution of social structures and then turn our attention to education, especially to the process of structural differentiation in schooling.

EVOLUTION OF SOCIAL STRUCTURES

Since the time of Herbert Spencer and other nineteenth-century social evolutionists, social scientists have claimed that modern institutional structures and individual roles are differentiated and specialized while traditional institutions and individual roles are highly diffused and unified. In fact, primitive societies are believed to be 'without distinction of parts'. Social evolution occurs when groups develop unlikenesses both in terms of social stratification and in terms of occupations (Spencer, 1967: 214). Spencer believed the first major social distinction occurred when a broad division between ruling and ruled groups developed. The next stage of evolution came about when those who were ruled divided into food-producing and handicrafts classes. Minor divisions within each of these groups then occurred, leading to further specialization and differentiation.

Traditional societies represent those which reach a degree of differentiation, especially in the urban centres such as we find in Feudal Europe. Some scholars, who concentrate on the study of traditional social environments, deal with urban life (e.g. Sjoberg, 1955, 1960), but most describe the less complex villages. Robert Redfield has indicated a striking sameness in all peasant villages; the social structure of villages in Greece and Feudal Europe vary little from the contemporary villages of Africa and Asia (Redfield: ch. IV). The peasants form a single pervasive group with little social stratification among the members. It should be stressed here that traditional village life, as we discuss it, is not synonymous with primitive existence, since peasant villages have always had some contact with elite strata and centres of intellectual thought which we usually associate with traditional urban areas. This association influenced the nature of village life and contributed to peasant life styles and social values (Foster, 1953: 164). It has also defined to some measure the social stratification which exists in traditional society, since the traditional elites maintained a peculiar life-style based on inherited occupational activities, mode of life, and political power (Weber, 1947: 429).

The traditional village is self-sufficient in terms of essential needs. In fact, in normal agricultural villages the household might well maintain itself with food and workshops under a single management, although most villages show some degree of household interdependence. At this level of development there is some division of labour but the primary characteristic of village life is that of diffuseness of roles rather than pronounced specificity.

The roles individuals assume and the functions institutions performed so overlap each other that it is difficult to distinguish precisely one role or institution from another. Even such particulars as land-use serve a wide variety of needs and purposes. One household property might serve as home, business, place of worship, farm, and government agency (Sjoberg, 1955: 436). The most common characteristic of traditional man is collective existence. Toennies (1957) has described in detail the role of kinship, neighborhood, and friendship in Feudal European society, and points out that symbiotic relationships bound people together in a life-long collective consciousness.

Diffuseness penetrated not only social roles and institutions but all sense of belonging and relatedness. Church, family, and economy retained some functional identity but they overlapped each other in terms of common membership, sphere of interest, and influence. The distinctions we now draw between these institutions are largely arbitrary, and they are usually established by modern scholars who attempt to translate their own life-styles into the traditional setting. In reality, spirituality was as much a part of family life and labour on the land as was attendance at church on Sunday. The land was not just a means of economic survival, but represented a spiritual intimacy and an avenue to express reverence toward the Creator. The family derived its identity as much from the home and soil as from genealogy. To speak of education in the traditional setting is to make reference to the entire network of processes which socialized and reinforced spiritual and interpersonal life and at the same time imparted whatever skills and knowledge were deemed important.

With the advent of modernity in Europe, the unity of which we have spoken was broken and structural differentiation took on a new quality. There was not just a shift of emphasis since institutions and roles took on their own distinctive character and even developed a degree of autonomy. By autonomy we do not mean isolation; the various elements which emerged were related in powerful ways to the whole. We mention political modernization to illustrate this process.

As political authority and roles became centralized and rationalized into the modern state, a functionally specific bureaucracy with specialized governmental institutions emerged which were intended to fulfil particular tasks.

The sovereign authority instituted a governmental structure which usually possessed specialized administrative functions, each unit having its own separate integrity and its own specialized professional staff. For example, modern military forces became a separate governmental unit consisting of a standing army with a highly trained corps of soldiers under the supervision of a professional corps of officers. The army does not interfere with and is not interfered by other governmental units. In contrast, medieval governments were characterized by a rather undifferentiated and diffused system (Parsons et al., 1962: 83-84). Even such fundamental modern functions as legislation and adjudication were diffused. In England, for example, judicial tribunals possessed many outright political powers, as did the *Justiza* of Aragon and the

French *Parlements*. Tudor England divided the legislative function among several institutions, and this system was later incorporated into the American constitution as a system of checks and balances. England moved, in the seventeenth century, toward a clear separation of powers whereby each function of government was assigned to a separate institution (Huntington, 1968: 109-21). In summary, modern government is characterized by legislatures which are responsible for rule-making, prime ministers and presidents who oversee rule application, the military which is charged to ensure the national defence, schools, which are expected to educate the citizenry, etc.

We have mentioned that differentiation reached an intermediate level in traditional Europe; however, with the advent of modernity, the very process of differentiation takes on a unique character for it is rapidly accelerated by two major forces. The first is the growing belief in the value of social progress, which accepts the claim that progression in social and biological organization results when forms move from the simple to the more complex. The Spencerian theory of social evolution may or may not be valid, but the very belief in its validity has tended to accelerate differentiation. The second force is an increase in organizational skill or of social competence. Skill in organizing has been aided by technology and communications developments and has resulted in a remarkable growth in the number, size, and power of organizations in the modern world.

Differentiation has advanced to the point that it is impossible for a single individual to comprehend every facet of most organizations. Some scholars have even maintained that the genius of America's industrial and economic capacity rests in its ability to extend organization beyond individual control into the realm of coordinated group control. Servan-Schreiber (1968) described this process in cogent fashion when he lamented the capacity of the United States to fuse the talents distributed through government, corporations, and universities into a coordinated whole to the point that America is threatening to turn Europe into a dependent colony.

Servan-Schreiber relies heavily on the analysis of John Galbraith who gives enormous weight to organizational talent being responsible for social and economic growth in the United States. Galbraith claims Americans are not 'inordinately sophisticated' and in fact most have 'common talent' which has the single advantage of being far more predictable than genius. The real accomplishment of modernity 'consists in taking ordinary men, informing them narrowly and deeply and then, through appropriate organization, arranging to have their knowledge combined with that of other specialized but equally ordinary men' (Galbraith, 1967: 73).

As science becomes linked to technology, the need for highly educated people throughout the industrial system becomes apparent, and specialization is fostered even more. In the production of the automobile, for example, metallurgists deal with the cooling system and engine block, engineers work on machining the crankshaft, and chemists decide on the composition of the finish or trim. The one is not interested in and only interferes with the work of the other if he brings his 'special' knowledge into the other's sphere of responsibility. The whole modern industry is dependent on the ability to 'divide and sub-divide tasks' and then bring 'knowledge to bear on these fractions' and finally to recombine the finished elements from these tasks into a whole finished product (Galbraith, 1967: 25). Dramatic consequences have followed such organization. Perhaps the most impressive example of such coordination is that of space travel where thousands of specialists have been able to combine their expertise to the single objective of putting a man on the moon.

Just as we observe differentiation in economic and political spheres, education also breaks away from the organismic and establishes its own integrity. In this section our task is to explore the differentiated educational structure in greater detail. At the most abstract level, we find education divided into two main spheres, known in contemporary jargon as non-formal education and formal education.

NON-FORMAL EDUCATION

So pervasive is formal education in the contemporary world that non-formal education has been defined as that education which exists outside its realm. Thus, Coombs and Ahmad (1974: 8) define non-formal education as 'any organized, systematic, educational activity carried on outside the framework of the formal system to provide selected types of learning to particular subgroups in the population'. Cole Brembeck

(1973: xvi) agrees that non-formal education 'deals with those learning activities that take place outside the formally organized educational system', and Rolland Paulston (1972: ix) also describes its 'structured, systematic, nonschool' nature. What none of these people stress, however, is that non-formal education in its present form is as much a creature of the modern age as formal schooling. We shall briefly describe the evolution of non-formal education into modernity by concentrating on the education of the handworker.

We reiterate that the crucial character of traditional life was the unity of existence. It is even an error to distinguish the craft guild as a separate entity though it did represent the major commerical enterprise of traditional Europe. As the mill and factory began to take form in the centuries just prior to modernity, the guild was unable to adjust to new imperatives. Adjustments of the guild would have necessitated not only receptivity to new technology but an entirely new way of coping with the world. We observe that the factory system grew up in competition with the guild and eventually replaced it as the dominant production process.

Karl Abraham points out that two factors are crucial in understanding the difference between the guild and the factory systems. First, since the people who manned the factory did not come from an 800 year craft tradition, the continuity of the past and especially the educational tradition of the guild was broken (Abraham, 1957: 82-83). We recall that this tradition included not only training an apprentice in a skill or craft but educating him toward a world view including norms of behaviour, an identity with the work, and a sense of belonging to a family in the broader sense of the term. In the guild the young neophytes were drawn into its practices and rituals and given a thorough and secret indoctrination in its functions and qualifications of practice. Having a virtual monopoly over performance in a given location, the guild was able to establish its own standards and though these were precise and the basis of pride, they were as much shrouded by ritual as by competence. The apprentice practised with a master for up to seven years before moving to the next stage of journeyman and finally, if worthiness was demonstrated, he too, was allowed to establish himself as a master. In the process he gained a sense of history, not in terms of knowledge, but in terms of custom and beliefs. The pride and standard required to be admitted as a journeyman and master contributed to his consciousness of the craft history.

Since it drew people from the land, the modern factory did not possess any of this tradition. Workers came to the factory, even in the earliest times, not out of its appeal and not because of the skills they possessed, but because the land could no longer sustain life and the factory provided hope for a new existence. The technical revolution had already extended itself to the agricultural sphere, permitting food to be raised in surplus without the need of large numbers of farm workers.

The guild system of long apprenticeship and lifelong belonging were not instituted in the factory. In its place came the wage system which was based on an arrangement whereby people dervied income from the sale of their labour. According to Boulding (1953: 89), the wage system as it evolved in early modernity was based on 'almost complete specialization between the management on the one hand and the wage earner on the other'. The traditional system, whereby each worker was able to become a journeyman and master, was dying in spite of the fact that these titles were sometimes carried over into the factory. The worker was expected to sell his labour to the management for the rest of his life. His labour was a commodity and represented an exchange relationship between labour and money. Management organized the labour in the same way it organized materials and machines and it maintained a relationship with the worker only to conduct business. The sense of belonging, the historical attitude, the pride in the work, the identity of the worker with the craft, may or may not have existed, but they were not a part of the contract; task performance was the critical factor which the worker was expected to give in exchange for wages.

The second factor critical to education in distinguishing the old from the new was the fact that the people who came to the factory did not constitute a unity but were strangers in terms of beliefs, customs and value priorities. Even the languages they spoke revealed different dialects and at times completely different modes of written or verbal communication. Whereas a pride of community and identity characterized the past, the new represented division and difference. The only unifying force was that of having a common enemy in the factory-owned and management. The emergence of social class consciousness can be traced to this largely negative force. The positive aspect of labour class consciousness was the emergence of a 'labor movement which was essentially a movement among wage earners to improve their position in society (Boulding, 1953: 89).

The labour movement ties itself to no traditional roots; its history is one of the modern era, although in this brief time it has evolved a tradition of its own based on the courage of confrontation to obtain better wages and working conditions. There has not been an attempt to develop a sense of community and unity in industry since the identity of labour is derived from separation and specialization, at least in the English-speaking countries. The labour movement does not represent a 'revolt against the wage system but an attempt to live with it and control it' (Boulding, 1953: 92).

If we were to look at the other types of modern workers who fill the slots of society as skilled 'employees', we would find a somewhat different history but a very similar consequence. Tradition having been broken, the employee comes into the organization with little investment except the willingness to sell his or her labour for the demands made on skills and time. The rewards have been great enough to quell the dislocation and sense of alienation and the organizational society has reaped enormous material advantages in the process.

Non-formal educational programmes instituted by industry during the nineteenth century had a single objective, which was to give the worker the skills necessary to carry out the job for which he was hired to do. The very nature of the factory system was to divide and subdivide the tasks into components. The tasks the worker performed were routine and simple, and the training was therefore highly specific and usually of little value in performing other tasks. This meant that training was neither difficult nor long, since industry in general was willing to participate in the non-formal training of the young only in so far as it pertained to work tasks. It was not deemed important to use skilled handworkers and little interest was shown by the factory system in establishing its own apprenticeship programme. Thus, during the nineteenth century the skilled crafts declined dramatically

As primary education became universal and young people gained enough education to become involved in social political affairs, pressure was applied to restore some form of occupational education that would extend beyond the narrow task-oriented training that was then available. The lack of apprenticeship opportunities in private industry led to the introduction of schools separate from business and industry, especially in French-speaking Belgium and France, which were intended to train the young handworkers. These schools became models for similar endeavours in other lands (Abel and Groothoff, 1959: 57). The major disadvantage of such institutions was the lack of a reality base and a serious work climate, since the tasks learners engaged in were like school lessons rather than real life responsibilities. In response to this problem Germany established a regulation, in 1897, whereby the apprentice would be placed at a work station for a major share of the week and only participate for a day in more theoretical training. The major model for this initiative came from George Kerschensteiner who became superintendant of Schools in Munich in 1895. Over fifty specialized continuation schools were established in the first ten years of his administration. He relied on the established handworker associations to provide inspectors and he even attempted to incorporate into the schools the peculiar atmosphere he had observed in the traditional craft programmes which still remained in Munich. The various master-apprentice relationships that existed were carried into the classroom. The peculiar instructional modes and instructor qualities were also incorporated as far as possible into the formal setting (Monsheimer, 1958: 433-34). Consequently, apprenticeship training in Germany came under the supervision of defenders of pre-industrial non-formal education more than modern industry. Abraham maintains such a restoration process was impossible for two reasons: (1) even those who attempted to maintain a genuine master-apprentice relationship were doing so in the context of a world which had lost its unity of existence, and (2) the people who had entered the crafts had such varied backgrounds and aims that it was impossible to operate on the basis of family-type relationships (Abraham, 1957: 96-97).

We might also add that formal schooling itself became an obstacle since the early years of the child's life were consumed in school and prevented extended direct participation in economic and skills training that would have naturally come in the earlier years. Apprenticeship training time was reduced to an average of approximately three years and it became necessary to incorporate vocational activities into the formal schooling programme to compensate for the loss in non-formal education that would have occurred had the child not been in formal school at all. Non-formal education is continually being absorbed into or linked with the formal process and thus is contributing to the expansion of the differentiated formal schooling qualities. Even though our discussion has concentrated on the handworker, it is clear that we would easily be able to extend the principle of differentiation if we look at the more advanced aspects of nonformal activities.

FORMAL EDUCATION

We have already demonstrated in Chapter 2 that formal education in the form of schools is a creature of the modern age. We do not wish to describe those earlier considerations which indicate that school systems are part of large bureaucratic systems; rather, we wish to deal with some obvious, but critical, structural features of the school unit itself. Their features are so commonplace that we fail to recognize that they are modern and subject to drastic revision as modernity comes to an end. We shall concentrate on three differentiation features of the schools. First, schools in modernity become fully separate, distinct institutions losing integral connection with other social institutions. Secondly, different types of schools themselves evolve clear divisions of function, clientele, and purpose. Thirdly, the schools develop a high degree of internal structural differentiation, mainly in terms of grade levels, courses of study, and ability groupings. We must once again pay attention to traditional environments to gain some comparative view.

Diffuse Traditional Schools

Although we say that schools are creatures of the modern age, we do not wish to imply that highly developed schools did not exist in traditional environments. Their definition as distinct, autonomous institutions has, however, probably been overemphasized by educational historians. In reality, schools were so much a part of the social unity of which we have spoken that it is often difficult to know whether to call an institution a school or not. Lawrence Cremin had done much to dispel the myth of schooling in early America and Renaissance England; he has substantiated with evidence a hypothesis put forth by historian Bernard Bailyn that traditional education was more a part of the total culture than in some special schooling institution (Bailyn, 1960). Cremin claims 'there was considerable blurring between households, churches, and schools all along the line' in Tudor England (Cremin, 1970: 173). He further claims that in colonial America the initial blurring of lines between institutions was even more accentuated than in metropolitan areas since 'schooling went on anywhere and everywhere, not only in schoolrooms, but in kitchens, manses, churches, meetinghouses, sheds erected in fields and shops erected in towns' (Cremin, 1970: 192-93). His belief in its accentuated integration in America might be a bit gratuitous since conditions similar to those in colonial America were found at that time throughout the Western world. For example, Boyd and King lament the fact that schoolkeeping in eighteenth-century England 'was usually regarded as a means of eking out a scanty livelihood at another trade', but they reveal at the same moment the integral relationship of schooling to life in general in declaring that 'schoolwork was often done in the living-room or the workshop of the teacher alongside the ordinary business of the house or the trade' (Boyd and King, 1972: 280).

Heinrich Meyer describes the school facilities in the Danish Oldenburg region during the seventeenth and eighteenth centuries in almost the same terms as does Cremin those in the colonies. The most typical educational arrangement was a circulation or travelling school. Usually a larger farm complex would host the school for a year, providing a room where the children were taught and a small unheated chamber where the teacher lived (Meyer, 1974: 34-36).

Even as late as the first half of the nineteenth century, continental European schools were much like those described by Cremin. Alfons Schagan determined that some communities in the Rhineland area at the time of the French occupation possessed school houses, but more often a community found a barrack room, apartment, or other accommodation in which to educate its young. Since the teacher was often forced to hold school in his own home, regulations were even distributed regarding sleeping and cooking arrangements wherever school was kept (Schagen, 1913: 19). Prussian statistical records indicate that in 1816 in the Magdeburg district fully one-third of the 469 country schools were conducted in private dwellings. There are also records in Saxony of school being kept in poor houses, sheep herding sheds, and village blacksmith shops (Öffentliche Volksschule, 1883: 7).

The school situation just mentioned were largely rural in nature, but it must be kept in mind that during this period over 80 percent of all Prussian and Saxon schools were rural. Bavaria maintained over 90 percent of its schools in rural settings at mid-century (Richter, 1930: 21-29).

Karl Heinz Günther and his colleagues in the German Democratic Republic have drawn our attention to the fact that the industrial areas of Europe were not much different from the rural in terms of schooling conditions. Children were just as likley to be placed in a factory-run school, conducted after they had spent a full day at work, as in any other type of instructional programme. Other children attended school on Sunday; in some communities as many as half the children did not even go to the formal school because no provisions were available (Günther et al., 1973: 236).

The integrated nature of schooling was even more revealing when we determine the backgrounds of the teachers. Cremin (1970: 193) finds that in early America 'pupils were taught by anyone and everyone including parents, tutors, clergymen, lay readers, preceptors, physicians, lawyers, artisans, and shopkeepers'. Meyer (1974: 16-17) documents shoemakers, tailors, shawlmakers, hat-makers, and seamen in the Oldenburg era prior to 1782, while Schagen (1913: 9) emphasizes the prevalence of sextons, grave-diggers and other underlings connected to local churches as well as craftsmen such as shoemakers, tailors, and clothmakers.

Advanced education was organized less haphazardly. It did possess a degree of teaching professionalism but it was as integrated into other social institutions as the lower schools. The dominant early links were with cathedrals and religious orders. Early universities were nothing more than religious teaching institutions (Paulsen, 1919: vol. I, 29). Even as sponsorship extended to secular authority, these religious links were usually retained in large measure since religion formed the basis of all intellectual life.

Just as the lower schools were integrated into other spheres, so too were the advanced schools. It was almost imperative that they be physically located where a church stood since the school day was interwoven into religious observance. St Paul's school was not only built in the churchyard of St Paul's in London, but the school itself was dedicated to the child Jesus. Erasmus reports: 'Over the master's chair is a beautiful image of the child Jesus, seated in a teaching posture. As the students enter and leave school, they salute him with a hymn. Above it hangs a representation of God the Father saying: Hear ye Him' (in Nugent, 1956: 40). The children were expected to 'prostrate' themselves three times a day to say prayers (Nugent, 1956: 40). Church pervaded the whole of school life, and 'going to choir' on Sunday was as much a part of the programme as reading Latin.

Both the lower and the advanced schools were committed to the building of faith. The Gotha School Statutes of 1642 dictated three morning hours of prayer, catechism, commandments study, verse reading, etc. and the afternoon schedule included choir singing plus daily rituals. The remaining time was devoted to reading and calculating (Dietrich and Klink, 1964: 54-71). Almost five hours were devoted to religious study and observation daily, whereas at times only a quarter of an hour was left for reading instruction.

School was integrated into community life in still another way. The Prussian *General-Land-Schul-Reglement* of 1763 suggests that those children who had to herd cows share the burdens and trade off herding for each other so that one child might visit school the first three days and the other the later three days (Dietrich and Klink, 1964: 133). Schooling was kept in such a way as to accommodate the activities of the community. The very schedule of the modern school reflects vestiges of such accommodation: we have summer vacation, harvest vacation, Christmas vacation, etc. which were originally designed to allow for farming and religious activities.

We have made reference to lower and advanced schools in our discussion, but we are compelled to stress that just as a blurring existed between traditional schools and other social institutions so did a blurring exist between school types themselves. Originally all schools were essentially Latin grammar schools although the name 'grammar school' only came into general use in the fourteenth century after the less prestigious and distinct 'song schools' and reading and writing schools emerged (D'Aeth, 1959).

An earlier distinction between 'school' and 'university' existed. The first intended to designate institutions giving Latin language training, and the second the disciplines of theology, law, and medicine; even then the university engaged in extensive language training, and the grammar schools often taught the disciplines. Further blurring is well illustrated in terms of the ages of the young people who attended. There were no fast entrance or completion ages. In 1692, for example, Caen College in France had an age range of nine through seventeen in its beginning class of 104 students. At the Oratorian College of Troyes in 1638/39 the age range in the beginning class was nine through twenty-four years. No single age group at Chalons in 1618 represented more than 12 percent of any given age group. Some children had completed their college courses by the time they were twelve or thirteen years old. The prestigious university did maintain a certain dignity and such precocity was rare; nevertheless, even it admitted young people as a rule from fourteen to twenty-one years of age (Aries, 1962: 189-240).

The grammar school often served as the preparatory school for the university because it usually admitted younger people. It also provided language training necessary for university work, but we can only use that criteria in a very general sense since a multitude of other possibilities existed to obtain some facility with Latin. Paulsen sees the boundaries between academic schools becoming even less distinct by the sixteenth century as the schools greatly extended their activities to include literature, philosophical studies and theology (Paulsen, 1919: vol. I, 328). The universities which maintained humanistic programmes were actually called an Academie, a Lyceum, or a Gymnasium at that time. For the next three centuries one could even speak of competition between them before the university won the place of advanced institution and the grammar school became the preparatory school for the university in the nineteenth century. The manner in which the preparatory institutions and the universities became two separate entities varied from nation state to nation state, although the distinction became well defined in all modern states.

The difference between what we now refer to as secondary schools and elementary schools was even less distinct. In fact the notion of elementary schools as separate institutions was almost non-existent prior to the Reformation. Scholars have even had difficulty distinguishing between schools that existed after the Reformation. This is in part a consequence of documentation difficulties, but also because primary schooling as a completely separate institution is an outgrowth of modernity. The Stralsunder School Statute of 1560, for example, directs the vernacular boys to meet with the 'Latin youth at a quarter before seven in the church and help with the conduct of the rituals connected with the early sermon. Afterwards they will go with them to the school and remain there until ten' where they engage in the study of basic skills and religious instruction. At three o'clock they go with the 'Latin youth all together in their own church, in order to sing the vespers' (Dietrich and Klink, 1964: 25-26). Four hours a day were therefore spent together and the separation between vernacular and Latin boys reflected a division of courses of study more than a separation of schools in the modern sense. Seaborne, in his study of school architecture in England, confirms a similar relationship in the 'grammar schools' of seventeenth-century England. It was not uncommon for the Latin and the English schools to be under the same roof and even in the same classroom. Chigwell, for example, had a screen or some similar device to separate the two groups when needed; only after the modern age arrived did the community establish a permanent partition between the two groups (Seaborne, 1971: 51).

Caution must also be exercised here because we have tended too often to assume that vernacular schools were elementary while the Latin schools were scholarly. In mid-eighteenth-century Prussia there were at least 400 Latin schools. The number of 'recognized *Gymnasien*' that existed in 1818 was set at 91, which means that almost 80 percent of the Latin schools had been 'transformed into elementary schools' once state regulations took over (Paulsen, 1919: vol. II, 290).

Cremin reminds us that in colonial America, although there were grammar and elementary schools which were designed to help children read, write, and cipher, it was very difficult to distinguish many things that went on as well as the quality of instruction that was reflected there (Cremin, 1970: 500). Boyd and King (1972: 280) find the same situation in England just prior to the modern age.

MODERN SCHOOL STRUCTURES TAKE FORM

As schooling came under the province of the modern world, especially the authority of nation states, educational possibilities were rationalized and organized into more cohesive systems. This is not to discount the fact that schools retained some elements of their traditional form and continued to cultivate their own values and intentions. We do observe, however, certain major tendencies in terms of external and internal structural alteration.

External Structural Differentiation

We find two major phases of modernity in which, externally, school structures underwent fundamental change. In the first phase, structure shifted from a diffused traditional condition to a clear horizontal dualistic system of schooling. In the second phase, the horizontal dualistic system tended to become vertically differentiated but horizontally unified.

Dualism of Schooling. As Western societies moved toward modernity, the schools not only established their own identity as separate social institutions, but they also established separate identity betweeen school types. The initial external structural form which emerged during the nineteenth century in almost all early modern lands was that of a tightly defined dualistic educational system. The elementary school served as the basic educational institution for the children of the common classes, while the grammar school served the elites. The teachers of these schools were drawn from their respective social classes and the programmes of studies were intended to instil the knowledge and virtues appropriate to each social class.

It is important to point out that social class consciousness as we know it is heavily loaded with modern industrial perspectives. We have seen that the lower schools of traditional Europe were so variegated that it would be impossible to make any clear cut generalizations as to their social class function. There is no question that the lower schools of traditional society took on definite class relationships as they moved near to modernity. We shall not bother to review the Poor Laws, the petty schools, the Society for Promoting Christian Knowledge in England, nor the charity schools which flourished throughout France in the seventeenth century, nor the great appeals for educating the poor after the time of Luther in Germany. However, the traditional lower schools were not as consciously social class oriented as in modernity. Recent analysis by Aries has demonstrated that even the French 'charity schools did not give rise to education reserved for the lower classes'. Rather, from their earliest origins, 'they attracted a well-to-do clientele of craftsmen, merchants, and burgesses, and were often competitive with the grammar schools in their ability to attract pupils' (Aries, 1962: 306). In no way could we link the holders of the large farming estates who were the typical hosts of even the small circulating schools in rural areas, with the industrial lower classes.

The higher schools of early modernity derived their form from the Latin grammar schools of traditional society and became crystallized as the elite wing of national education. They were defined very early in modernity as schools for the gifted, and although there was some chance for pupils from the poor classes to enter, the private tutoring and preparatory institutions were designed specifically to prepare pupils for the higher schools. In fact, in lands such as England, France, and Germany these preparatory schools were often attached directly to the grammar school. A sharp division existed between the social classes which was reinforced by the schools.

Comprehensive Schooling. We have seen that the external structural modernization process began by differentiating explicitly between two major horizontal parallel institutions. Two major forces are responsible for the breakdown of this system. The first force came through the impact of science and technology which obliterated the distinct social class structure that was so dominant in early modernity. With the rise of a middle class, accompanied by reduced upper class and increased lower class status, the differences between social levels was greatly reduced. Schelsky (1957: 13) claims this process manifested itself not so much through money and possessions as through a merging of 'cultural life style' brought about by scientific innovation and mass production.

New schools, which we simply describe as more practically oriented middle schools, emerged serving the needs of the rising middle classes. This process has been traced in our chapter on higher learnings and it should suffice here to say that they challenged the exclusive split between elites and masses and served as a levelling force on both.

The second major force, which overlapped the first, was directly related to political impulses. Even though authority was consolidated to the nation state, it was in no way unified in terms of the policies and programmes that were established. We saw that France moved quickly in forming elite schools but lagged in its energy to provide education for the masses. We saw that Prussia was the most thorough in establishing state schools for both elites and the masses, while England was slow getting involved in either. The United States was the one early modern country which opted to stress primary education, and in the process, literally by-passed the phase of dualism which was universal in nineteenth-century modern Europe. However, even in Europe political forces came to cater more and more to an ideology of equal opportunity and national unity as reflected in a comprehensive school structure. The structural reforms of the twentieth century have concentrated, therefore, on breaking down the dualism of early modernity, and laying elementary, middle, and higher schools vertically in such a manner that the schooling process becomes one of passing from one institution to another in regular progression. We shall briefly review the major vertical levels of schooling that emerged.

Early Childhood Education. The idea of a school for the very young was entertained as early as the seventeenth century by men such as Comenius. He recognized that the first years were critical if the child was to obtain a sense of natural sciences, arts, and the things of the spirit (Comenius, 1874). The writings of Rousseau and Pestalozzi, over a century later, revived the modern vision of Comenius. For Rousseau the father becomes the teacher of the boys and for Pestalozzi the mother serves as teacher for all children. An important purpose of their writings was to produce manuals for child-rearing. The family had taken on a distinct role in the budding period of modernity and it was no longer deemed appropriate to turn the baby over to a wet nurse or to assume that the process of early education would happen naturally. The family had already taken on much of its modern form in that it did not fit completely into the organic whole of the past. The occupation of the father had moved him into spheres of life that were no longer intimately related to ongoing family life. The land, the Church, and work were becoming separate segments of life. Such atomization was even characteristic of the family which itself was becoming a differentiated, specialized social unit. The burden of child-rearing in this new institutional form fell on the shoulders of the parents from the time the child was born until it entered school or went to work.

Early childhood education traces its early modern history to two sources. The first interlinks schooling for small children with the modern family, and the second interlinks it with industrial society. It is a mistake to attribute the first view as traditional since the traditional family itself was only part of a multiple network which included a vast array of relatives, tribal members, and friends. In Europe, according to Aries, the family existed 'as a reality', but paradoxically it did not exist as a concept until the eighteenth century (1962: 405-406).

We presently give recognition to Froebel for developing early education schools in Germany but we often overlook the fact that he was a strong defender of the family as the primary institution of education for the very young. The Kindergarten was meant to serve as a model to fathers and mothers showing how, especially through the cultivation of play, the children were to be reared. 'Our educational center should not replace the family,' he declared as early as 1823, 'on the contrary, we are attempting to build the truly educated family, as the centerpoint for the child.' At a later date he suggested, 'even though we have established an educational center, we are working toward its eventual destruction, dissolution, and obsolescence' (Froebel, 1862: 351).

The Kindergarten was much more than a centre to help the child learn; it was a centre to educate the mother and help the family to fulfil its new function in society. Froebel's original conception found receptivity in many lands. The United States, through the influence of refugees such as Carl Schurz who fled the reactionary forces following the 1848 revolution, was influenced to the degree that many private nursery schools were established. In England, France, Belgium and Switzerland some receptivity was also shown.

The second source of early childhood education reflects a different orientation. As industrialism expanded, modern working parents came to rely on the Kindergarten to provide custodial care for their children. Early examples of this thrust are found in the work of Charles Fourier in France and Robert Owen in Scotland and later America. Both were social reformers and they recognized the social potential of early childhood education. Their social philosophies gave priority to the happiness of the community rather than to the individual. The important difference between Fourier and Owen was the latter's ability actually to establish successful experiments of his ideas.

At New Lanark in Scotland, where Robert Owen transformed the community into a model industrial town at the beginning of the nineteenth century, the infant school was viewed as the first level of a inified though many-sided educational process that would extend throughout life. Owen's orientation was much different from that of Froebel, since his school relieved the family mother of the child-care burden. The role of the mother was to support the school as the primary early education institution and contribute to the whole community rather than just to her family (Owen, 1897: Appendix C). The school at New Lanark contained much of his plan; the little ones were in the school all morning and in the afternoons they were together for free, but supervised, activity. The programme at New Harmony in America, where he moved, was even more revolutionary; by the time the child was three years of age it was involved in a daily nine-hour programme including observation of Nature, work in building and gardening, and participation in activities such as music and dance.

In 1819 Owen's ideas were transported to London where a model infant school was established and soon the infant school movement was under way. By 1836 over 90,000 three to seven-year-olds were attending almost 3,000 schools (Turner, 1970: 158), and by 1870 they were incorporated into the national school system. Consequently, England, which had lagged behind all other modern nations in terms of a national system, came to maintain 'obligatory education' for a younger age group than anywhere else in the world (Turner 1970: 165).

Even the English were, however, persuaded to make a distinction between the very young and those over five years of age. At the turn of the century the number of three to five-year-olds in school was radically reduced to less than 15 percent of an age group. Nursery schooling now exists in England but has never been as dominant as it was in the last decades of the previous century (Roberts, 1972).

As did England, countries such as Germany (in 1872) and Switzerland (in 1870) usually brought early childhood education under its state jurisdiction. France has maintained *écoles maternelle* for over one hundred years and now sends over 90 percent of its four-year-olds to school.

In summary, Froebelian ideas are still found in the literature and in practice, but more often early childhood education is justified on the basis of child care either for parents who are away from the home because of work or who are not capable of fulfilling their responsibilities. The Owen model appears to have become dominant especially in those lands having a socialist orientation. The German Democratic Republic has been as conscientious as any country in the world in making places available for young children. Their purpose is singular. In 1959 that country took on the dual task of giving all three to six-year-old children a 'thorough socialistic education and preparation for school' (Krecker, 1971: 371).

Early childhood education has become commonplace and even pervasive in some areas of the modern world, but it has played almost no role in the struggle for a unified schooling structure. Only after the common primary school was established has extensive early childhood education emerged as a national commitment.

Common Primary Schools. The United States, which by-passed the dualistic phase of modern education, was the first to introduce common schooling on a large scale. We have already seen that the grammar school lost its viability before the country overcame its colonial status. The grammar school was replaced largely by the academy, a private institution, which served as a transition school for advanced learning. 'Perhaps the most that can be said of any given academy', said Cremin while discussing eighteenth-century America, 'is that it offered what its master was prepared to teach, or what its students were prepared to learn, or what its sponsors were prepared to support, or some combination or compromise among the three' (Cremin, 1970: 505).

When the surge for public schooling came during the 1830s and 1840s, the academy was already in decline. Americans flooded to Europe to find models for the school which would serve them best. Calvin E. Stowe brought home the news that in Prussia the 'best school districts that have ever been organized exist' (1930: 307). Alexander Dallas Bache spent two years in Europe and was unequivocal that Prussian primary education was the 'most perfect of the centralized systems' (1839: 172). Henry Barnard, superintendant of common schools in Connecticut, observed that the Prussian schools had 'commanded the admiration of intelligent educators in every part of Christendom' (1854: 87). And the father of the American common school, Horace Mann, claimed: 'Among the nations of Europe, Prussia has long enjoyed the most distinguished reputation for excellence of its schools' (1844: 72). Although there was resistance to the Prussian Volksschule, because it was designed to indoctrinate the masses toward monarchy, it was ultimately adopted as the school model designed to support and strengthen the new American Republic (Rust, 1968: 86-97).

Secondary education emerged in a totally different form than in Europe since it developed mainly by extending the eight-year common school. Since education was locally administered, such a process was sporadic and fragmented. Whenever a community demanded more schooling, school boards usually met this need by adding additional courses of study to the common school curriculum. By the end of the century both primary and secondary education presented a full unified twelve-year course of studies. In contrast to the United States, in early modern Europe the common school was a vital though unsuccessful political issue. It was not a new concept since several centuries earlier the most visionary prophet of modern education, Comenius, had conceived of a four level unified education programme leading from birth through higher education. In 1819 a national unified school plan had been seriously proposed by Prussian Minister of the Interior, Johann Süvern, but such a plan was much too premature in Europe (Scheibe, 1965: 7-10).

Throughout the nineteenth century the liberal political forces, including the elementary school teachers, united in advocating some kind of unified school which would help all people develop a sense of intellectual independence and which would at the same time bind people of all social classes together. In the last quarter of the century specific proposals for integration began to take shape. However, Scandinavia was the only major Western European area which was successful during that century. The Swedish government actively engaged in discussions about a common school, and legislative bills were introduced as early as 1867; in 1894 a three-year foundation school was adopted. In 1928 the common school was extended to four, in 1950 to six and in 1962 to nine years. Japan, which modernized economically within a generation, shifted during this brief time from a dual to a common school design. In 1872 it copied the dual system of Prussia in its initial attempt to modernize its educational system (Nbakamori, 1974: 573), but by 1881 the first three years had already been instituted as a common experience, shifting to four years in 1890, and moving finally to six years in 1907 (Kaigo, 1965: 64).

Russia moved decisively in an attempt to establish a unified schooling programme. A month after the October Revolution in 1917 a proclamation was issued outlining the task of education, the first and most important being the establishment of a universal common school. A month later a decree was issued withdrawing all teaching institutions from Church control. One year after the Revolution the All Russian Executive Committee ratified a plan for common schools which would consist of a nine-year, secular, free, general, obligatory education. By 1920 over 12,000 of the 54,000 existing primary schools had achieved a five-year common programme (Günther et al., 1973: 506), but the enormous task for Russia lay ahead. The majority of the population was still living in almost primitive conditions and the scientific-technological forces which had been an important factor in Europe were essentially non-existent. In spite of this, by 1930 almost all children were receiving at least four years of common schooling and the larger cities had committed themselves to a seven-year common schooling experience. In 1943 a universal seven-year schooling programme was mandated and this was extended to eight years in 1957. Today, the state is attempting to institute a ten-year middle school for all; however, its goal is still hindered by the enormous size of the land, cultural differences, and an economic level of development that is not well balanced (documentation in Anweiler and Meyer, 1961).

We wish now to return briefly to Western Europe which perpetuated the early modern dual school structure almost until the present day. The first major breakthrough for a unified common school occurred in Germany, which, after the collapse of the monarchy at the end of the First World War, called a conference of 600 educators to design a comprehensive school reform plan. The Education Law of 1921 was a consequence of this conference and it stipulated that a common school was to become a reality by 1925 (Article 146; 2). The Germans were able to unify teacher qualifications since all Volksschule instructors were thereafter required to pass the leaving examination of the Gymnasium. However, National Socialism overtook the country before common schooling could be genuinely adopted. It was therefore 1945 before all young people of Germany found themselves beginning school together at the age of six and remaining for four years before they separated into their dual schools. This structure remains in most of the German states to this day.

The French also maintained complete separation between elementary and secondary schools until 1925 when some common primary schools were established; however, preparatory classes continued to dominate the scene until the mid-1930s when, through the efforts of Jean Zay, a common primary school law was passed. In 1937 a six-year common primary school became a reality, the last year serving as an observation class which would determine if a child was to go on to classical, modern, or technical secondary school. In England a very similar programme was initiated in 1944; the primary school became standard for all children until the age of eleven, when they were channelled to a secondary modern, technical, or grammar school.

As we come to the end of modernity, we find national patterns along a continuum between the early modern structure and the mature modern structure. At the one extreme, countries such as Japan, the United States, and Canada attempt to provide comprehensive education from the beginning of primary school until the end of secondary school. Scandinavia, Norway and Sweden provide up to nine years of extended basic education, while Russia, East Germany, Czechoslovakia, and other Eastern European lands offer an eight-year general education before placing children in appropriate differentiated secondary schools.

Intermediate and Secondary Schools. As we would expect, the intermediary institution is found in countries that have adopted an extended unified schooling policy. In Sweden, where comprehensive education has been national policy since 1948, the eight-year common schooling experience is broken down into a three-year primary school, a three-year middle school and a two-year general secondary school before the children separate into a general continuation, vocational or academic programme.

The United States, which has maintained an extended common schooling programme longer than any other country, adopted the idea of an intermediate or junior high school at the turn of the century because efficiency-minded educators felt that eight years of primary schooling could be shortened. In 1912, the Committee on Economy of Time in Education recommended to the National Education Association that primary schooling be reduced to six years so that children might move on to more exalted secondary schooling. By the time the junior high was a reality, its existence was argued on psychological rather than academic grounds. This period in the pupil's life seemed to mark a radical transition from childhood to adolescence and the junior high school became an intermediary institution intended to help the youth move more easily from one stage of life to another (Spaulding et al., 1935).

A number of countries continue to provide a minimal four- to six-year primary school experience and then separate the children into general, vocational technical, and academic schools. This was the general case in Europe until the past two decades, although many nations have since adopted the comprehensive secondary school ideal, which places all of these tracks in one institution. The comprehensive school usually provides a two- to four-year observation period in which the children are carefully monitored to make certain they have been appropriately tracked. France, for example, provides a four-year *cycle d'observation et d'orientation* above its five-year primary school which receives all children and places them in loosely defined general and practical sections based on the child's ability. The children are provisionally placed in order for adjustments to be made for late bloomers and misjudged cases. However, The Netherlands, Belgium, England, West Germany, Italy, Spain and other countries are still dominated by the separation of children into different schools following primary school. All of these countries have plans or policies which dictate comprehensive education. London, for example, defines all its post-primary institutions as comprehensive schools but in actual practice a large number of them are nothing more than secondary modern or grammar schools. The socialist governed states in West Germany are also moving quickly toward comprehensiveness but the nation as a whole could not yet be so characterized.

As we move to the upper levels of the schooling continuum, we find quite a different situation evolving in mature modernity. Even in countries such as Russia, which established the unified schooling principle from the beginning, differentiation of schools has occurred, especially in the past two decades. The rhetorical question raised by the All Russian Education Commission in October, 1918 was: 'What does it mean to have a unified school? It means, that a complete system providing an unbroken ladder from kindergarten to the university exists in the form of a common school.' It would also mean that 'all children are obliged to enter the same school type . . . and all have the right to climb this step ladder to the highest step' (Anweiler and Meyer, 1961: 74).

In spite of this, a wide array of academic and vocational schools have emerged, especially since Khrushchev's 1958 proclamation that education and life be drawn more closely together. Special schools for music, graphic arts, and dance are catering to the best talents in Russia. Since 1948 schools have existed which are designed to provide training in English, German, French, and Spánish to students who show interest and talent for language. Within the framework of the general middle school programme, schools have emerged which 'specialize' in one discipline or another. Mathematics-physics boarding schools, directly linked with universities, have been instituted which furnish intensive training to young people who have completed nine years of general schooling (Mitter, 1969). Add to this the full array of vocational and polytechnical institutes which exist, not only in Russia, but in all lands of the modern world and we are able to get some sense of the explosion of specialized schooling at the upper levels.

Internal Structural Differentiation

In spite of the fact that modern countries have tended toward comprehensive schooling, differentiation has continued within the unified school structures themselves. Internal structural differentiation in modernity has taken place vertically with the establishment of age grade levels and it has taken place horizontally in the form of streaming and discipline specialization in unified schools.

Age Grading. Grouping is almost as old as recorded history itself; still, we are able to draw clear distinctions between traditional and modern modes. The Latin grammar schools of the Middle Ages set the model for traditional schools as they were typically divided into three levels: (1) *Tabulistae,* in which the alphabet and some Latin words were memorized; (2) *Donatistae,* in which elementary grammar was learned; and (3) *Alexandristae,* in which advanced grammar, according to the standard of Alexander de Villa Dei, was studied (Paulsen, 1919: vol. I, 23).

In spite of the fact that there was grouping in the grammar schools and universities, there was no concept of a faculty of teachers having separate groups in their own rooms or buildings. In the extreme case the learner worked with a single teacher in a common room with all other learners and was attached to a group which sat in a special place. It was the teacher's role to work with each learner individually and it was the learner's role to engage in the communal life of the school and to master the material of the particular group to which he was attached. Since the tasks were individually monitored, it was possible for the learner to move on to the next group as soon as he had learned the material. In this arrangement it was possible to pass through the various groups at different speeds.

Such a process was so common in Prussia that the school law of 1763 stipulated that

> should the children, either through their own ability or the applied industry of the schoolmaster, learn the required material before the thirteenth or fourteenth year they would receive a leaving certificate from the inspector when certified by the minister and schoolmaster (Dietrich and Klink, 1964: 133).

By the sixteenth century advance schooling had evolved a complex grading programme in some isolated, but important, instances. The schools of the Brethren of the Common Life appear to have been the first to have developed age graded instruction, although Bowen feels the original graded school was developed at the town school in Zwolle, Holland (Bowen, 1975: vol. II, 174). At any rate the Low Countries' schools established the first models which were subsequently copied and spread so that by the end of the sixteenth century grading was common in the continental grammar schools.

Phillipe Aries has given us a good account of specific aspects of grading as they occurred mainly in the French schools of that period.

These characteristics included grouping according to grammar level, assigning a master to each level, and providing separate rooms for each master (Aries, 1962: 176-88).

To suggest that these elements were innovations means that they did not exist in any systematic form prior to that time. We recall that the three major levels found in earlier periods were based on language competence, but the later innovation took into consideration literature, historical study of writers, rhetoric, composition, etc. Between 1465 and 1498 Alexander Hegius at Deventer had organized such an elaborate programme that it would have taken twenty-five years to complete.

The institution which served as the major model for grammar schools of that period was undoubtedly that run by Johannes Sturm. In the sixteenth century Sturm began his schooling at Deventer and after attending several universities he was invited to direct a school in Strasbourg in 1537. Copying much of the Brethren of the Common Life schooling tradition, which he had experienced as a youth, including grading, he set up a highly trivium-oriented programme which followed an eight-year, a nine-year, and finally a ten-year course of studies. Sturm spelled out in precise terms the studies to be learned each year emphasizing that each pupil should remember that 'to retain that which has been won is no less an art than the winning of something itself' (Raumer, 1877: 217-50). Sturm believed the best time for a youth to begin studies was at the age of six. He was to remain at a grade level, or 'class' as it was coming to be called, for one year. Grade level placement was almost exclusively dependent on the level of development the student had attained in grammar school.

There were, of course, other schools during the period which evolved graded programmes. In fact, Valentin Trotzendorf set up a school programme in Silesia six years before Sturm went to Strasbourg. He organized his school into six classes, each class being subdivided into three parts for disciplinary purposes (Raumer, 1877: 173). In 1552, Heronymus Wolf relied on Sturm's organization principles in setting up a Gymnasium in Augsburg. The first major structure which he adopted was a five-grade programme, each grade lasting one and one-half years. The lowest class was also divided into three divisions: the ABC group, the (Latin) reader group, and the (Latin) writing and memorizing group. In 1576 Wolf reorgnized the school into nine grade levels. The young boys were expected to enter school in their seventh year, when possible, and remain in each class for one year so that they would complete their programme of studies by the age of sixteen (Raumer, 1877: 192-208).

The Jesuits also adopted a graded structure for their Latin schools (Bowen, 1975: II, 419). The *Ratio Studiorum* outlines a highly rationalized course of studies divided into five levels for 'inferior' or elementary studies and three upper grammar classes. One half year was devoted to each elementary level and two years to each upper level requiring nine or ten years to complete the entire process.

The second pre-seventeenth century innovation of schooling structure which Aries discusses is the notion of several masters in the same grammar school. To have several classes does not preclude the possibility of having but a single master. One reason for the necessity of retaining but one master and perhaps an assistant was the initial size of grammar schools. In England, as grammar schools proliferated during the sixteenth century, they were usually very small. It has been estimated that about 12,000 boys were attending the 361 grammar schools which existed at the close of the sixteenth century; this averages out to no more than 33 boys per school (Brown, 1933: 7). Eton, which was established in 1440, was originally intended to have a size of 20 scholars although school rosters which are still available show an enrolment of 198 boys in 1678. If we contrast this figure with the 500 scholars at the time of the Industrial Revolution, we get some sense of the change in school size. Manchester Grammar School had maintained an enrolment of between 87 and 276 boys over five-year spans as late as the eighteenth century. By the end of the nineteenth century, it maintained 730 pupils in a single year, growing to over 1,000 just before the First World War.

In England during the sixteenth century even the larger schools were inclined to rely on a master and perhaps one assistant. St Paul's school, which was set up for 153 boys, made provision for a master, a sur-master, and a chaplain. Eton, even though it had established six classes, or forms as they were known in English grammar schools, retained a master to teach the upper three and an assistant to handle the lower three forms.

On the Continent the practice of hiring a number of teachers for the prominent schools was introduced even earlier. Undoubtedly, one of the reasons Deventer became a model for newer organizational design was the fact that during Hegius's time the school reached an exceptional enrolment of 2,220 pupils and it became necessary to devise a different structure to cope with that number. Sturm copied the practice of hiring several teachers, maintaining that the ideal was to have a teacher for each grade level. Wolf also hired teachers for different classes (Raumer, 1877: 197).

The process of placing new teachers was slow and usually corresponded with the development of a positive school reputation. Trotzendorf was the only teacher at Goldenberg for seven years before he was able to gain a sufficient reputation to expand the number of teachers. Fully devloped, his school called for six special people: (1) a schoolmaster; (2) a teacher of philosophy and literature; (3) a teacher of astronomy; (4) a grammarian and rhetorician; (5) a music teacher; and (6) a catechism instructor (Loeschke, 1856: 25).

The final innovation which found some footing by the sixteenth century was the practice of providing separate rooms for the different grades. This feature was not universally adopted at that time since the typical mode of school-keeping was to gather all pupils in a single room under the supervision of the master and his assistant.

The idea of dividing the learners into separate rooms met with resistance for pedagogical as well as practical reasons. The schools run by the Brethren of the Common Life never accepted the practice and expanded the size of the rooms as far as possible. It must be remembered that the entire school spent an enormous amount of time together and separate rooms would have interfered with these communal activities. For example, the Hessian School Law of 1618 stipulated that 'each and every class shall be together' to practise piety in (1) daily public prayer, (2) singing of psalms, (3) reading of bible chapters, (4) reading sections of the catechism, and (5) explaining the gospels and Sunday sermons, as well as other matters. The purpose and aims of each of the eight classes are fully outlined, these being divided into two sections: activities common to all classes and activities related to specific classes (Vormbaum, 1863: 184-88). If masters were added, the groups often remained in the same room. Sturm reflected a sentiment that was un- doubtedly widespread: 'It is better to gather the classes together in a single place than to disperse them over several. It would be senseless, if one had ten sheep, to assign a sepherd and a field to each sheep, when a single meadow is sufficient' (in Aries, 1962: 185).

This idea was carried to extremes as schools grew. We might recall the monitorial system of early modernity in England and America which continued the practice of one large room with a single master and up to 1,000 children under his charge. Such a practice was not considered strange since England continued to maintain single-room schools much longer than did the Continent. In fact, during the eighteenth century, as schools proliferated, we find that England established multiple schools in the same facility in preference to grading the same school. Separate schools for boys and girls became common, but even when the number of pupils of the same sex expanded beyond the capacity of one schoolmaster, a new school was added in lieu of dividing the old (Seaborne, 1971: 125).

We conclude that although grading, multiple teacher faculties, and separate classrooms had become somewhat common in the advanced schools by the end of the sixteenth century, these innovations were resisted by many, and as we shall soon see, were non-existent in the lower schools.

One of the major reasons for resistance against segmentation and specialization was the knowledge that individual flexibility and freedom of entrance and movement was only possible as long as a close, intimate relationship was maintained. This relationship was already in danger of deteriorating in the sixteenth century, as schools expanded in size. However, large schools, with their differentiated structure, were still exceptions to the general tradition.

During the seventeenth century, we find the beginnings of modern instruction as exemplified by the proposals of Comenius, who professed to have discovered a method to teach everyone everything. Comenius realized the single most pervasive problem in the equation was how to teach everyone. He envisaged schools of the future that would overcome the intimate individual environments of his generation and become institutions in which 'a single teacher is able [simultaneously] to instruct a hundred pupils'. To accomplish this the subject matter of the school was to be brought into a detailed and explicit order of presentation, and the times of presentation were also to be ordered 'so that every year, every month, every day, every hour possesses its own lesson' (Comenius, 1954: 95). Comenius claimed it was necessary to move from individual to group instruction. The new instruction would use the sun as its model. 'The sun does not deal individually with every single object, such as with a tree or an animal; instead it radiates, warms, and softens the whole earth' (1964: 120). The sun was not the only model for Comenius. The teacher was also expected to perform 'as an officer, who does not conduct his exercises with every single recruit, but rather with all at once on the exercise ground' (1954: 128-29).

Comenius anticipated the model of mass education which required not only graded groups but graded instruction. The whole house of learning was to be assembled from bottom to top, brick upon brick. The insight of Comenius was also that of Pestalozzi, whose methodology also involved group teaching; the teacher would raise questions in the entire group and would even encourage exchange of impressions on the part of the students. Although this approach was more open-ended than that advocated by Comenius and demanded great skill in classroom management, it also required that all children be at a similar level of development. In other words, it was deemed important that a degree of homogeneity was necessary if group instructional programmes were to be successful.

The new class instruction as conceived by Comenius and Pestalozzi assumed certain conditions in school organization. It would be necessary for the young to begin school at about the same age and then progress through the school within one age group.

It is possible to conceive of organizational schemes which would account more adequately for differing abilities or differing rates of progression. At that time, however, organizational skill was still at a primitive stage of development and a complex plan would likely have resulted in breakdown. Even Comenius turned to the simpler scheme of age groups moving in uniform cadence.

As the state became the regulator of schooling, it also defined, in explicit terms the age at which a child was to enter school. It further defined the number of grades a child would pass through in order to complete the course of studies. A teacher and a separate room were instituted for each class, and the teacher was required to have a standardized educational background. Vertical differentiation meant that a genuine step-ladder arrangement existed with each step having a separate, unique function in the total process.

So far in our discussion of grading we have concentrated on grammar schools; therefore, it is necessary to describe the establishment of grading in the lower schools. In the sixteenth century when vernacular education was instituted the three levels found in earlier grammar schools were usually adopted. The Gotha school regulations of 1642 divided the learners into lowest, middle, and highest classes and stipulated in precise terms the reading programme, scriptures, catechism sections, etc. that were to be learned in each group (Dietrich and Klink, 1964: 59-67). The Prussian *General-Land-Schul-Reglement,* over one hundred years later, once again prescribed three divisions: ABC pupils, spelling learners, and readers. This grouping is only oriented to reading instruction, but we have seen that the greater part of the day was devoted to communal activities (Dietrich and Klink, 1964: 140).

As we enter the modern age, we find once again that the Prussian school laws carried the three level grouping into its structure. The law of 1872 stipulated that the eight-year Volksschule should be divided into three groups: lower (two years), middle (three years), and upper (three years). Even when the Volksschule possessed multiple classes the three level concept was retained; 'whenever a Volksschule has four classes, it shall form two middle levels, whenever there are six classes, each level shall maintain two classes' (in Scheibe, 1965: 28-30). The one-room schools were also directed to divide into three levels. These schools usually only hired but a single teacher and they were not allowed to have over 80 children on their rolls. If they admitted more children, the law stipulated that it was necessary for the schools to either divide the children and conduct half-day instruction or hire a second teacher (Scheibe, 1965: 28). The figure of 80 children is not to be taken lightly. Johannes Tews gives figures from six typical cities in Germany in 1882 showing an average of 68 pupils per teacher. By 1886 this figure had risen to 76 (Tews, 1914: 194), but by 1911 the pupil-teacher ratio had been reduced to 55.5 in Prussia and by 1923 to 40, enabling the Prussians to realize the goal of age-grading (Müller, 1930: 105).

We have concentrated on Germany because it acted as the model for primary education more than any European country. Of course, there were variations to that model. At the turn of the century, Denmark, for example, grouped the elementary school as follows: Grade 1, 7-10 years; Grade II, 10-12 years; and Grade III, 12-14 years.

However, it moved with the other modern countries toward an age-graded school during this century and the process is now complete in all but the most remote areas.

The United States typically set up two major divisions for its early common school but through the efforts of men such as John D. Philbrick, superintendent of schools at Boston in the middle of the nineteenth century, age-grading became the ideal toward which progressive educators worked. America has not been without enormous problems in achieving its ideal, however, because until very recently it has been mainly rural. The small one-room school house was the dominant institution until this generation. As recently as 1930 the average primary school had 93 pupils on its roll and 149,000 of the 248,000 primary schools were still one-teacher institutions. That figure has decreased rapidly until less than 5 percent of the schools in America remain one room (U.S. Bureau of the Census, 1973).

Since the general evolution of primary school size was so slow during the nineteenth century, age-grading was only an ideal. By the twentieth century the primary schools had joined the secondary schools in organizing a step-ladder programme of studies. That ladder system often included a new section for nursery or infant children. In fact, in England the earliest physical division of rooms in elementary schools was usually designed to accommodate infants (Seaborne, 1971: 155).

Even as the age-graded objective was being realized, however, another major factor of grouping had come to occupy the best minds engaged in education. Age-grading created the necessity for uniform progress up the ladder. The dual system of education had served as an intermediary solution since the 'gifted', those pupils in the secondary school, could move at a more rapid rate than the rest of the children. But even this arrangement was not sufficient to quell the problems. Herbart recommended that the first two years in the Gymnasium be observation years in which those who were unable to keep up the pace fall into their proper station at the Volksschule. He also recommended 'drill classes' to help the slower pupils (Herbart, 1919: 149).

After the turn of this century, a number of unique grading plans were devised to account for differing rates of progress. Thus, the Dalton Plan of Helen Parkhurst, the Winnetka Plan of Charleton Washburne, the Jena Plan of Peter Peterson and many others attempted in one way or another to homogenize the groups that existed so that progress of one pupil would not impede progress of the other. More recently modular scheduling programmes have been introduced in the United States which provide for variations in group size, instruction time, and achievement levels. The Germans continue to retain the child at a grade level if he or she fails a part of it. The English have attempted to resolve the problem of differential progress by establishing A, B, C streams in which the grades or standards are subdivided according to achievement level so that age-grading is retained but mastery expectations are altered depending on the stream. Such a design brings us directly in line with our next item of inquiry.

Internal Horizontal Differentiation. Internal horizontal differentiation has a fairly recent history but it has become so important that when we speak of differentiation in current educational reforms, we usually have it in mind. This is because unified or comprehensive schooling has reduced radically the number of school types at least before the upper levels of secondary school. Now differentiation usually refers either to general grouping within the school in the form of academic, technical, and general streams or to specialized grouping within streams or specific disciplines. Pupils are usually placed in streams and course specializations according to some combination of ability, achievement, interest, and inclination. We wish to provide some historical context for internal horizontal differentiation since its intent has been altered in modernity.

Although he in no way intended his programme to symbolize modernity, we see the first seeds of modern internal horizontal differentiation in August Hermann Francke's *Paedagogium* in Halle toward the end of the seventeenth century. The most fundamental aspects of his programme were embedded in the traditional world since he maintained that the ultimate objective of education was pietism and devotion to God. He rejected new ideas such as play in school and perpetuated the traditional practice of up to four hours of religious study and observance each day.

His ideas did, however, include novel aspects which would ultimately dominate modern education. The first was that newer languages and the sciences could be used as adequately as the classics 'in the service of God and one's fellow man'. The second aspect was that since the boys possessed such different intellectual abilities and backgrounds, they were to be guided into different subjects of study 'according to their special and separate capacities so that the groups that would be formed would be similar in nature' (Francke, 1885: 208).

Each of the major subjects of Latin, Hebrew, theology, Greek, history, geography, and arithmetic was organized into at least three different classes with as many levels of competence. The classes were set up in sixteen week cycles, and if a boy was unable to reach the standard set in any cycle, he could repeat it as many as three times (1885: 218). It was also not necessary for a boy to take all of the twenty possible subjects in the school. His capacity and the purposes for which his parents sent him to school would determine the subjects he would study (1885: 234).

Francke further insisted that no student was capable of studying more than three subjects during a given cycle. His design was to have the student remain in a subject course as long as it took him to complete it, at which time he would be permitted to move to another subject (1885: 228). Such an arrangement had highly traditional overtones since it meant that students of all ages and levels of past experience were found in a subject of study at any given time. His programme also reflected the memorization tradition of the past in that he stipulated that the boys not forget their previous subjects by devoting every Wednesday and Saturday to repetition (1885: 229). Even though the 'subject course' system conceived by Francke anticipated schools in the mature modern age, it was seen more as an anomaly of early modernity since the age-grading system became universally accepted. The reason for this was mainly organizational; as the number of pupils increased, a more manageable system than Francke had conceived was necessary.

The most important early theoretical reason for rejecting a subject course structure was the traditional unity of studies. There were disciplines in early schools and even people who specialized in one study or another, but the overwhelming orientation was toward a unity of knowledge and a sense of common spirit within the intellectual community. The most pervasive force for retention of this unity in the advanced schools was its religious relationship. If a man taught astronomy, it was in the context of his main commitment, which was to God and Church. We recall that the concept of a unified studies programme was retained even as advanced education entered the modern world. Such an aim fitted very well within the age-graded concept since all were expected to engaged in the same work. The problem of capacity differences in the advanced schools was handled pragmatically. In many countries if a pupil failed any part of the total programme he would simply return to the same grade level for another year.

Even though age-gradedness dominated vertical differentiation, an internal horizontal differentiation emerged which ultimately destroyed the concept of unified studies. We have already traced this external process in Chapter 3 when we described the emergence of middle schools which reflected modern language and science-mathematics orientations. An internal differentiation process was also at work which was masked since the number of studies a pupil tended to engage in was not expanded during the nineteenth century. In Germany, for example, the leaving examination of 1810 and 1898 covered approximately fifteen subjects. All pupils studied all subjects until the last two years when some specialization was permitted in one of three areas: languages; maths and science; history and geography. Emphasis with the general learnings was so strong that if the pupils had not attained the necessary general standard when they began the last two grades, they were not allowed to specialize until they had reached it. In other words, the intent of the elite school was to help all the youth who attended the school obtain a general education and any specialization was subordinate to that intent.

Quite a different orientation was emerging in the middle school; not so much with the students as with the teachers. These schools had adopted the practice of hiring teachers who themselves were not in possession of a general education. Once a faculty becomes fragmented it is not a long step before a similar programme for students becomes the norm. Three major factors appear to have contributed to the presence of specialized teachers in all higher schools. The first was the growth of the number of schools. The universities were ill-prepared to train the required number of people, and teachers without a general education were allowed into service. The second was the re-orientation in emphasis on the part of the middle schools to include more and more science; this further increased the shortage of qualified teachers possessing a general education. The third was a shifting meaning of a general education itself. The Prussian Gymnasium leaving examination of 1898, for example, reveals a striking shift in orientation during that century. Students were examined in fifteen subjects. Those studies in 1898 carried over from 1810 were philosophical propadeutic, German, Latin, Greek, Hebrew, French, history, geography, and physics. Mathematics had been subdivided to pure and applied programmes. Theology, pedagogy, and natural history, which existed in 1810 were dropped, while English, chemistry-minerology, and botany-zoology were added (Blättner, 1960: 156). The teachers capable of teaching the new subjects were no longer fully prepared to see the relationship of their subject to some overarching general or liberal education experience. Although we do not wish to discuss the universities, we might note that they were the first to specialize. The teachers who studied at the university and then moved back to the secondary school were subject-matter specialists; therefore, it became a fiction that students exposed to a cluster of specialists would receive a general or liberal education.

Internal horizontal differentiation in early modernity meant less a study of more and varied subjects than a fragmentation of studies or the establishment of subject-matter autonomy. The curriculum for students was usually uniform in a particular type of school and internal horizontal differentiation was not yet considered to exist.

The unification of the schooling structure during the twentieth century brought with it a new problem. Since the upper level of common schools, the middle schools and the advanced schools, reflected different curricula, their unification signalled the breakdown of uniform study and the introduction of subject-matter streams. These streams replicated in many respects the curricula of the different school types that existed. Twentieth-century internal structural differentiation becomes little more than a replication of nineteenth-century external structural differentiation. We find the Europeans thus moving toward institutional unification but perpetuating the social distinctions of the early modern age.

Quite a different picture emerges in the secondary schools of modern Russia and the United States. The Russian orientation, coloured by political overtones, stressed a general education for all, which meant that until recently a largely uniform curriculum was imposed on all pupils. Differentiation has until now taken on a largely secondary position in comparison with the stress on uniformity of studies. The Russians unsuccessfully experimented in the 1960s with specialization variations in the last two years of the middle school. This is not to suggest that differentiation is not evolving, for the talented are being channelled into the special schools we mentioned earlier. 'Optional' courses are available in most middle schools but these are restricted almost exclusively to parallel and additional work related to the required studies in mathematics, literature, physics, Russian language, and chemistry (Mitter, 1969: 121).

The reasons for emphasis of a uniformity of studies in Russia can be traced to the revolutionary attempt to overcome social differences through education. A unified school does not necessarily ameliorate class differences. One of the major findings of social science research, as we shall see, is that internal horizontal differentiation has facilitated the perpetuation of social class distinctions in the school itself. The Soviet Union has attempted to intervene in this process by requiring a uniform course of studies and by practising some reverse discrimination: the children of workers and farmers are given some advantages for advancement.

The United States has moved to the other extreme of the spectrum, since there is little to find in terms of universally required subjects. The elective tradition in the United States, at least beyond primary school, has necessitated an enormous proliferation of courses. At one time Robert M. Hutchins was led to suggest that it would take a person 45 years to complete all the possible courses which are taught somewhere in American high schools. Such an estimate was not too far off the mark since the Department of Health, Education, and Welfare recently issued a listing of 292 different courses offered in American high schools in 1960-61. The number of courses has undoubtedly increased since that time.

In summary, the differentiation process in modernity has attempted to organize the school in such a way as to build homogeneous groups to facilitate group instruction. As technology has advanced, schools have been able to embark on more sophisticated plans, building smaller cells of instruction, usually within the framework of established practice such as age-grading and streaming. Individualized instruction could be described as nothing more than the most extreme expression of organizational complexity. Even in socialist countries, which demand uniformity for ideological reasons, differentiation has also become as common as anywhere since age-grades, classes, disciplines, specialized schools, and curricular hierarchies, are taken for granted. Schools of modernity are not unlike factories; the units of the schools are broken down into ever simpler components and organizational genius is able to integrate them together to produce giant educational mills which process the raw material of society.

PROTEST AGAINST THE SCHOOL

Of all the protests against modernity, that which has been the most shocking to educators and even the general public has been the protest against the school institution itself. This has been the most acute in the United States because of the intransigent belief on the part of so many that America is the land of the free, the happy, the humane, and the belief held so dearly that schools are a model reflection of society and are therefore happy, open, and free institutions. The United States commitment to education has been so great that approximately one-third of the population is engaged in full-time teaching or learning, while only two-fifths of the population is engaged in non-education occupations. Futurologists, less than a decade ago, were proudly pointing to their education charts predicting that by the turn of the century at least 40 percent of the population would be engaged in the schooling enterprise (von Hentig, 1972: 50).

Such optimism is already a fragment of past memory. The major protests against schooling have come from (1) those who claim the school as an institution is anti-human, and (2) those engaged in national development who find that underdeveloped countries are unable to pay for modern schooling.

Humanistic Education

In the early 1960s, at the time education commissions and ministries throughout the Western world were actively engaged in plans to extend schooling to more and varied elements in society, a small stream of literature began to appear, especially in the English-speaking countries, suggesting that some thing was radically wrong with the school. In America, books with exotic titles such as *Our Children are Dying, Death at an Early Age,* and *How Children Fail,* described in diary fashion the destructive forces to which the United States was subjecting its children daily. A growing sense of outrage began to boil throughout the land, and almost overnight the humanistic education movement was born.

The first direct action parents took was to withdraw their children from the public schools in order to set up their own educational enterprises. The major problem confronting them was to find a viable alternative to the school. Paul Goodman (1963) was responsible for popularizing a book written in 1959 by A.S. Neill describing his work at Summerhill in England. Neill's book soon became a bible for a whole movement. *Summerhill* is attractive because it describes supportive relationships between Neill and the children; yet it fails to explain how the schooling part of his institution was actually conducted. The book was ideal for its time, however, because in the first stages of the movement parents were inclined to express outrage toward the school. Any positive descriptions of educational alternatives would have interfered with parental indignation.

Soon hundreds of 'free schools' sprang up based on Summerhill, each taking on a form according to its founders' conception of Summerhill. They did, however, have common characteristics including: extensive free play, small group or individual activity, adult 'facilitators' rather than teachers, children of different age levels in the same group, open process oriented structures, meagre physical surroundings, disregard for order, no formal lines of authority, reduced concern for dress and cleanliness. This initial thrust has sustained itself to this day. Other courses of action have recently received greater attention such as the so-called alternative school movement which has entered the public school system.

Conventional schools have tended to adjust to the protests by instituting innovative programmes. Of course, an innovation orientation is not just the result of contemporary protests. One of the major characteristics of post-Second World War modern education is its reform orientation. The term 'school reform' itself has taken on slogan character in this period as the mature modern countries have accepted the prospect of continual change in school systems. To be maturely

modern is almost synonymous with being receptive to constant innovation, which has been accelerated as we have reached the final stages
of modernity.

In the United States, where the first two decades after the war were
viewed as 'one of the largest and most sustained educational reform
movements in American history', reform was almost exclusively
directed toward the goings on in the classroom (Silberman, 1970: 158).
New curricular programmes became the order of the day; teaching
methods moved to inquiry rather than presentation; team teaching
replaced the isolated self-contained classroom; teaching machines,
paraprofessionals, and television invaded the programme; non-
gradedness and modular schedules replaced the lock-step schedule of
the past. In spite of all these innovations, the problems of the schools
continued to grow until the entire structure was under attack.

In Europe the reform movement focused on setting up schooling
that would place children of all social classes in the same environment. In the Soviet Union, particular concern was shown toward
articulating school studies with the work world. However, almost
every aspect of education was undergoing some form of revision. At the
same time that the elite dominated dual system was being replaced in
Europe, the period of compulsory education was being extended,
and new curricular programmes of study were being instituted. In
West Germany, which was relatively mild in terms of its efforts, over
300 different reform categories are listed in a recent document
(Schmidt and Lützenkirchen, 1969).

It is important to note the relationship of the reforms to the
alternatives orientation of today and to suggest its impact on the
present schooling crisis. The reforms which we have just mentioned
are exclusively within the modern framework. The participants
of these reforms are not identified with the present so called
'alternatives in education' movement, the main reason being that
they are almost exclusively oriented toward changing the school to
meet the increased demands of a mature technological society. The
school has been reformed in order that modernity might be more
completely realized. Nevertheless, the modern reform orientation of
the recent past has itself been a vital factor in the emergence of the
alternatives movement.

The purpose of any educational reform is to meet the problems that emerge in society and to create a better educational system. During the recent past, reforms have been piled upon reforms until a sense of insufficiency has emerged with regard to all aspects of education. Certain reforms have undoubtedly resulted in improvement of schooling, but change and innovation have so accelerated that we are usually unable to make quality assessments before the next reform is set in motion. Consequently, the reform process has led to a general distrust of the more stable criteria of what is good because it has multiplied data, theories, proposals, and criticisms. As reforms are added to reforms, we reach a point of social chaos; we approach a condition of relativity which is no longer productive since it lacks any standard. Rather than improving schooling, accelerated reforms simply contributed to a sense of randomness whose value is seen only in its Hawthorne effect, not in its inherent improvement. Modernity is caught in its own trap of self-destruction since change acceleration can only culminate in chaos and anarchy. The reforms are, therefore, contributing to rather than reducing the problems of modern schooling.

Ronald and Beatrice Gross have identified the source of the basic humanistic revolt against schooling in the United States; they note that recent innovations are attempts to maintain the basic philosophies and aims of conventional schooling, while the concern for humanistic educators centres on a new role for education. That role would reorient education toward human beings and human concerns rather than the society, the state, the economy, or the school itself (Gross and Gross, 1969: introduction).

Bonnie Barrett Stretch, in writing one of the earliest comprehensive statements on free schools in the United States, accurately identified the main thrust of the revolt against public schools. It has reached a point that is

> no longer against outdated curricular or ineffective teaching methods, the concerns of the 1950s and 1960s. The revolt today is against the institution itself, against the implicit assumption that learning must be imposed on children by adults, that learning is not something one does by and for oneself, but something designated by a teacher (Stretch, 1970).

The teacher in this case symbolizes the institution. The goals of school, the tasks assigned, the activities engaged in, are seen as being institutional rather than as personal and human.

With this pressure the public sector gave way even further and allowed 'alternative schools' to emerge as a part of the public system. The schools which have emerged within the public sector are usually rather similar to the free schools, though there are some striking innovations in the former. The most dramatic being the so-called 'school without walls'. Community High School in Ann Arbor, Michigan, began in 1972, Metro in Chicago in 1970. The most prominent school of this type is the Parkway school in Philadelphia which began in 1969 with 140 students and quickly grew to over 500 students. Besides the more conventional humanistic aims of self-responsibility and self-directedness, as well as humanization toward tolerance, friendliness, and respect for each other, Parkway's unique function is to bridge the gap between the world of work and culture and the monolithic school. The school is structured around 'tutorial groups' which have one faculty member, at least one college intern, and fifteen students which function as a unit in providing traditional courses of study as well as relationships with over 200 institutions on the Benjamin Franklin Parkway in downtown Philadelphia. Art is studied in the museum, economics and maths at the bank, mechanics at local garages, child development at child care centres, and bacteriology at the hospital (Bremer, 1970). There are other versions of public alternative schools. The 'school in a school', such as at Innovative Program School at University High School in Los Angeles, does have its own facilities and programmes on the main campus but students are also able to participate in the main school activities.,

Even though the free school movement is largely an American phenomenon, other mature modern countries have experienced their own version of alternative humanistic education. Yet, there are difficulties in these lands not encountered by the people in the United States; education ministries are usually so dominant that the protest is unable to find outlet in the form of real physical alternatives. Still, we find actual institutions having taken form, usually with public funds and within the framework of public sponsorship.

Denmark is the one European country which has become broadly engaged in alternative schools. In 1970 approximately 5 percent of all pupils were attending some 162 free schools that had been identified by the ministry of education (Richmond, 1973: 163). The Experimental Gymnasium in Oslo, Norway has functioned for almost a decade having been initially inspired by young people who wished to learn in an environment which encouraged personal initiative and mutual trust. This school has since become a model for other alternative schools in Denmark and Sweden (Hague, 1973). In Germany, a group of parents, some willing teachers, and a progressive school council in Hannover were able to establish a primary alternative school called Glocksee School in which teachers are addressed informally; no grades, examinations, or retentions are given; basic skill activities are complemented by emotional and aesthetic expression; children are allowed to act as facilitators in learning alongside professional teachers; children of all social classes are encouraged to work together in an attempt to reduce social tensions; and parents are drawn into the entire learning process (Ramseger, 1975: 158-59). England, which has a tradition of public support for private schooling, has also experienced a limited number of alternative schools, the most prominent being the White Lion Street School in London (Moorsom, 1973).

Since almost all of its support has come from within the ranks of the educated and fairly well off, one of the major problems of the humanistic education movement has been its social class bias. Some exceptions are to be found, but even if schools are located in or cater for working class areas, they are initiated by educated people who wish to help the lower classes. Schooling is still, for many, their major hope of upward mobility. However, this element of modern support for schooling is also rapidly coming to an end as the general public becomes aware that schools have failed in this task.

There is growing empirical evidence that schools have done little to ameliorate the socio-economic inequities in many societies. In England the Plowden Report was conclusive in pointing out that schools reflect the socio-economic background of parents (Central Advisory Council on Education, 1966). In the United States, the Coleman Report of 1966 also provided conclusive evidence that public schools have not overcome the social and racial inequities which exist in the country (Coleman, 1966). A recent review of research on the determinants of schooling effectiveness by Rand Corporation shows that 'socio-economic status of a student's family – his parents' income, education, and occupation – invariably prove to be significant predictors of his educational outcome' (Averch, 1972: 148). The recent studies on educational achievement in mathematics, reading comprehension, literature education, etc. in a dozen or more countries show that the majority of the variance in school achievement is explained by family background factors, while school factors often play a minor role in predicting achievement level (Thorndike, 1973).

These studies simply confirm what is obvious to most scholars, but recent interpretations go even further than simple confirmation in that the school has been found to not only fail to break down social class barriers, but to actually reinforce the social class structure which exists (Hollingshead, 1947). In the United States one might argue that such a condition is not serious enough to warrant alarm, simply because the standard of living of most people is higher than anywhere else in the world, the school system is open enough to allow most young people to finish high school; and almost half the young people attend some form of higher education. In other words, the odds are about fifty-fifty that a person will begin some form of higher education. These are high enough to give serious consideration to defence of the system. However, the situation changes radically in the less developed areas of the world which are attempting to emulate such models.

Even with the best of intentions, schools are unable to play an equalizing role, because less wealthy countries do not have the resources to keep the majority of children in formal schools for any reasonable length of time; therefore, their resources pay for the education of the elite. According to Reimer, in Bolivia 'half of all public allocations for schools are spent for one percent of the population. The ratio of educational expenditures on the upper and lower tenths of the population, respectively, are about three hundred to one' (Reimer, 1971: 6).

While the ratio of higher education students to population in the United States is about 40 to 1 (in California it is almost 20 to 1) that ratio is 5,000 to 1 in Argentina. Under these conditions schools provide no statistical chance of equalizing access to societal rewards. The more probable situation is that schools are intended to act as reinforcers of the status quo, which is not at all egalitarian. Two scholars working in Latin America, Everett Reimer and Ivan Illich, have become the dominant critics of schools maintaining, as did Hollingshead in the late 1940s, that schools are instruments of oppression, that they are maintained by the ruling class to protect their status and power. Thus, they see schools in Latin America as instruments which perpetuate a class society and prevent social integration (Reimer, 1971; Illich, 1970).

The Schooling Crisis in the Developing World. During the past two decades much literature has emerged, mainly by educational planners and change agents, who were concerned that a more rapid modernization process take place in the developing nations. As a consequence of several studies such as those cited in the first chapter of this book showing relationships between education and economic development, an assumption was usually made that education could be used as an intervening variable; that is, it was believed that greater investment in schooling would result in more rapid economic and social growth. We notice that education in the equation just cited was translated as schooling. The faith expressed was that a larger system of formal schooling would increase skills and the standard of living, both individually and nationally. Following a period of unparalleled investment in schooling, a new framework began to take shape. Ironically, it came into the public eye in 1967 through the initiative of a former grade school teacher, Lyndon B. Johnson, who dramatized education world-wide by calling together approximately 150 ministers of education, university presidents, and scholars for an International Conference on the World Crisis in Education. The International Institute for Education Planning (IIEP), a UNESCO organization headquartered in Paris, was called on to provide a working paper for the conference. At the time Phillip H. Coombs, an economist, was the director of IIEP and he undertook with his colleagues to present an economist's view of the world situation in education. The picture they presented was of a world which had engaged in a 'sharp increase in popular aspirations in education', accompanied by a rapid expansion of schooling which resulted in an 'acute scarcity of resources'. They also suggested that an inherent inertia of educational systems and society continued to perpetuate 'traditional attitudes, religious customs, prestige and incentive patterns, and institutional structures', which have acted as a block in 'making the optimum use of education and of educated manpower to foster national development' (Coombs, 1968: 4).

The vision of Coombs was that modernity would not be fully realized by the underdeveloped world unless radical measures were taken. A strictly economic assessment of formal schooling forces one to conclude that it is one of the most expensive educational processes possible. The return in investment is also so intangible as to defy input-output measures that might hint at optimum investment options. It is therefore almost impossible to determine how better to allocate limited resources.

Coombs himself proposed a possible solution, which he defined as non-formal education. He built his case for non-formal education on observations which he had made of out-of-school programmes in industrial countries. Harold Clark, for example, had initiated studies in the United States in which he identified educational programmes in the 200 largest industries which were as large as all of higher education in the United States put together (Clark and Sloan, 1958). The military was also found to engage in an enormous educational enterprise. Approximately seventy-five percent of an American soldier's time was found to be in an instructional-learning capacity (Clark and Sloan, 1964). Although commercial businesses were not yet engaged in research to any degree, their educational programmes were also found to be impressive (Clark et al., 1962). The enterprises just mentioned engage in such enormous educational activities because it is the only way to survive in the competitive climate of modernity.

Coombs described similar activities in Europe and Russia pointing out that formal schooling is but a part of the educational process in industrial areas. He suggests that the developing countries have little option except to turn to these new forms if they expect to 'catch up, keep up, and get ahead' (Coombs 1968: 138).

Efforts have since been made to illuminate the advantages for national development of non-formal education. Descriptions of unusual non-schooling educational programmes in dispersed places such as mainland China, Tanzania, Cuba, and Peru have begun to flood the scholarly world. Cuba has become a prominent example of what can be done. In 1961 there was an all-out campaign against illiteracy in that country. Within one year the percent of the adult population which could not read was reduced from 25 to 3.9 percent according to state statistics. Cuba accomplished the task by closing the schools and sending all teachers and over 100,000 students into rural areas where they lived with and taught the people to read (Bowles, 1971). Formal schooling was actually viewed as a hindrance to full literacy and it was necessary to cease schooling operations to accomplish this priority goal.

Tanzania has become another focal point since Julius Nyerere rejected the elitist school model his country had inherited from the English and turned instead to a new conception of education which attempted to provide 'knowledge, skills, and attitudes which will serve the student where he or she lives'. Education for self-reliance resolved to break down the barriers between school and community and turn everyone who knew something into teachers and everyone who wanted to learn something into students (Nyerere, 1969).

The major push for alternatives came from funds out of the United States, especially from the Agency for International Development (AID), which became heavily committed to exploring alternative ways to invest the Federal government's foreign aid funds. Michigan State University, the University of California, and the University of Massachusetts alone received millions of dollars to search for and provide information about non-formal activities.

Three major types of efforts have recently been sponsored by AID and other agencies. The first type is the more extensive since it deals with the inventories of what actually exists in specific countries or world regions in terms of non-formal educational programmes. IIEP had already initiated such activity by the time Coombs had delivered his report to the conference called by President Johnson. In 1967 Janet King (1967) published a brief survey of non-formal programmes in Tanzania. Fougeyrollas et al. (1967) did a similar inventory of Senegal. These were fairly superficial studies and considered only the more obvious programmes sponsored by the government and international agencies, but they did demonstrate that inventories could be taken. In 1971 James R. Sheffield and Victor P. Diejomaoh published an extensive survey of African areas including 37 case studies of specific training programmes. Cole S. Brembeck and his staff at the Institute for International Studies, Michigan State University, have established the most active centre for mapping school education in many areas of the world.

The second type of activity has been to actually develop non-formal education schemes. This effort has received minimal attention, mainly because of the sound assumption that we ought to find out what exists before we try to develop something new. There are some noteworthy exceptions. Paulo Freire (1971) has gained world-wide attention for his radical literacy programmes in Brazil and Chile. Freire is an articulate, abstract thinker who has been able to inspire the peasants to move from what he calls the 'culture of silence', which is imposed by the Third World elites and the metropolis dominators, to a state of consciousness of their 'dehumanizing reality'. Literacy is much more than learning certain written symbols; for Freire it is an act of knowing. 'The literacy process', he argues, 'must relate *speaking the word to transform reality*, and to man's role in this transformation' (Freire, 1970: 213). The learner is helped to understand the world around him and to become capable of changing it. This process represents nothing less than engaging in an act of liberation.

One of the best known university based community development endeavours is an attempt by David Evans and other staff members at the University of Massachusetts to engage the peasants through fluency games, simulation games, media based exercises, and expressive activities (D. Evans, 1975: 169-84).

The third type of activity has been to engage in evaluation efforts of non-formal programmes. Rolland Paulston (1972), for example, looked at four such programmes in Peru; using eight key variables as a basis he ranked their successfulness. The more typical study, however, is to compare formal and non-formal educational outcomes. These have some history in the industrial areas of the world, mainly in terms of economic gain due to schooling; the developing areas have only recently become subjects of such study.

The Latin American Centre at the University of California, Los Angeles, has engaged in some assessment of the work world and education in Latin America and was forced to conclude that even though there may be a greater pay-off for some out-of-school activities, they are not viewed by young people and employers as viable alternatives to formal schooling (LaBelle, 1975a: 51). The evidence as to the potential of non-formal education in national development is as yet almost non-existent. There are, however, strong indications that it may end in disillusionment as great as that now shown toward formal schooling. For example, UNESCO's literacy programme, which has relied heavily on non-formal adult education activities, had ended in failure. In 1965 there were 735 million illiterates in the world and UNESCO's efforts were able to reach at best one million people. By

1975 this figure had risen to 800 million (*Herald Tribune*, 1976).

Non-formal education will probably not provide the salvation promised by so many planners, but the impact of the issue being raised appears to have a more important potential. The major mistake modern developers make is that they disregard the evidence that schooling is a pervasive and vital element in the network of modernity. The school cannot be eliminated from the equation of modernity any easier than other vital political, economic, and social aspects. If the web of modernity is as tightly interwoven as we have been forced to conclude, the breakdown of the school might signify that the fabric of modernity itself is coming unravelled. It would appear that development experts find themselves unwittingly contributing to the crisis of modernity.

6

TRANSITION TO POST-MODERNITY

The major obejctive of this book has been to outline, within the context of school and society, the emergence and evolution of certain critical economic, intellectual, political, and social dimensions of modernity and to demonstrate that in mature modernity each of these has reached a point of crisis.

In describing the emergence of modernity, we traced the transformation of the Feudal, traditional world to the modern world. We observed that a social and cultural revolution occurred which was so fundamental that it eventuated in a transformation of an interconnected network of institutions, values, and thought structures. In Western Europe and the United States this process was slow enough to mask its revolutionary consequences. More recent modernizing revolutions have often been brought about through violence and force. Marxism, for example, is distinguished mainly in its radical modernizing ideology in that it has attempted to shatter traditional institutions and life-styles.

In tracing the evolution of modernity, we find that it did not emerge in a piece but that it originated as a fragmented blueprint, a skeletal concept, or set of ideals toward which the world worked. Modernization could be described as a process of giving flesh to an outline or bringing into reality ideals either vaguely or clearly held in the minds of the people. We are, therefore, able to observe that modernity itself progressed through a number of stages during which cumulative change occurred.

In the present period we find that even while the Third, Fourth, and Fifth World areas are striving to attain modernity, the mature modern nations have reached a juncture in their own history during which they are passing through a new social and cultural revolution. Perhaps the claim that they are on the brink of a new age is premature, because there have been abortive revolutions in the past; still, the seriousness of the crisis cannot be discounted. Ever greater numbers of people no longer accept modern age assumptions. The past modes of interpreting and explaining the world are no longer held as valid.

The present day not only involves conflict of thought and values but institutional malfunction. The human tendency is to rely on the existing institutions as long as they provide solutions to problems and satisfy needs, but when these fail to function adequately they eventually give way to new political, social, and economic institutions. Thomas Kuhn, in describing political revolutions as a metaphor of scientific revolutions, says their success 'necessitates the partial relinquishment of one set of institutions in favor of another, and in the interim, society is not fully governed by institutions at all' (Kuhn, 1962: 97).

This is what we find today in the mature modern world. From Berlin to New York to Tokyo we find dysfunction, disruption, and fear. A garbage collectors' strike can throw the largest cities of the world into disarray; a handful of people, either because of ideology or hatred, can terrorize nations; a protest movement against food prices can run entire industries into bankruptcy. Social disturbance is also common in our schools. The university student disruptions are such common knowledge they need not be elaborated. More surprising is the level of anger and defiance vented in so many primary and secondary schools. Some of America's high schools have reached such a point of anarchy that armed guards patrol the hallways and doors are locked between class periods. Professional journals no longer just highlight teaching methods and educational theory, but they struggle with issues such as 'civil war in the high schools' (Dececco and Richards, 1975).

These are indisputable signs of social disintegration and evidence that social institutions are no longer as capable of performing their basic functions. We have reached a stage in which institutions struggle for survival as much as they struggle to govern.

TOWARD SYNTHESIS

Some critics tend to emphasize the dysfunctionality of modern institutions while others seek to defend and shore up the old. In the political realm, scholars such as Robert Heilbroner (1974) contend that stronger national governments are our major hope to resolve the world crisis. In contrast, men such as Frederick C. Thayer, suggest that any variation of the old system is nothing more than a replay of hierarchy and competition which he sees as the heart of our crisis. Since the nation state justifies itself on the basis of its ability to compete with other nation states for territory, markets, power, and influence, we must bid farewell to the nation state.

> We will find that the only overall system which must survive is the planet itself, and that the significant sub-systems are small face to face groups bringing *selves* together. Intermediate groupings may persist (cities, nation-states, regional groupings), but their linking responsibilities will be designed only to endure the viability of important systems – small groups and Earth. The important conceptual shift will remove the nation-state from the status as an organization 'above' other organizations (Thayer, 1973: 179).

We could explore the same polarization in the other spheres of modernity. Technologists claim the solution to the ills of our age is more technology; those at the other extreme demand that we must abolish the entire technostructure. There are claims that we could solve the ills of our present educational crisis by resorting to more excessive schooling structures; an opposing ideology desires to destroy the schools altogether.

These extreme positions are not the only alternatives being proposed. In fact, one of the dimensions of our current crisis is the existence of too many alternatives and the sense that they are increasing in numbers. In stable societies it might be possible to agree with Einstein that 'at any given moment out of all conceivable constructions a single one has always proved itself absolutely superior to the rest' (in Pirsig, 1974: 108). But in time of crisis and transition alternatives have a tendency to multiply until we reach a stage of indeterminacy and relativity. We reach a point which Alvin Toffler describes as 'information over-load' or 'tyranny of over-choice' which only adds further fuel to the crisis since it psychologically dulls our capacity for adaptability (Toffler, 1970: 325-42). Joseph Pearce (1973: 13) suggests that 'a mind divided by choices, confused by alternatives, is a mind robbed of power'. The social forces become as an engine out of phase, working against itself, using up enormous energy, accomplishing little, and destroying itself.

We have yet to transcend the period of crisis but we can predict that as a new age emerges, we shall again find stability. George B. Leonard reminds us that productive human action is always guided by a positive vision which takes shape in the form of a myth or 'story'. The myths of the modern age are dying and have not yet been replaced by another 'bold positive vision sense of density appropriate to the times' (Leonard, 1974: 15). Following the period of transition, we predict that a new story line will emerge having its own cultural values, in-tellectual assumptions, and organizational structures; it will once again guide mankind positively and productively.

The final outcome of the process of transition will not be a simple extension of the old but a reconstruction of the world. Data, vocabu-lary, and even institutions may be much the same as in modernity but they will be reorganized into new relations and place in such a frame-work that the post-modern world will assume a new gestalt. A new consciousness will emerge, not in the mystical, but in a perceptual, experimental sense. It may be that the framework of the new age is already available, but if this is the case, the crisis of transition only manifests it as one more alternative among the many. It may also be that considerable time will be required before the form of the new age takes shape. If this is the case, we might at least take comfort, with Karl Mannheim, that such a 'socially disorganized intellectual situation' allows us to see our own world from perspectives that were not tolerable before (Mannheim, 1936: 85). Whatever the new vision becomes we can assume, if the history of modernity has a lesson to teach, that it will take the form of a concept or ideal toward which to strive rather than the form of immediate substance, with institutions and actual living conditions. In other words, once the conceptual skeletal structure emerges, cumulative change will proceed throughout the new age giving it flesh and substance.

Given countless alternatives, we might well inquire if there is some process by which a new design or gestalt can find footing. Historians of modernity have indicated that, at least in the early modern countries, political modernity was initiated by a central elite. It was then extended gradually to greater spheres of people (Eisenstadt, 1966: 55-58). There is also a generational factor in that at least scientific revolutions are usually brought about by 'men so young or so new to the crisis-ridden field that practice has committed them less deeply than most of their contemporaries to the world view and rules of the old system of thought' (Kuhn, 1962: 143). The new vision is rarely accepted by those having conflicting positions; Max Planck explains that 'a new scientific truth does not triumph by convicing its opponents and making them see the light, but rather because its opponents eventually die, and a new generation grows up that is familiar with it' (Planck, 1949: 33-34). This is even more the case in terms of political and social mind sets.

The structure of post-modernity is primarily a question of value priorities; however, we can postulate definite criteria by which it will emerge. Most of the perceived advantages of the modern world will be accommodated within the new framework, and it must provide satisfaction of needs not met by modernity. It is for this reason that it appears possible to subscribe to a dialectical process. It is not the intention of this book to focus on the manner of social change, but we admit to an underlying social historical theory of social change which maintains that the forces which bring about evolutionary as well as revolutionary social processes are dialectical in nature. We claim to recognize in all phenomena the existence of contradictory, mutually exclusive, opposite tendencies. The tension between these tendencies, the struggle of the old and new, the positive and negative, the past and future, constitute the process of development. Synthesis is analogous, for instance, to the phenomenon of biological mutation since evolution is not altogether continuous but is characterized by intermittent qualitative changes.

In a dialectical sense, we are now facing the extremes of modernity and their inherent contradictions. These should lead to a new synthesis, retaining much of modernity and restoring much of the traditional world. Once again, this new context will not be a patchwork of the modern and the traditional worlds but will have a unique gestalt. At the present time we are faced with a multitude of alternatives, but the essential tension between their polarized extremes is the substance of evolution and should eventuate in a productive synthesis of all social and educational spheres, providing for viable future alternatives.

ALTERNATIVES IN EDUCATION

During the present transition period, the term 'alternatives in education' denotes criticism of the prevailing order of things educational and the need for a look into the future to suggest new paths, new structures, new patterns. In the recent past two extreme educational tendencies have emerged. On one hand we find people predicting a 'schooled society', while on the other we encounter proposals for a 'deschooled society'. The tension between these extremes provides the main dialectic framework for the emergence of edcuation in post-modernity. We shall attempt to portray in skeletal form what advocates of the two positions are saying about the future.

The Schooled Society

A schooled society is one which depends on schooling to satisfy a large share of its educational requirements; that is, intentional, systematic teaching and learning tends to become an integral part of the schooling enterprise. If a schooled society were to evolve, our concept of school would change somewhat. The distinction between non-formal and formal schooling would disappear since out-of-school activities would become a part of schooling, either through administrative arrangements or some central accounting or transcript agency which would be responsible for credentials and certificates.

We would like to elaborate on a proposed description of a schooled society. The European Cultural Foundation has adopted an ongoing project entitled, Education for the 21st Century (Schwartz, 1974); it anticipates that by the year 2000 schooling of one kind or another will continually service Europeans almost from the time of birth until the end of life. Their proposal breaks down schooling into four major periods: preschool education, basic school, compulsory tertiary education, and adult education.

Pre-school education will occupy the lives of the children until they are approximately five years old. Pre-schools are not intended to replace family education, but to serve as a strong schooling complement to parents by educating the young and by preparing the adults to assume their roles as fathers and mothers. The European Cultural Foundation believes the better nursery schools of today are already capable of accomplishing these goals. The major change necessary will be a positive societal attitude toward universal, systematic, and extended nursery schooling.

The second phase of education will take place in the 'basic school', which children will attend until they are at least sixteen years of age. It will consist of two cycles, the first six and the second five years in duration. The first cycle has three objectives: (1) to stimulate pupil awareness of the technical and social environment; (2) to give pupils competence in mathematics, in oral expression in foreign languages, in the mother tongue, and in graphic expression having to do with artistic and physical activities; and (3) to provide cultural and sporting activities. Structurally, age-grading will give way to family grouping as is now found in the British infant school. Learning will take place mainly through a process of discovery and personal inquiry.

In the second cycle the concentration is on intellectual training. The children will explore the key concepts of the major fields of endeavour, and will be expected to integrate and interrelate knowledge through multi-disciplinary studies. Education will be individualized, taking into account the personality of each child. Independent attitudes and potential abilities will be developed through a wide range of personal choice and study contracts. One of the unique innovations anticipated by the European Cultural Foundation is the awarding of a common secondary schooling certificate which will be recognized throughout Europe.

The compulsory tertiary cycle consists of either a college or a vocational stream. The European Cultural Foundation does not draw a sharp distinction between these streams but suggests that a separation be made. Consistent with its desire to move toward a schooling society, it maintains that if students do not attend college, they are 'obliged before leaving school to follow a vocational course lasting two years'. In fact, *no one shall leave the school system without receiving vocational education'*. This principle has caused the Foundation to recommend compulsory schooling until the age of 18 (Schwartz, 1974: 71).

Following the period of compulsory education, some students will enter the university and others will engage in general adult education. It is at this point that the European Cultural Foundation talks in terms of rights to schooling rather than duty to schooling. Because of their commitment to lifelong education, they recommend that some type of 'improvement contract' be established whereby certain advantages accrue to those who, either on a part-time or a full-time basis, avail themselves of further schooling at regular intervals. The European Cultural Foundation is so committed to the concept of parallel alternating work and study programmes for adults that it would require lifelong schooling in professions such as teaching and medicine.

In order to realize a schooled society, the European Cultural Foundation anticipates that 'school buildings' must play a dominant role in the process, but that schooling will also extend to 'non-school' public and private sectors. Libraries, museums, cinemas, laboratories, auditoriums, office building space and other kinds of facilities readily available in every community will become active educational centres. It also anticipates that television equipment and computer terminals will provide administrative and instructional assistance.

The Deschooled Society

The concept of a deschooled society differs radically from any modern conception of formal education. Ivan Illich and Everett Reimer are the most popular advocates of deschooling and their proposal departs from progressive liberalism of modern Western societies and revolutionary Marxism found in so many newer modern lands.

These men are most eloquent when criticizing the ideology of schooling, but they encounter difficulty when attempting to clarify what a deschooled society would look like. Since they do not distinguish between the types of learning environments which would correspond to various schooling levels, and since most of their examples refer to mature adult situations, it is difficult to imagine how their deschooled society would adjust itself to the education of six-, eleven-, or fifteen-year-olds. We speculate that the lack of detail is not a matter of over-sight, but that vagueness is inherent in their orientation, which shifts the emphasis from schools and programmes toward educational resources. Such a reorientation necessitates that institutional design and programme structure remain essentially undefined. The reason for this becomes clear when we look at two deschooling concepts.

The first of these concepts has to do with institutions. Illich maintains that there are two major opposing types of institutions. 'Manipulative insitutions', can be described in positive form because they set up strict definition as to who enters, what happens, and under what conditions people may leave (1970: 78). These include the military, the jail, and the modern school. These are considered manipulative because institutional ends are paramount and people in them are treated as objects and coerced to behave according to the institutional requirements.

Since so many modern structures are manipulative, Illich has mistakenly been condemned for wanting 'deinstitutionalized schools in a deinstitutionalized society' (Pearl, 1973: 113). On the contrary, he simply wants to deinstitutionalize environments that are manipulative and rely more heavily on what he calls 'convivial-institutions', which are 'distinguished by spontaneous use' (Illich, 1970: 79). These do not impose themselves on their users but are available to be used or not according to the needs and interests of the users. For example, people do not have to be coerced to take advantage of institutions such as parks, water and sewage systems, and sidewalks. They also are not required to use libraries, museums, or other educational facilities. The process of liberation away from manipulation must come by replacing modern schools with 'new formal educational institutions' which are convivial in nature (Illich, 1970: 108).

The concept of appropriate educational institutions is paralleled by the nature of state involvement in the learning process. The major distinction which Illich draws in his conception of learning processes themselves might be characterized as 'prescriptive' in contrast to 'proscriptive' learning (discussed at length by Holt, 1972). Prescriptive learning is that which exists in contemporary modern societies since teachers and administrators tend to define how learners should behave.

Illich envisages proscriptive learning processes which depend on authorities to set definite boundaries but which allow learners the greatest possible freedom within these boundaries. The parent, for example, relies mainly on proscription when telling a child it is not allowed to do something, go somewhere, or play with certain other children; however, the child does have unlimited personal choice within these boundaries.

A society in which convivial institutions and proscriptive learning processes predominate would require a shift of obligations. In modernity the individual is forced to attend manipulative institutions and follow prescribed routes leading to 'job' certificates. In post-modernity the obligations would shift to authorities who would

> provide all who want to learn with access to available resources at any time in their lives; empower all who want to share what they know to find those who want to learn it from them; and, finally, furnish all who want to present an issue to the public with the opportunity to make their challenge known (Illich, 1970: 108).

Illich sees these formal obligations being accomplished by the establishment of four 'opportunity networks', which provide a countless array of services in terms of things and people (1970: 112-13). Everett Reimer is more explicit than Illich about what learning environments would look like, but his description comes very close to that of a school. In fact, he admits that a school 'provides an excellent model for the organization of educational resources'. The important difference between his proposed structure and a school is that it must 'be used in reverse' (Reimer, 1971: 94). These men give highest priority to information reference services which facilitate access to processes for formal learning. The focus here is on 'things' or objects which in the past have been the monopoly of the school. These resources would remain in schools, but their intention is to make them also available in such institutions as toolshops, libraries, laboratories, and gaming rooms, especially for self-directed learning. The following account by Illich (1970: 121) gives a hint of their vision:

Some storefront learning centres could contain viewing booths, for closed-circuit television, others could feature office equipment for use and for repair. The jukebox or the record player would be commonplace, with some specializing in classical music, others in international folk tunes, others in jazz. Film clubs would compete with each other and with commercial television. Museum outlets could be networks for circulating exhibits of works of art, both old and new, originals and reproductions, perhaps administered by the various metropolitan museums.

The second priority would go toward identifying those people who possess a special skill and are willing to demonstrate its practice. The third priority would go toward peer matching services which would help fellow learners share their own past experiences or present problems with each other. The final priority would make provision for 'educators, who, by virtue of experience, can facilitate the use of the more essential learning resources' (Reimer, 1971: 94-95).

This description, in the abstract, reverses the priorities we usually attach to schooling in that material resources and non-teachers take on a much greater educational role than do peer groups and teachers. It is crucial, however, to note that the 'essential learning resources' spoken of by Reimer are those learnings which are universally valued. This suggests that some arrangement similar to schooling would probably play a large role in the beginning stages of life. As the learners matured, the priorities would shift more and more toward self-educational resources and skills models.

This being the case, we are able to come to an opportune conclusion. If we consider the actual workings of the envisaged educational enterprises in both the schooled and deschooled societies, we find that the distinctions between them tend to blur and in many respects fade away. The extreme tendencies do not represent linear movement away from each other but a convergence in terms of structure and function. Granted, a fundamental philosophical difference does persist which hinges on a commitment to prescribed as opposed to free learning. In the schooled society a good deal of the learning is compulsory, which reflects an attitude that man is not inclined to voluntarily learn certain critical things. In the deschooled society man is seen as being willing and inclined to engage freely in learning if given the opportunity. It is, of course, futile to expect a reconciliation between philosophical points of view. If we turn to actual practice in post-modern education, especially with regard to some of the crucial issues discussed in this book, the distinctions are not so apparent. We do not intend to provide a blueprint of the future, but it might be of value to suggest certain practical educational tendencies.

Lifelong Education

Implicit in both schooling and deschooling concepts is the assumption that lifelong learning will become a reality. Paul Lengrand (1970) has declared that lifelong learning not only encompasses formal education from birth until the end of life, but it includes the totality of human activities. That is, permanent education is related not only to work but leisure, not only to cognitive development but to effective learning. It is involved with physical activity, consumption, and politics. Henri Hartung (1966) agrees with Lengrand that lifelong education encompasses human development in its totality, including the interactive processes between the individual and his material and social environments; he also indicates that if lifelong education is to achieve its fullest meaning, it must contribute to the inner, spiritual, humanistic development of the personality.

The above description of lifelong learning is in full accord with schooling and deschooling projections. Its present popularity not only emanates from post-modern conceptions but is a consequence of disparate and diverse points of view throughout the world. Great thrust in this direction comes from the developing world. We tend to attribute this to the developing world's interest in achieving the status of modernity. To a significant degree this is indeed the case; however, lifelong education is actually more compatible with traditional than modern educational practices.

Interest in lifelong education has been shown by people who have been affected by the growing crisis of modernity. Modern adults, shaken in their ability to maintain stability and cope with the period of transition, are demanding some type of systematic process through which their capacities and talents can be extended.

Lifelong education has also been fostered by a number of formal agencies. The Council of Europe has declared that permanent education is fundamental to an integrated educational policy in Europe (Council of Europe 1971). On the world-wide scale UNESCO has actively engaged in encouraging lifelong education. The fundamental recommendation of the Faure Report on 'The World of Education Today and Tomorrow' is that lifelong learning is a 'master concept for educational policies in the years to come in developed and developing countries' (UNESCO, 1972a: 182). The Unesco Institute for Education in Hamburg has recently devoted a major share of its resources to inquiries into lifelong education. Important monographs have appeared under the editorship of R.H. Dave which outline its full possibilities in schools and curriculum (Dave, 1973; 1975).

Scores of individual countries have accepted lifelong education as a foundation principle. Permanent education is central to the present reform in Yugoslavia (Dragomiv, 1968). In Japan, the limits of school education and the necessity of establishing a policy of permanent education has also become apparent (Dave and Stiemerling, 1973: 122). In Peru the educational reforms of the last decade have also been based on the principle of lifelong education (Bizot, 1975).

Since lifelong education is a principle having both vertical and horizontal dimensions, it is impossible to outline programme specifics. We must assume, however, that as attitudes change, the necessary programmes and organizational structures will evolve to satisfy them.

Administrative Diffusion

We cannot disagree with Karl Deutsch (1969: 125) that the 'nation state is still the most powerful instrument for getting things done'. The problem, of course, is that much of the getting-done has been of a unitary nature which forces all processes into some ideological mould. Furthermore, we can anticipate that the state will remain the most powerful entity in terms of functions performed, including schooling. The most likely major shift has to do with values and quality factors. Even though administrative functions will be performed by national bureaucracies, we will no longer be inclined to give the nation state our soul. The state will no longer be able to dictate how to handle individual learning styles, cultural variation, or matters of personal taste. It will also no longer define basic values of high culture or civilization having to do with language, world view, or spiritual commitments, since they will transcend national boundaries. Post-modern nations will continue to administer funds, facilities, and time blocks, but the decisions as to what to do with these resources and the determination of their quality will be, in part, coopted by bodies outside formal state administrations. It is not Utopian to suggest that diffused authority can function. In fact, we have a number of examples of such administrative arrangements in the modern world, albeit found in the national context, which have fostered diversity within a unitary system.

Holland, for example, in spite of being one of the smallest countries in Europe, must accommodate itself to important differences in the population. Geographically, there are jealously guarded regional differences, but the most important division is religion. The country is almost equally divided between Catholics (41.2 percent) and Calvinist Protestants (40.4 percent) with an important minority declaring no religion (18.4 percent). The government constitutionally declares itself responsible for establishing and maintaining schools for those who wish to take advantage of them. It also makes constitutional provision for private groups to establish and maintain their own schools at public expense under minimal conditions. If a group of people, usually having some common interest or value system, such as political ideology or religion, can raise but 15 percent of the estimated building costs of a proposed school and can convince authorities that a minimum required number of children are prepared to attend (for example, fifty children per primary school), then the government and municipality are compelled to provide the remainder of the building costs and all other costs including salaries. As a consequence of this provision, 80 percent of all pre-schools, 70 percent of all primary schools, and 60 percent of all secondary schools are private. The remarkable outcome of this provision for diversity is that a common trust and national cohesion rather than fragmentation appears to be fostered. Unusual alignments often emerge as religion and ideology are submerged in favour of pragmatic considerations having to do with life-style, curricular focus, or geographical convenience.

A much different arrangement exists in Yugoslavia which is valuable to observe since it is a federal republic consisting of six major nationalities (42 percent Serbs, 22 percent Croatians, 9 percent Slovenes, 5 percent Macedonians, 3 percent Montenegrins, and 7 percent Bosnians). Five major languages are spoken which are confounded by the existence of Latin written forms in some languages and Cyrillic forms in others. Besides these major groups, 12 percent of the population identify themselves as Albanians, Turks, Bulgarians, and Rumanians. The country provides a prototype of federation possibilities that might exist on a larger regional level. It is dominated by a pervasive political ideology but the differences between groups necessitate shared responsibility and radical decentralization of some decision-making elements.

Since 1971, the republics have obtained rather strong independence, mainly because the dominant Slovenes and Croatians wish to avoid sharing their wealth. Yet the centralized administration redistributes a good share of the income throughout the country.

Education in the republics has also undergone a radical decentraliz-ation process in that school-to-school differences are fostered through self-governance bodies in each school. The school self-governance programme, which is replicated in commercial and industrial firms, has been practised for many years. The more typical model for the governing school council is a tripartite arrangement: one-third of the membership representing teachers and other school personnel; one-third representing the public, including parents, businesses and industry, political parties, and social organizations; and one-third representing the pupils, at least at the secondary level.

Public representation to the council is especially critical because each school has the possibility to draw financial and industrial groups into the governance structure. This arrangement encourages access to funds beyond the minimum money allocation awarded by the state and inspires local, practical, self-interest programmes.

The school council usually divides itself into a 'restricted council' consisting of school personnel, and a 'council of the whole'. Each school receives special funds from the republic based on the number of teachers in the school; the 'restricted council' determines what portion of these funds each teacher shall receive as salary. The 'council of the whole' selects the school leader from among the school statutes.

In Yugoslavia, self-governance usually does not lead to a radical breakdown of the schooling tradition but to a greater sense of community and pupil commitment to school even though schooling is conducted in a rather conventional manner.

We find yet another type of structure in the military regime which has ruled Peru since 1968. The unique innovation in that country is the introduction of 'nuclearization'. The ultimate aim of the government is to establish approximately 1,000 small social units of from two to four thousand inhabitants called 'Communal Education Nuclei', within which schools, factories, parishes, clubs, associations, cooperatives, farms, medical facilities, and other more specialized or local units function. These units are integrated at the local level in such a way that they all become a part of the educational process: 'Priests . . . transforming their pulpits into dicussion stands; police commissioners undertaking literacy campaigns together with teachers; cultural clubs functioning within the agricultural cooperatives; industrialists promoting campaigns of social education, etc.' (Pacheco, 1972: 534). According to Peruvian President Velasco, this plan attempts to allow 'men, freely organized, to intervene in all spheres of decision making and exercise directly, or with a minimum of intermediaries, all forms of power in its economic, cultural, social and political dimensions' (in Pacheco, 1972: 533-34).

The United States does not possess a history of school administration which has encouraged diversity. One of the major functions of the school has been to Americanize the immigrants and to bring races and cultures together. Recently, however, creative proposals have emerged which suggest ways of administering the schools toward pluralism. The Fleischman Report on school reform in the state of New York has recommended that all state funds bypass the local school districts and be channelled directly into individual schools. Large urban school districts are also addressing direct local needs by establishing community advisory councils for each school. These are much more than the old parent-teacher associations since they have legal powers and consist of formal elected community representatives.

Voucher proposals have a long history, dating from the time of Adam Smith, who suggested that schooling be placed on the competitive market; they have experienced a rebirth in the past decade with proposals being made by conservatives such as Milton Friedman and have been joined by moderates such as James Coleman and liberals such as Christopher Jencks. Through vouchers, Catholics see a possibility of saving their parochial school; Blacks reorganize a way to establish greater Black identity; business sees a new source of business investment. The most attractive and the most feared element of vouchers is the responsibility it places on the shoulders of parents who decide if a school is providing an adequate education for the children. There are a number of voucher proposals but they all have one thing in common: each demands that governments get out of the business of dictating what goes on in schools. Rather than perpetuating their own ideologies as to what constitutes an appropriate public school programme, administrators would begin to serve as agents helping parents find and place their children in suitable educational environments.

Jencks, whose proposal has been implemented on an experimental basis, sets up Educational Voucher Agencies comparable to school district administrations which issue a voucher, or an edu-credit card to parents. The parents cash their voucher in for a certain amount of training each year at any approved school. The school in turn is reimbursed with public funds according to the number of vouchers it collects. An institution becomes an approved school by agreeing to abide by certain minimal rules established by the Educational Voucher Agency. Under the Jencks plan these include: agreement not to charge the parents additional tuition fees; acceptance of all applicants as long as places are open; agreement to make public a wide variety of specific information about facilities, faculty, programme, and student composition; maintenance of open accounts of the way money is spent in the school; and assurance against racial or religious discrimination (Areen and Jencks, 1971). Experiments using the Jencks plan have so far been public school based. We can anticipate that even more flexible arrangements will emerge allowing a child to attend more than one institution at a time or engage in legitimate non-school environments. The ultimate fate of vouchers is unknown but the idea provides but another example of diffuse authority relationships.

Helmut Becker describes the coming relationship between central and local bodies in the following manner: 'What is needed is at the same time greater rationalization at the centre and wider autonomy at the base' (in Schwartz, 1974: 174). Thus, the central body would provide programme and curricular models, information, evaluation service, and would engage in legislation which it deems is universally important. The central government cannot control interest, but it can help prevent inbreeding and parochialism and can encourage growth by facilitating the making of fully informed decisions on the part of the people and by coordinating universal interests that emerge.

Educational Integration

The third concept which we anticipate is the priority given to personal integration. By stressing personal integration we do not discount the extension of diversity and choice in structures; we merely place human considerations over specialized disciplines and organizations. Some tendencies are such a part of common discourse that they are already conceptually acceptable.

Psychological Integration. We are rapidly moving away from conventional education which has divided the individual personality into physical, intellectual, emotional, and spiritual segments. In school, physical needs have been met in health and physical education courses; intellectual needs have been met in 'solid' subjects; spiritual needs have been met by rituals at the beginning of the day. We are finally rediscovering that the whole child is simultaneously involved in all of these activities.

Psychological integration demands radical modification of modern learning environments and some inroads are being made. The British infant school has been exemplary in breaking down the fixed points of learning and bridging subject matter distinctions. The child, in all his or her complexity, can thereby incorporate direct personal needs and personality uniqueness into the learning process. In the United States, George I. Brown has approached the problem from a theoretical point of view, having established a 'confluent education' centre at the University of California, which attempts to facilitate the flowing together of effective and cognitive learning. Drawing from contemporary humanistic psychology and more especially gestalt psychology as developed by Frederick Perls, Brown has embarked on a wide range of projects. His book, *Human Teaching for Human Learning* provides a fair overview of techniques which have been developed for young children, adolescents, and adults.

Since modern education has stressed the cognitive side of the person, we find special attention presently being given to the construction of intensely interpersonal educational processes. Encounter groups among adults and Glaser circles for the young children are found, which help participants share feelings and deal with one another as emotional beings. These activities are so often initiated in reaction to the one-sidedness of conventional education that they are as one-sided as their cognitive counterparts; they are, however, helping us to come to a new awareness of ourselves in all our complexity and should help pave the way toward processes which recognize and encourage full human growth.

Role Integration. We are beginning to integrate the specialized roles human beings have been expected to play in modernity, including those associated with job, family, school, and social organizations. The current trend represents more than mere coordination of these roles; it also hints at their diffusion into various differentiated institutions. We can anticipate that institutional specialization will be radically reduced and institutions will begin to expand their spheres of responsibility so that they provide integrated environments able to satisfy human rather than role needs.

The most revolutionary aspects of schooling in this context is that it will cease to exist in an isolated, separate institution and will tend toward integration into all spheres of society. Some separate, school-like institutions will likely continue, especially those serving children in their earlier years, but these will share the educational burden with many other institutions since they will not be in a position to satisfy all intellectual, spiritual, and social learning needs. Therefore, a multiplicity of institutions and instructional forms must emerge which will allow the individual to engage, simultaneously in a variety of educational processes.

Those processes which veer most markedly away from standard modern educational conceptions include interpersonal and self-instructional opportunities. Dave has coined the term 'inter-learning' to stress that a different style of group learning is gaining prominence (Dave, 1975: 46-49). This learning is that which has no hierarchical structure or teacher-student relationships and defines every member of the group as a learner. The learning process is dependent on immediate group needs rather than some demands or requirements beyond the boundaries of the group itself and is, therefore, free flowing and spontaneous.

John I. Goodlad predicted almost a decade ago that self-instructional learning will soon occupy a large portion of education. Electronic instruments such as television and the computer have already advanced to the stage that they are able to serve as a private tutor of every modern child (Goodlad, 1968). We anticipate that technology will continue to expand in terms of its ability to contribute to education; however, it will be more judiciously applied than in some mature modern lands and will be restricted largely to instruction which can best be engaged in on an individual basis. Essentially all schooling that demands hierarchical learning will move beyond the lock-step structure of the modern era, since it will be capable of adjusting and tailoring itself to private individual needs. Technology already has the capacity to bring formal education into a multitude of physical settings, including the home, work place, recreational centres and church.

We might mention that within the context of genuine multiple learning options, compulsory education, which is one of the most difficult theoretical problems to reconcile between the schooling and deschooling advocates, is actually losing much of its modern meaning. Already in the United States, except for the extreme cases of young people on the fringe of society, to drop out of formal school is usually nothing more than to drop into another educational environment. A young man might leave school and join the military only to find the majority of his time is spent in a classroom, or he might go to work in industry only to discover that a large amount of his time is spent in systematic learning environments related and unrelated to his job. If these processes were incorporated into formal education, a young man choosing such options would actually only engage in a process of lateral educational transfer. Under these conditions compulsory education itself takes on blurred significance.

A final aspect of role integration is related to associations among people of all ages. We are already tending toward 'family grouping' in the present schooling structure; this is but a small step toward a conscious, systematic, and deliberate establishment of educational environments involving all age groups. Of course, peer grouping is included in the age spectrum, but its intent will be altered since most of the hierarchical learning, such as reading and mathematics, which required age-grading, will be absorbed into individual learning environments.

Reality Integration. Those integration elements which we have mentioned are already acceptable to much of mature modernity. There is one other integration imperative which has yet to find its way into public consciousness. We have chosen to describe this as a movement toward a multi-reality universe.

We are moving quickly to a stage in which we will be willing to accept the value of ideological truths while demanding that no ideology become exclusive. We observed that the greatest thrust of the modern age was in science, but we are beginning to recognize that no ideology, including that of science, has a monopoly on legitimate access to truth. Science is already being placed in new perspectives. Recent public opinion poles in America indicate that between one-fourth and one-half of all Americans are now exploring ways of gaining truth through non-scientific avenues. One pollster described these efforts in the following manner: 'We are seeing an expanded concept of rationality, one that does not equate reason with technocratic reason. It embraces other ways of knowing, experience and direct involvement, and the feelings. It is not antiscience, but goes beyond science' (in Harris, 1976: 68).

We would not say the new explorations will go beyond science in the sense that it will be replaced. Science promises to continue providing a legitimate but not the only avenue to reality. 'Science offers us an aspect of reality', delcares Polanyi, 'and may therefore manifest its truth inexhaustibly and often surprisingly in the future' (1968: 69). However, every system of thought has margins of error, spaces of ignorance, and accepted truths which do not fit other systems. In this study we have looked at modernity from four closely related but different discipline perspectives, and even within these conventional modern social science modes of inquiry, we find that the overlay necessary to mould modernity into a single comprehensive concept is missing. The discipline lenses through which we observe a phenomenon sets its structure and colours its truth.

Just as various scientific disciplines provide valid glimpses of realities, the truths of other human spheres such as literature, poetry, history, politics, philosophy, and law have their own validity. These are not always consistent with the truths of science; moreover, to turn every system into a science only destroys its potential unique contribution.

The fully integrated individual will learn in a variety of institutions, each fostering its own thought system and each giving its own partial contribution to lifelong learning. It would be a mistake to suggest what these major systems might look like. We prefer to mention a limited number of examples of multi-reality situations in the present world.

The introduction of acupuncture into the Western world view, with its own unique assumptions, will likely be only partially accommodated within the realm of rationalist science. The truths of acupuncture are dependent on its own historical and spiritual theory of the universe and of man. It would be a mistake to force it into Western medical theory, for both would suffer in the process. Each system is at once legitimate and limited; although they overlap each other in many respects, each is indeed unique.

A second example deals with the relationship between subjective and objective man. There are those who contend that the dominant elements of the traditional world are subjective, inner, and spiritual while rationality plays a subservient role. In contrast, the objective, material, rational elements are so dominant in the modern world that even spirituality is subject to objective scrutiny. We now find people such as Robert Ornstein who attempt to explain that these two forces are nothing other than cultural emphasis of brain hemispheres. In this theory the right hemisphere is responsible for the creative, visionary, dreaming, and subjective aspects of human thought, while the left is the source of logic and reason. Such a theory is not yet validated but it serves well by way of analogy. It would be difficult to suggest that one brain hemisphere is more important than the other. Each hemisphere in its own realm provides the individual with advantages and disadvantages. The integrated person recognizes and appreciates both.

A final example is taken from Eastern tradition known as Kundalini. The lotus ladder, consisting of seven intervals from the base of the spine to the top of the head, is central to an elaborate body of doctrine and practice of Kundalini Yoga. Through rigorous discipline a symbolic serpent, slumbering at the base of the spine is moved to raise its head and pass up through the seven centres or chakras, each representing a higher level of consciousness. The first four chakras have been described as having certain characteristics in common with elaborate Western psychological theories. The first chakra level concentrates on a materialistic, survival of the fittest orientation similar to well known authoritarian personality types. The second level concentrates on sensual gratification as well as reproduction; it is best represented by Freudian theory which forces all human motives into sexual themes. The third level is 'primarily connected with power, with mastery, with ego control' (Ram Dass, 1974: 29). This position is best represented by the Adlerian 'will to power', and probably symbolizes the best of Western industrial accomplishments. The fourth level is the beginning of what we have come to describe as 'higher consciousness' character- ized by more mystical and religious oriented psychologists such as Carl Jung. The higher chakras are continuations of psychic evolution but we will not elaborate on them, since, as Joseph Campbell has suggested, 'no formal Western systems of psychology correspond to any of the next three chakras' (1975: 78).

The major insights we might draw from the above example are two- fold. In the first place, it is possible that the psychological orientation of individuals provides the substance of the universe which they are prone to perceive. Freud was inclined to interpret the highest mani- festations of religious experience and the lowest level of consciousness in terms of a single identifiable level of consciousness in Kundalini Yoga. He was 'stuck', if you will, at one level, whereas the other giants of psychology just mentioned were stuck at other chakra levels. Their elaborate theories were valid from a certain perspective but incomplete and distorting from another. Each level is of value since everyone seeks to survive, experience eros, exercise control, and have flights of the spirit, but an integrated full life is best achieved if we see and experience the universe from various vantage points.

Secondly, the psychological orientation of the modern age appears to have set definite limits of reality perception. In the above example of the Kundalini, it is striking that the variations of orientation in modernity are concentrated on the lower continuum of Eastern psychic evolution. The modern age has tolerated and encouraged reality per- spective variations but within a narrower band than is tolerated and encouraged in certain other cultures. By moving to a multi-reality orientation it should be possible to become more inclusive in terms of legitimate explorations of the universe.

One of the thrusts of the emerging age will be to understand any system as a perceptual vantage point and to avoid a single angle of vision. Each of these visions has the potential of illuminating the others and of illuminating the whole. The mistake of modernity is that it has interpreted a single vantage point as the only source of truth. By moving into other reality spheres we will be able to gain comparative perspective and thereby realize fuller human potential.

REFERENCES

ABEL, H. and H. GROOTHOFF (1959) Die Berufsschule: Gestalt und Reform. Darmstadt: Carl Winter.

ABRAHAM, K. (1957) Der Betrieb als Erziehungsfaktor. Freiburg: Lambertus.

ADAMSON, J. (1929) The Extent of Literacy in England in the Fifteenth and Sixteenth Centuries. London: Bibliographical Society.

ALMOND, G. and J. COLEMAN (1960) The Politics of the Developing Areas. Princeton, N.J.: Princeton University Press.

ANDERSON, C.A. (1965) 'Literacy and Schooling on the Development Threshold: Some Historical Cases', p. 347 in C.A. ANDERSON and M.J. BOWMAN (eds) Education and Economic Development. Chicago: Aldine.

ANDERSON, R. (1959) Japan: Three Epochs of Modern Education. Washington, D.C.: U.S. Department of Health, Education, and Welfare.

ANTON, H. (1965) 'Modernität als Aporie und Ereignis', pp. 7-13 in H. Stephan, Aspekte der Modernität. Göttingen: Vandenhoeck und Ruprecht.

ANWEILER, O. and K. MEYER (1961) Sowjetische Bildungspolitik seit 1917: Dokumente und Texte. Heidelberg: Quelle und Meyer.

AREEN, J. and C. JENCKS (1971) 'Education Vouchers: A Proposal for Diversity and Choice, Teachers College Record (February).

ARIES, P. (1962) Centuries of Childhood (translated from the French by R. BALDICK). New York: Vintage.

ARISTOTLE (1962) The Politics of Aristotle. New York: Oxford University Press.

ARMYTAGE, W.H.G. (1970) Four Hundred Years of English Education. Cambridge: Cambridge University Press.

ASHTON, T. (1948) The Industrial Revolution: 1760-1830. London: Oxford University Press.

AVERCH, H. et al. (1972) How Effective is Schooling? A Critical Review and Synthesis of Research Findings. Santa Monica, Ca.: The Rand Corporation.

BACHE, A. (1839) Education in Europe. Philadelphia: Lydia Bailey.

BACON, F. (1876-1890) The Works of Francis Bacon. J. SPEDDING, R. ELLIS and D. HEATH (eds). London, Longmans, 7 Volumes.

BAILYN, B. (1960) Education in the Forming of American Society. Chapel Hill: University of North Carolina Press.

BARNARD, H. (1854) National Education in Europe. Hartford: Case Tiffany.

BARNARD, H.C. (1947) A History of English Education from 1760. London: University of London Press.

BARRAU, T.H. (1857) Du rôle de la famille dans l'éducation. Paris: L. Hachette.

BARRACLOUGH, G. (1964) An Introduction to Contemporary History. New York: Penguin.

BARTH, P. (1967) Die Geschichte der Erziehung. Donaustadt: Wissenschaftliche Buchgesellschaft.

BELL, D. (ed.) (1967) Toward the Year 2000: Work in Progress. Boston: Beacon Press.

BENEDICT, R. (1934) Patterns of Culture. New York: Houghton Mifflin.

BERGER, P. and T. LUCKMANN (1966) The Social Construction of Reality. Garden City, N.Y.: Doubleday.

BERSTEIN, J. (1975) 'I.I. Rabi', The New Yorker (13 October): 47-110, and (20 October): 47-101.

BIRCHENOUGH, C. (1930) History of Elementary Education in England and Wales. London: University Tutorial Press.

BIZOT, S. (1975) 'Educational Reform in Peru' in Experiments and Innovations in Education, pamphlet No. 16. Paris. UNESCO.

BLÄTTNER, F. (1960) Das Gymnasium. Heidelberg: Quelle und Meyer.

BOAS, F. (1911) The Mind of Primitive Man, New York: Macmillan.

BOBBITT, F. (1912) 'The Elimination of Waste in Education', Elementary School Journal, 12.

BOBBITT, F. (1913) 'The Supervision of the City Schools', in the Twelfth Year-book of the National Society for the Study of Education I. Bloomington, Ind,: Indiana University Press.

BOULDING, K. (1953) The Organizational Revolution. New York: Harper.

BOULDING, K. (1964) The Meaning of the 20th Century, New York: Harper and Row.

BOWEN, J. (Vol. I, 1972; Vol. II, 1975) A History of Western Education. London: Methuen, 2 Volumes.

BOWLES, S. (1971) 'Cuban Education and the Revolutionary Ideology', Harvard Educational Review, 41 (November).

BOWMAN, M. and C.A. ANDERSON (1967) 'Concerning the Role of Education in Development', pp. 113-31 in Readings in the Economics of Education. Paris: UNESCO.

BOYD, W. and E.J. KING (1972) History of Western Education. London: Adam and C. Black.

BRACY, J.H. et al. (1969) Black Nationalism in America. Indianapolis: Bobbs-Merrill.

BREMBECK, C.S. (1973) Nonformal Education as an Alternative to Schooling. East Lansing: Michigan State University.

BREMBECK, C. and T. THOMPSON (eds.) (1973) New Strategies for Educational Development. Lexington, Massachusetts: Lexington Books.

BREMER, J. (1970) The Parkway Program. Philadelphia: Philadelphia Public Schools.

BRIM, O. Jr and S. WHEELER (1966) Socialization after Childhood. New York: John Wiley.

BRINTON, C. (1963) The Shaping of the Modern Mind. New York: New American Library.

BROWN, J. (1933) Elizabethan Schooldays. Oxford: Basil Blackwell.

BRUBACHER, J. (1967) A History of the Problems of Education. New York: McGraw-Hill.

BRUNER, J., J. GOODNOW and G. AUSTIN (1956) Study of Thinking. New York: John Wiley.

BROWN, G.I. (1971) Human Teaching for Human Learning. New York: Viking Compass.

BURCKHARDT, J. (1958) The Civilization of the Renaissance in Italy. New York: Harper.

BUTTS, F. (1955) A Cultural History of Western Education. New York: McGraw-Hill.

CALLAHAN, R. (1962) Education and the Cult of Efficiency. Chicago: University of Chicago Press.

CAMPBELL, J. (1975) 'Kundalini Yoga: Seven Levels of Consciousness', Psychology Today (December): 76-78.

CARLISLE, N. (1818) A Concise Description of the Endowed Grammar Schools in England and Wales. Vol II. London: Baldwin, Cradock, and Joy.

CASTENEDA, C. (1972) 'Sorcerer's Apprentice', Psychology Today (December): 103.

CENTRAL ADVISORY COUNCIL ON EDUCATION (1966) Children and their Primary Schools. London: HMSO.

CHARLTON, K. (1965) Education in Renaissance England. London: Routledge and Kegan Paul.

CHO, K. (1956) 'Christian Civilicism of Traditional Japanese Ethics in the Meiji Period'. Tokyo: International Christian University (Mimeograph).

CIPOLLA, C. (1969) Literacy and Development in the West. Baltimore: Penguin.

CLARK, H. and H. SLOAN (1958) Classrooms in the Factories. Rutherford, New Jersey: Dickinson University.

CLARK, H, H. SLOAN and C. HERBERT (1962) Classrooms in the Stores. Sweet Springs, Mo.: Roxbury Press.

CLARK, H. and H. SLOAN (1964) Classrooms in the Military. New York: Bureau of Publications, Teachers College.

COHEN, Y. (1969) 'The Shaping of Men's Minds', p. 36 in Comparative Educational Anthropology. New York: Random House.

COLEMAN, J.S. (1966) Equality of Educational Opportunity. Washington, D.C.: U.S. Government Printing Office.

COMENIUS, J. (1874) Die Mutterschule. Halle: Pfeffer.

COMENIUS, J. (1954) The Great Didactic (edited and translated by W.M. KEATINGE). New York: Russell.

COOMBS, P.H. (1968) The World Educational Crisis. New York: Oxford University Press.

COOMBS, P.H. and M. AHMED (1974) Attacking Rural Poverty, How Nonformal Education Can Help. Baltimore: Johns Hopkins.

COUNCIL OF EUROPE (1971) 'Permanent Education: Fundamentals for an Integrated Educational Policy'. Strasbourg: Council of Europe (Mimeographed).

CREMIN, L.A. (1964) The Transformation of the School. New York: Vintage.

CREMIN, L.A. (1970) American Education, The Colonial Experience: 1607-1783. New York: Harper Torch Books.

CUBBERLEY, E. (1916) Public School Administration. Boston: Houghton Mifflin.

CURTIS, S.J. (1948) History of Education in Great Britain. London: University Tutorial Press.

CUTRIGHT, P. (1963) 'National Political Development: Measurement and Analysis'. American Sociological Review, 28 (March): 25.5.

D'AETH, R. (1959) 'The Grammar School in the Age of Science'. Inaugural Lecture at the University of Exeter.

DAHRENDORF, R. (1964) Gesellschaft und Demokratie in Deutschland. München: R. Piper.

DAVE, R. (1973) Lifelong Education and School Curriculum. Hamburg: UNESCO.

DAVE, R. (ed.) (1975) Reflections on Lifelong Education and the School. Hamburg: UNESCO.

DAVE, R. and N. STIEMERLING (1973) Lifelong Education and the School. Hamburg: UNESCO.

DECECCO, J. and A. RICHARDS (1975) 'Civil War in the High Schools', Psychology Today (November): 51-56.

DEUTSCH, K. (1961) 'Social Mobilization and Political Development', The American Political Science Review, LV (September): 493-514.

DEUTSCH, K. (1969) Nationalism and its Alternatives. New York: Knopf.

DEWEY, J. (1899) School and Society. Chicago: University of Chicago Press.

DEWEY, J. (1916) Democracy and Education. New York: Macmillan.

DIETRICH, T. and J. KLINK (1964) Zur Geschichte der Volksschule. Bad Heilbronn: Klinkhardt.

DIVOKY, D. (1971) 'New York's Mini-Schools', Saturday Review (December 18): 60-61.

DOBBS, A. (1919) Education and Social Movements: 1700-1850. London: Longmans, Green.

DUNKEL, H.B. (1970) Herbart and Herbartianism: An Educational Ghost Story. Chicago: University of Chicago Press.

EASTERLINE, R. (1965) 'A Note on the Evidence of History', pp. 422-29 in C. ANDERSON and M. BOWMAN, Education and Economic Development. Chicago: Aldine.

EGGLESTON, S.J. (ed.) (1974) Pre-School Education in Europe. A Council of Europe Publication. Braunschweig: Georg Westerman.

EISENSTADT, S. (1966) Modernization: Protest and Change. Englewood Cliffs, New Jersey: Prentice-Hall.

ELIOT, C. (1898) 'Can School Programs Be Shortened and Enriched?' Educational Reform: 151-76.

ELLUL, J. (1964) The Technological Society. New York: Vintage.

EVANS, D. (1975) 'An Approach to Nonschool Rural Education in Ecuador' in T.J. LABELLE (ed.) Educational Alternatives in Latin America. Los Angeles: UCLA Latin American Center: 169-84.

FAURE, E. (ed.) (1972) Learning to Be. Paris: UNESCO.

FINKLE, J. and R. GABLE (1971) Political Development and Social Change. New York: John Wiley

FINN, J. (1960) 'Technology and the Instructional Process', pp. 382-87 in A.

LUMSDAINE and K. GLASER (eds) Teaching Machines and Programmed Learning. Washington, D.C.: NEA.

FISHMAN, J. (1972) Language and Nationalism. Rowley, Mass.: Newbury House.

FLITNER, W. (1941) Die Vier Quellen Des Volksschulgedankens, Hamburg: Der Hansischer Gildenverlag.

FOHR, P. (1969) 'Compulsory Schooling for Nomads', West European Education 1 (Summer): 12.

FOSTER, G. (1953) 'What is Folk Culture?' American Anthropologist, LV, No. 2, part 1 (April-June): 164.

FOUGEYROLLAS, P., F. SOW and F. VALLADON (1967) L'Education des Adultes au Sénégal. Paris: UNESCO/IIEP.

FREIRE, P. (1970a) 'The Adult Literacy Process as Cultural Action for Freedom', Harvard Educational Review 40 (May): 205-25.

FREIRE, P. (1971) Pedagogy of the Oppressed. New York: Herder and Herder.

FRIEDENBERG, E. (1959) Vanishing Adolescence. Boston: Beacon Press.

FRIEDENBERG, E. (1963) Coming of Age in America. New York: Vintage.

FROEBEL, F. (1840) Kommt, lasst uns unsern Kindern Leben. Leipzig: Obraldruck.

FROEBEL, F. (1862) Gesammelte pädagogische Schriften (edited by Richard LANGE). Berlin: Enslin.

FOSTER, P.J. (1965) Education and Social Change in Ghana. Chicago: University of Chicago Press.

GALBRAITH, J. (1967) The New Industrial State. New York: Signet.

GAY, J. and M. Cole (1967) The New Mathematics and an Old Culture: A Study of Learning Among the Kpelle of Liberia. New York: Holt, Rinehart and Winston.

GOOD, H. (1960) A History of Western Education. New York: Macmillan.

GOODLAD, J.I. (1968) 'Learning and Teaching in the Future', Today's Education: NEA Journal (February): 49-51.

GOODLAD, J.I. et al. (1975) The Conventional and the Alternative in Education. Berkeley: McCutchan.

GOODLAD, J.I. M. KLEIN, et al. (1974) Looking Behind the Classroom Door. Worthington, Ohio: Charles A. Jones.

GOODMAN, P. (1956) Growing up Absurd. New York: Random House.

GOODMAN, P. (1963) Compulsory Mis-Education. New York: Random House.

GRANBARD, A. (1974) Free the Children. Radical Reform and the Free School Movement. New York: Vintage

GROSS, R. and B. GROSS (1969) Radical School Reform. Boston: Simon and Schuster.

GUIZOT, F. (1860) Memoires pour servir a l'histoire de mon temps. Vol. 3. Paris: Michel-Lévy fréres.

GULLIVER, J. (1956) 'Norwich Free Academy, with an Account of Recent School Movements in Norwich, Connecticut', Journal of Education, II; 665-94.

GUMBERT, E.B. and J. SPRING (1974) The Superschool and the Superstate:

American Education in the Twentieth Century, 1918-1970. New York: John Wiley.

GÜNTHER, K. et al. (1973) Geschichte der Erziehung. Berlin: Volkseigener Verlag.

HABER, W. et al. (eds) (1954) Manpower in the United States. New York: Harper.

HAGEN, E. (1962) On the Theory of Social Change. Homewood, Illinois: Dorsey Press.

HAGUE, T. (1973) 'The Experimental Gymnas, Norway', in Case Studies of Educational Innovation. Vol. 3: At the School Level. OECD: Paris.

HAINES, G. (1957) German Influence upon English Education and Science: 1800-1866. New London, Connecticut: Connecticut College.

HALL, J. (1965) 'Changing Conceptions of the Modernization of Japan', pp. 7-14 in M. JENSEN, Changing Japanese Attitudes toward Modernization. Princeton, N.J.: Princeton University Press.

HALLS, W.D. (1965) Society, Schools and Progress in France. Oxford: Pergamon.

HARBISON, F. and C. MYERS (1964) Education, Manpower, and Economic Growth. New York, McGraw Hill.

HARRIS, T. (1976) 'The Religious War Over Truth and Tools', Psychology Today (January): 67-68.

HARTUNG, H. (1966) Vers une éducation permanente. Paris: Fayard.

HARTZ, L. (1955) The Liberal Tradition in America. New York: Harcourt Brace.

HARVEY. F. (1966) 'Literacy in the Athenian Democracy', Revue des Etudes Greques, 79.

HEILBRONER, R. (1975) An Inquiry into the Human Prospect. New York: W.W. Norton.

HENTIG, H. von (1971) Cuernavaca oder: Alternativen zur Schule? Stuttgart: Klett.

HENTOFF, N. (1966) Our Children are Dying. New York: Viking.

HERSKOVITS, M. (1973) Cultural Relativism. New York: Vintage.

HERBART, J. (1919) Pädagogische Schriften. (edited by O. WILLMAN and T. FRITZSCL) Vol. 3. Leipzig: Osterwieck/Harz.

HILL, C. (1967) Reformation to Industrial Revolution. Harmondsworth: Penguin.

HOLLINGSHEAD, A.B. (1947) Elmtown's Youth. New York: John Wiley.

HOLMAN, H. (1898) English National Education. Glasgow: Blackie.

HOLT, J. (1966) How Children Fail. New York: Dell.

HOLT, S. (1972) Freedom and Beyond. New York: Dell.

HOOYKAAS, R. (1968) 'Science and Reformation', in S.N. EISENSTADT ed.) The Protestant Ethic and Modernization. New York: Basic Books.

HOSTETLER, J.A. and G.E. HUNTINGTON (1971) Children in Amish Society: Socialization and Community Education. New York: Holt, Rinehart, and Winston.

HUNTINGTON, S. (1968) Political Order in Changing Societies. New Haven: Yale University Press.

HUNTINGTON, S. (1971) 'The Change to Change', Comparative Politics; 3 (April): 283-322.

HUSEN, T. (1967) International Study of Achievement in Mathematics: A Comparison of Twelve Countries. Stockholm: Almquist and Wiksell.

HUSEN, T. (1972) 'Does More Time in School Make a Difference?', Saturday Review (29 April): 32-35.

HUXLEY, T.H. (1895) Collected Essays. London: Macmillan.

ILLICH, I. (1968) Commencement Address at the University of Puerto Rico.

ILLICH, I. (1970) Deschooling Society. New York: Harper and Row.

JAMES, W. (1943) Pragmatism. New York: Meridian.

JENCKS, C. (1972) Inequality: A Reassessment of the Effect of Family and Schooling in America. New York: Basic Books.

KAIGO, T. (1965) Japanese Education: Its Past and Present. Tokyo: Society for International Cultural Relations.

KARIER, C., P. VIOLAS and J. SPRING (1973) Roots of Crisis: American Education in the Twentieth Century. Chicago: Rand McNally.

KATZ, M. (1971) Class, Bureaucracy, and Schools; the Illusion of Educational Change in America. New York: Praeger.

KAUFMANN, G. (1888) Die Geschichte der Deutschen Universitäten. Stuttgart: J.G. Gottäsche.

KEATINGE, M. (1931) Comenius. New York: McGraw-Hill.

KERR, C. et al. (1964) Industrialism and Industrial Man. New York: Oxford University Press.

KING, J. (1967) Planning Non-Formal Education in Tanzania. Paris: UNESCO/ IIEP.

KOZOL, J. (1968) Death at an Early Age. New York: Penguin.

KOZOL, J. (1972) Free Schools. New York: Bantam.

KRAMER, D.G. (1876) A.H. Francke's pädogogische Schriften. Langensaltze: Hermann Beyer.

KRECKER, M. (1971) Quellen zur Geschichte der Vorschulerziehung. Berlin: Volk und Wissen.

KUHN, T. (1962) Structure of Scientific Revolutions. Chicago: University of Chicago Press.

KUHN, T. (1963) 'The Essential Tension', p. 343 in C. TAYLOR and F. BARRON (eds) Scientific Creativity. New York: John Wiley.

KUHN, T.S. (1970) 'Reflections on my Critics', in Criticism and the Growth of Knowledge, edited by I. LAKATOS and A. MUSGRAVE. Cambridge: Cambridge University Press.

KVARACEUS, W. (1965) 'Teacher and Pupil in the Technological Culture of the School', Phi Delta Kappa (February): 269-72.

LaBELLE, T. (1975a) Educational Alternatives in Latin America. Los Angeles: UCLA Latin Amrican Center Publications.

LADURIE, E. (1966) Les Paysons de Languedoc. Paris: SEVPEN.

LAING, R.D. (1967) The Politics of Experience. New York: Ballantine.

LAKATOS, I. and A. MUSGRAVE (1970) Criticism and the Growth of Knowledge. Cambridge: Cambridge University Press.

LASCH, C. (1975) 'The Family and History', New York Review of Books, 22 (November 13) 33-38.

LEACH, A. (1911) Educational Charters and Documents: 598-1809. Cambridge: Cambridge University Press.

LENGRAND, P. (1970) An Introduction to Lifelong Education. Paris: UNESCO.

LEONARD, G. (1974) 'How We Will Change', Intellectual Digest (June).

LERNER, D. (1958) The Passing of Traditional Society. New York: Free Press.

LERNER, M. (1957) America as a Civilization. New York: Simon and Schuster.

LIPSET, S. (1959) 'Some Social Requisites of Democracy: Economic Development and Political Legitimacy', American Political Science Review, 53 (March): 69-105.

LIPSET, S. (1963) Political Man: The Social Bases of Politics. Garden City, N.Y.: Doubleday.

LÖSCHKE, K.J. (1856) Valentin Trotzendorf nach seinem Leben und Wirken. Breslau: Grass, Barth und Comp.

LOWE, R. (1862) Speech on the Revised Code of the Regulations of the Committee of the Privy Council on Education. London: House of Commons (13 Feb.)

MacLEISH, A. (1968) 'The Great American Frustration', Saturday Review (13 July): 14.

McCLELLAND, D. (1961) The Achieving Society. Princeton, N.J.: D. Van Nostrand.

MANN, H. (1844) 'Mr. Mann's Seventh Annual Report, Education in Europe', Common School Journal, VI.

MANNHEIM, K. (1936) Ideology and Utopia (translated from the German by L. WIRTH and E. SHILS). New York: Harcourt, Brace and World.

MARCUSE, H. (1964) One Dimensional Man. Boston: Beacon.

MARCUSE, H. (1966) Eros and Civilization. Boston: Beacon.

MARROU, H. (1956) History of Education in Antiquity. New York: Mentor.

MEDLIN, W.K. (1960) Soviet Education Programs. Washington: U.S. Dept. of Health, Education, and Welfare.

MEDLIN, W. K. (1964) The History of Educational Ideas in the West. New York: Center for Applied Research in Education.

MEYER, A. (1967) Educational History of the American People. New York: McGraw-Hill.

MEYER, H. (1974) Zur Geschichte der Oldenburgischen Schule. Oldenburg: Heinz Holzberg.

MILLS, C.W. (1959) The Sociological Imagination. New York: Grove.

MITCHELL, J. (1935) 'A Model for the Maintaining of Students and Fellows of Choice Abilities at the College in Cambridge', Publications of the Colonial Society of Massachusetts, 21: 311.

MITTER, W. (1969) 'Einheitlichkeit und Differenzierung als Problem der Sowjetischen Schulreform', in Bildungsreformen in Osteuropa. Stuttgart: Kohlhammer.

MITZEL, H. (1970) 'The Impending Instructional Revolution', Phi Delta

Kappa (April): 434-39.

MONSHEIMER, O. (1958) 'Die Berufsschule zwischen Gestern und Morgan', Gewerkschaftliche Monatschrift403-13.

MOORSOM, S. (1973) 'Free Schools', Where? (May): 148-51.

MÜLLER, R. (1930) Die Preussische Volksschule im Volksstaate. Osterwieck: Lickfeldt.

NBAKAMORI, Z. (1974) 'Pestalozzi, Herbart und der Herbartianismus in Japan', Pädagogische Rundschau, 28 (July): 572-78.

NEILL, A. (1960) Summerhill: A Radical Approach to Child Rearing. New York: Hart.

NUCHTER, F. (1915) 'Klasseneinteilung und Vorrückungssysteme in Amerika', Deutsche Schule, 19: 97-98.

NUGENT, E.M. (ed.) (1956) The Thought and Culture of the English Renaissance. Cambridge: Cambridge University Press.

NYERERE, J.K. (1969) Nyerere on Socialism. Oxford: Oxford University Press.

DIE ÖFFENTLICHE VOLKSSCHULE IM PREUSSISCHEN STAAT (1883) Denkschrift 13. Ergänzungscheft zur Zietschrift des Königlichen Preussischen Statistischen Büros.

OETTINGER, A.G. (1969) Run, Computer, Run. New York: Macmillan.

OLIVER, J.W. (1956) History of American Technology. New York: Ronald Press.

OWEN, R. (1857) The Life of Robert Owen, written by Himself. London: E. Wilson.

OZBEKHAN, H. (1968) 'Toward a General Theory of Planning', pp. 47-155 in E. JANTSCH, Perspectives of Planning. Paris: OECD.

PARKER, I. (1914) Dissenting Academies in England. Cambridge: Cambridge University Press.

PARSONS, T. et al. (1962) Toward a General Theory of Action. New York: Harper and Row.

PAULSEN, F. (1908) German Education Past and Present (translated from the German by T. LORENZ). London: Allen and Unwin.

PAULSEN, F. (1919) Geschichte des Gelehrten Unterrichts. Leipzig: Viet und Comp.

PAULSTON, R. (1972) Non-Formal Education: an Annotated International Bibliography. New York: Praeger.

PEARCE, J. (1973) The Crack in the Cosmic Egg. New York: Pocket Books.

PEARL. A. (1973) 'The Case for School America', pp. 112-17 in I. ILLICH et al., After Deschooling, What? New York: Perennial Library.

PESTALOZZI, J. (1958) 'Buch der Mutter', in E. DEJUNG and W. ZÜRICH (eds), Pestalozzi: Sämtliche Werke. Vol. 15, Zürich: Füssli.

PIRSIG, R.M. (1974) Zen and the Art of Motorcycle Maintenance. New York: Bantam.

PLANCK, M. (1949) Scientific Autobiography and Other Papers. New York: Philosophical Library.

POINCARE, H. (1914) Science and Method. London: Thomas Nelson.

POLANYI, M. (1958) Personal Knowledge. New York: Harper Torch.

POLANYI, M. (1968) 'On the Nature of Science'; in W. COULSON AND C. ROGERS (eds), Man and the Science of Man. Columbus, Ohio: Charles E. Merrill.

PRESTHUS, R. (1962) The Organizational Society. New York: Alfred A. Knopf.

PROJEKTGRUPPE 'FREIE SCHULE FRANKFURT' (1975) 'Konzeption der Projektgruppe', Informationsdienst des Sozialistischen Lehrererbundes (15 January): 29; 44, Sozialistisches Büro: 605 Offenbach, Postfach 591.

PROST, A. (1968) Histoire de l'enseignement en France, 1800-1967. Paris.

RAM DASS (1974) The Only Dance There is. Garden City, New York: Anchor.

RAMO, S. (1960) 'A New Technique of Education', in A. LUMSDAIN and R. GLASER (eds), Teaching Machines and Programmed Instruction. Washington, D.C.: National Education Association.

RAIT, R. (1912) Life in the Medieval University. Cambridge: Cambridge University Press.

RAMSEGER, J. (1975) Gegenschulen. Bad Heilbronn: Julius Klinkhardt.

RASHDALL, H. (1936) The Universities of Europe in the Middle Ages' Vol. I., Oxford: Clarendon.

RAUMER, K. von (1877) Geschichte der Pädagogik, Band I. Güttersloh: Bertelsmann.

REBLE, A. (1951) Geschichte der Pädagogik. Stuttgart: Ernst Klett.

REDFIELD, R. (1960) Peasant Society and Culture. Chicago: University of Chicago Press.

REIGART, J. (1916) The Lancastrian System of Instruction in the Schools of New York City. New York: Teachers College, Columbia University.

REIMER, E. (1971) School is Dead: Alternatives in Education. New York: Doubleday.

REISNER, E. (1922) Nationalism and Education Since 1789. New York: Macmillan.

RICHMOND, W.K. (1973) The Free School. London: Methuen.

RICHTER, J. (1930) 'Sächsische Volksschule', Monumenta Germaniae Paedagogica, 59.

RIGGS, F. (1961) 'Modernization and Political Problems: Some Developmental Prerequisites', p. 61 in W. BELING and G. TOTTEN, Developing Nations: Quest for a Model. New York: Van Nostrand Reinhold.

ROBERTS, A. (1972) 'A New View of the Infant School Movement', British Journal of Educational Studies, 20: 154-64.

ROBINSON, J.H. (1904-06) Readings in European History. Boston: Ginn.

ROSE, H. and S. ROSE (1969) Science and Society. Harmondsworth: Penguin.

ROSTOW, W. (1960) The Stages of Economic Growth. Cambridge: Cambridge University Press.

ROSZAK, T. (1969) The Making of a Counter Culture. Garden City, New York: Anchor.

ROUSSEAU, J. (1962) The Emile of Jean Jacques Rousseau (edited and translated by William BOYD). New York: Teachers College Press.

RUST, V. (1967) German Interest in Foreign Education Since World War I. Ann Arbor: University of Michigan, School of Education.

RUST, V. (1968) 'The Common School Issue — A Case of Cultural Borrowing', in W. CORRELL and F. SÜLLWOLD (eds) Forschung und Erziehung. Donauworth: Auer.

RUST, V. (1972) 'Anti-Authoritarian Education in West Germany', Intellect (November): 130-33.

SAPIR, E. (1964) Culture, Language, and Personality. Berkeley: University of California Press.

SCHAGEN, A. (1913) Josef Görres und die Anfänge der Preussischen Volksschule am Rhein 1814-1816. Bonn: Marcus und E. Webers.

SCHEFFLER, I. (1967) Science and Subjectivity. Indianapolis: Bobbs-Merrill.

SCHEIBE, W. (1965) Zur Geschichte der Volksschule. Bad Heilbronn: Klinkhardt.

SCHELSKY, H. (1957) Schule und Erziehung in der Industriellen Gesellschaft. Würzburg: Werkbund.

SCHELSKY, H. (1961) Der Mensch in der Wissenschaftlichen Zivilisation; Köln: Westdt. Verlag.

SCHILLER, F. (1907) Studies in Humanism. London: Macmillan.

SCHLEE, E. (1894) 'Das öffentliche Schulwesen in den Vereinigten Staaten von Nordamerika'. Beilage zum Jahresbericht des Altonaer Realgymnasiums.

SCHMIDT, H. and F.J. LUTZENKIRCHEN (1969) Bibliographie zur Schulorganisation. Weinheim: Julius Beltz.

SCHNEIDEWIN, M. (1897) Die Antike Humanität. Berlin: Weidmannsche Buchhandlung.

SCHWARTZ, B. (1974) Permanent Education. The Hague: Martinus Nijhoff.

SCIENCE COMMISSION (1875) Nature.

SEABORNE, M. (1971) The English School: Its Architecture and Organization 1370-1870. London: Routledge and Kegan Paul.

SERVAN-SCHREIBER, J. (1968) The American Challenge. New York: Atheneum.

SILBERMAN, C. (1970) Crisis in the Classroom. New York: Random House.

SJOBERG, G. (1955) 'Pre-Industrial City', American Journal of Sociology 60 (March): 436.

SJOBERG, G. (1960) The Pre-Industrial City. Glencoe, Ill.: Free Press.

SKINNER, B. (1968) The Technology of Teaching. New York: Appleton-Century-Crofts.

SMALL, W. (1914) Early New England Schools. Boston: Ginn.

SNOW, C.P. (1964) The Two Cultures and a Second Look. Cambridge: Cambridge University Press.

SPAULDING, F., O. FREDERICK and L. KOOS (1935) 'The Reorganization of Secondary Education'. National Survey of Secondary Education Monograph 5 USOE Bulletin 17, 1932, Washington, D.C.: Government Printing Office.

SPENCER, H. (1897) Education. New York: Appleton.

SPENCER, H. (1867) The Evolution of Society (edited and with an introduction by R. CAMEIRO). Chicago: University of Chicago Press.

STEINHILBER, H. and C. SOKOLOWSKI (1966) State Law on Compulsory Attendance. Circular 793, Washington, D.C.: U.S. Government Printing Office.

STOWE, C. (1930) 'Report on Elementary Public Instruction in Europe', in E. KNIGHT, Reports on European Education. New York: McGraw-Hill.

STRETCH, B.B. (1970) 'The Rise of the "Free School"', Saturday Review, 53 (20 June): 76-79, 90-93.

STRUKTURFORDERUNG IM BILDUNGSWESEN DES LANDES NORD-RHEIN-WESTFALEN (1972) Kollegstufe NW, Heft 13. Ratingen: Aloys Henn.

TAYLOR, F. (1911) The Principles of Scientific Management. New York: Harper and Row.

TAYLOR, J. (1912) 'Measurement of Educational Efficiency', Educational Review, 44 (November): 350-51.

TEWS, J. (1914) Ein Jahrhundert Preussischer Schulgeschichte. Leipzig: Quelle und Meyer.

THAYER, F. (1973) An End to Hierarchy! An End to Competition. New York: New Viewpoints.

THOMPSON, V. (1961) Modern Organization. New York: Knopf.

THORNDIKE, R.L. (1973) Reading Comprehension Education in Fifteen Countries. Stockholm: Almquist and Wiksell.

TILDEN, W.A. (1930) Famous Chemists. London: Routledge.

TINDEMANS, L. (1972) 'Regionalized Belgium: Transition from the Nation-State to the Multinational State', Chronicles 151-152 (August/September), published by the Ministry of Foreign Affairs.

TOENNIES, F. (1963) Community and Society (translated and edited by C. LOOMIS), New York: Harper and Row.

TOFFLER, A. (1970) Future Shock. New York: Bantam.

TURNER, D. (1970) '1870: The State and the Infant School System', British Journal of Educational Studies, 18: 151-65.

TYACK, D. (1967) Turning Points in American Educational History. New York: Xerox.

ULICH, R. (1961) The Education of Nations. Cambridge, Mass.: Harvard University Press.

ULICH, R. (ed) (1965) Three Thousand Years of Educational Wisdom. Cambridge: Harvard University Press.

UNESCO (1972a) Learning to Be. Paris: UNESCO.

UNESCO (1972b) Literacy: 1969-1971. Paris: UNESCO.

U.S. BUREAU OF THE CENSUS (1960) Historical Statistics of the United States, Colonial Times to 1957. Washington, D.C.: U.S. Government Printing Office.

U.S. BUREAU OF THE CENSUS (1973) 1970 Census of the Population: Educational Attainment. Washington: Government Printing Office.

VARRENTRAPP, C. (1889) Johannes Schulze und das Hohere Preussische Unterrichtswesen in seiner Zeit. Leipzig: B.G. Teubner.

VEBLEN, T. (1921) Price System. New York: B.W. Heubsch.

VORMBAUM, R. (1863) Evangelische Schulordnungen. Bände I, II, III, Güterslch: Bertelsmann.

WALLACE, A. (1973) 'Schools in Revolutionary and Conservative Societies', p. 231 in F. IANNI and E. STORY (eds), Cultural Relevance and Educational Issues. Boston: Little, Brown.

WARD, B. (1966) Spaceship Earth. New York: Columbia University Press.

WEBER, M. (1947) The Theory of Social and Economic Organization. New York: Free Press.

WEBER, M. (1968) Economy and Society. New York: Bedminster.

WEHLER, H. (1975) Modernisierungstheorie und Geschichte. Göttingen: Vandenjoeck und Ruprecht.

WEINBERG, I. (1967) The English Public Schools. New York: Atherton.

WHITEHEAD, A.N. (1926) Science and the Modern World. Cambridge: Cambridge University Press.

WHORF, B. (1956) Language, Thought, and Reality. Cambridge, Mass.: MIT Press.

WINN, H. (ed.) (1929) Wycliff: Selected English Writings. London: Oxford University Press.

WOODY, T. (1928) 'Entrance of Women into the Teaching Profession', Educational Outlook, II (January, March): 72-88; 138-63.

YENGO, C. (1964) 'John Dewey and the Cult of Efficiency', Harvard Education Review, 34 (Winter): 33-53.

ZÄNDER, U. (1975) Qualifikationsanforderungen und Sekundarschulreform in der UdSSR, in the series on Qualifizierung und wissenschaftlich-technischer Fortschritt. Ravensburg: Otto Maier.

ZILLER, T. (1884) Allgemeine Pädagogik. Leipzig: Matthes.

Val. D. Rust is Associate Director of the Göttingen Study Center of the University of California and Associate Professor of Comparative and International Education at the University of California, Los Angeles, USA.

Notes